CIVIL RELIGION AND POLITICAL THEOLOGY

BOSTON UNIVERSITY STUDIES IN PHILOSOPHY AND RELIGION

General Editor: Leroy S. Rouner

Volume Eight

Civil Religion and Political Theology

Edited by
Leroy S. Rouner

UNIVERSITY OF NOTRE DAME PRESS
Notre Dame, Indiana 46556

Library of Congress Cataloging-in-Publication Data

Civil religion and political theology.

(Boston University studies in philosophy and
religion ; v. 8)
Includes bibliographies and index.
1. Christianity and politics.   2. Civil religion—
United States.   I. Rouner, Leroy S.   II. Series.
BR115.P7C387   1986   261.7   86-11242
ISBN 0-268-00757-8

Contents

Preface

Boston University Studies in Philosophy and Religion is a joint project of the Boston University Institute for Philosophy and Religion and the University of Notre Dame Press. While the Studies may eventually include occasional volumes by individual authors dealing with critical issues in the philosophy of religion, it is presently focused on an annual volume edited from the previous year's Institute lecture program. The Director of the Institute, who also serves as editor of these Studies, chooses a theme and invites participants to lecture at Boston University in the course of the academic year. These public lectures are on Wednesday evenings, chaired by faculty from the various schools and departments within the university which jointly sponsor the Institute. There is a critical respondent to each paper and general discussion by the audience. The papers are then revised by their authors, and the editor selects and edits the papers to be included in these Studies. In preparation is a volume on civil rights and the world's religions.

The Boston University Institute for Philosophy and Religion is a Center of the Graduate School and is sponsored jointly by the School of Theology, the Department of Philosophy, and the Department of Religion of Boston University. The Institute receives regular financial support from the Graduate School. This year our budget has been supplemented by generous grants from the Old South Fund, the Lilly Endowment, and the Humanities Foundation of Boston University. As an interdisciplinary and ecumenical forum it does not represent any philosophical school or religious tradition. Within the academic community it is committed to open interchange on questions of value, truth, reality, and meaning which transcend the narrow specializations of academic life. Outside the university community it seeks to recover the public tradition of philosophical discourse which was a lively part of American intellectual life in the early years of this century before the professionalization of both philosophy and religious studies.

This volume's concern with social philosophy will be reflected in several succeeding studies in this series on human rights and the world's religions. Our commitment to a renewal of the philosophy of religion, outlined in the Introduction to Volume 7, includes relating theory to practice. This volume and its immediate successors explore living religion in its social and cultural context.

Civil Religion and Political Theology focuses on the Christian tradition, despite our conviction that religious and cultural pluralism is now the inescapable context for all work in the philosophy of religion. Our forthcoming volumes on human rights will each deal with all of the great world religious traditions. Human rights is a much clearer concept than civil religion, however, and there is little agreement even on a definition of civil religion. A genuinely comparative study of civil religion therefore seemed conceptually out of reach. Because the topic is of critical importance, however, we have tried to clarify what civil religion is in relation to Christianity, how it functions in American society especially, and what its relevance may be for the coming world civilization. The complex relationship between civil religion and political theology is inescapable.

Our hope is that this volume may illuminate the way living religion actually functions in its culture, and thereby lead to a better understanding of this complex phenomenon, both within the academic community and beyond.

Acknowledgments

Once again I have the privilege of thanking those who have helped prepare this book. Our authors have been gracious in response to my insistence that clarity and conciseness should be hallmarks of a consistent style in this series. Even extensive revisions were accomplished with a patient cooperation for which I am especially grateful. Irena Makarushka and Rosalind Carey did the first round of copy editing with their usual care and attention to detail, and my Administrative Assistant, Barbara Darling Smith, was once again responsible for final preparation of the manuscript for the publishers. Last year I described Barbara as a legend in her own time. This year she is even better than that. Suffice it to say that there could be no series without her.

Carole Roos reviewed the manuscript for the University of Notre Dame Press, and she and Barbara ironed out the last details. Gregory Rockwell oversees the publication process with a keen eye for detail. Editor Ann Rice maintains a relaxed and reassuring good humor in spite of an annual October deadline for the Institute's publication party. The books always arrive on time, and each year we have one more reason to be proud of our association with the University of Notre Dame Press. Jim Langford, Director of the Press, has helped us with this series in ways too numerous to mention. Not only was Jim willing to publish this series and able to market it successfully, he has been an intellectual colleague and spiritual companion in planning these volumes and in helping us articulate critical issues in the philosophy of religion. Our gratitude to him is enormous, and continues to grow.

Contributors

ROBERT N. BELLAH is Ford Professor of Sociology and Comparative Studies at the University of California at Berkeley. He studied at Harvard and received his Ph.D. in Sociology and Far Eastern Languages in 1955. He was recipient of a Fulbright Research Grant in 1960 which allowed him to study in Tokyo. Among his awards are the Sorokin Award of the American Sociological Association (1976) and the Guggenheim Fellowship (1983–84). From 1975–78 he was Director of the National Endowment for the Humanities summer seminars for college teachers. He has lectured and taught at Harvard and Princeton. In addition to numerous articles, his books include *Religion in America* (1968), *Beyond Belief: Essays on Religion in a Post-Traditional World* (1970), *The Broken Covenant: American Civil Religion in Time of Trial* (1975), and, most recently, *Habits of the Heart: Individualism and Commitment in American Life* (1985).

JOHN B. COBB, JR., is Ingraham Professor of Theology at the School of Theology at Claremont and Avery Professor of Religion at Claremont Graduate School, as well as Director of Process Studies there. Born in Kobe, Japan, Professor Cobb received M.A. and Ph.D. degrees from the University of Chicago. Among his books are *A Christian Natural Theology* (1965) and *The Structure of Christian Existence* (1967). More recently he coauthored (with David Ray Griffin) *Process Theology: An Introductory Exposition* (1976) and (with L. Charles Birch) *The Liberation of Life: From the Cell to the Community* (1981).

JAMES H. CONE is the author of numerous articles and several books, including *Black Theology and Black Power* (1969), *A Black Theology of Liberation* (1970), *God of the Oppressed* (1975), *My Soul Looks Back* (1982), and *For My People: Black Theology and the Black Church* (1984). A number of his books have been translated into other languages. He received his B.A. from Philander Smith College (1958), B.D. from Garrett Theological Seminary (1961), M.A. and Ph.D. from Northwestern University (1963, 1965). In addition he holds an L.L.D. from Edward Waters College (1981) and an L.H.D. from Philander Smith College (1981). As visiting professor he has taught at Barnard College, Drew University, Princeton Theological Seminary, and Howard School of Religion. He is Charles A. Briggs Professor of Systematic Theology at Union Theological Seminary.

YARON EZRAHI studied at Hebrew University of Jerusalem where he received his B.A. in Political Science and Philosophy in 1964 and an M.A. in Political Science in 1966. His A.M. and Ph.D. in Political Science are from Harvard University. Among his many awards and grants are the Fulbright Travel Fellowship (1966), the National Science Foundation Grant at the Center for Advanced Study in the Behavioral Sciences, Stanford (1977), and a combined grant from the Center for Advanced Study in the Behavioral Sciences and the Russell Sage Foundation for organizing a conference on the changing status and functions of professional authority in modern liberal democracies (1984–85). Author of many scholarly articles and essays, he is also now writing *Descent of Icarus: The Idea of Politics as Technique and Its Decline in Modern Democracy* and *The Legacy of Utopia: Science and the Changing Rhetoric of Democracy*. In 1984–85 he was Visiting Professor at Duke University. At present he is Senior Lecturer in Political Science at Hebrew University.

MATTHEW L. LAMB studied at the Trappist Monastery in Georgia, at the Pontifical Gregorian University in Rome, where he obtained an S.T.L., and at the University of Münster, where he received his doctorate in Theology. He is the author of over sixty articles, and his books include, among others, *History, Method, and Theology* (1978) and *Solidarity with Victims* (1982). He edited *Creativity and Method: Essays in Honor of Bernard Lonergan* (1981). Having taught at the University of Chicago Divinity School and at Marquette University, he is now Associate Professor of Theology at Boston College. He has been the recipient of several awards, including the Merit Scholarship from the Government of Nordheim-West-falen and the Walsh-Price Fellowship at the Maryknoll School of Theology.

THOMAS A. McCARTHY holds a B.S. in Mathematics and Philosophy from the College of the Holy Cross (1961) and an M.A. and Ph.D. in Philosophy from the University of Notre Dame (1963, 1968). His many awards include a Fulbright Research Fellowship (1963), the Alexander von Humboldt Fellowship (1975–76, 1978, 1983), and a Guggenheim Fellowship (1985). He is author of *The Critical Theory of Jürgen Habermas* (1978) and translator of numerous works, including those by Jürgen Habermas titled *Legitimation Crisis, Communication and the Evolution of Society*, and *Reason and the Rationalization of Society* (volume 1 of *The Theory of Communicative Action*). In addition, he is general editor of *Studies in Contemporary German Social Thought* for MIT Press. Having taught at the University of Munich (1968–72) and Boston University (1972–85), he is now Professor of Philosophy at Northwestern University.

JOHANN BAPTIST METZ is Professor of Fundamental Theology at the University of Münster. He is also a member of the board of the University of Bielefeld and its Center for Interdisciplinary Studies, a member of the Foundation and the Committee of Directors of the international journal *Concilium*, and a temporary member of the Vatican Office *pro non credentibus*. His many books include *Poverty of Spirit* (1968),

Theology of the World (1969), *Followers of Christ* (1978), *Faith in History and Society* (1980), *The Emergent Church* (1981), and, with Karl Rahner, *The Courage to Pray* (1981). He is main author of the Document of the German Synod of Bishops, "Our Hope: A Confession of Faith for This Time" (1976).

MARGARET R. MILES is the author of *Augustine on the Body* (1979), *Fullness of Life* (1981), and, most recently, *Image as Insight* (1985). In addition she has written numerous articles, essays, and reviews for scholarly journals and is associate editor of the *Harvard Theological Review*. She is Professor of Historical Theology at Harvard Divinity School. Among her many awards are the National Endowment for the Humanities Summer Stipend (1982), a Guggenheim Fellowship (1982–83), and a Rockefeller Fellowship at the Study and Conference Center in Bellagio, Italy (1983). She holds a B.A. and an M.A. from San Francisco State University (1969, 1971) and a Ph.D. from the Graduate Theological Union at Berkeley (1977).

JÜRGEN MOLTMANN was educated at the University of Göttingen where he received his Ph.D. in 1955 and his Habilitation in 1957. He is also the recipient of several honorary degrees and the Elba Library Prize. He is Professor of Systematic Theology at the University of Tübingen. Among his many books are *Theology of Hope* (1967), *The Crucified God* (1974), *The Church in the Power of the Spirit* (1977), *The Future of Creation* (1979), *The Trinity and the Kingdom* (1981), and *On Human Dignity: Political Theology and Ethics* (1984).

RICHARD JOHN NEUHAUS is a "Pastor on Assignment" in the Lutheran Church and worked in a low-income section of Brooklyn for over seventeen years. His works and writings have been the focus of interest for many publications, including *Time, Newsweek, Harper's,* and *The New York Times Magazine*. He studied in Ontario, where he was born, as well as in Nebraska and Texas; his theological training is from Concordia Theological Seminary in St. Louis. The Religious Heritage Foundation of America has awarded him the Faith and Freedom Award (1982), and Pope John Paul II recognized his work with the Religious Freedom Award (1983). His many books and publications include *In Defense of People* (1971), *Time toward Home: The American Experiment as Revelation* (1975), *Christian Faith and Public Policy* (1977), and, most recently, *The Naked Public Square* (1984).

LEROY S. ROUNER is Professor of Philosophy and Philosophical Theology at Boston University, Director of the Institute for Philosophy and Religion, and general editor of Boston University Studies in Philosophy and Religion. He graduated from Harvard College (A.B., 1953), Union Theological Seminary (B.D., *summa cum laude*, 1958), and Columbia University (Ph.D., 1961). He was Assistant Professor of Philosophy and Theology at the United Theological College, Bangalore, India, from 1961 to 1966. He is editor of the Hocking Festschrift, *Philosophy, Religion, and the Coming World Civilization* (1961), and (with John Howie) of *The Wisdom of William Ernest Hocking* (1978), as well as author of *Within Human Experience: The Philosophy of William Ernest Hocking* (1969). He was Visiting Professor of Philosophy at the University of Hawaii in 1982.

JOHN F. WILSON studied at Harvard College (A.B., *magna cum laude*, 1954), and at Union Theological Seminary (M.Div., *magna cum laude*, 1957, and Ph.D., 1962). In addition to many articles, he has written several books, including *Church and State in American History* (1965), *Pulpit in Parliament* (1969), *Public Religion in American Culture* (1979), and, most recently (with Thomas P. Slavens), a *Research Guide to Religious Studies* (1982). He has been the recipient of many awards, including the Fulbright Fellowship (1958), the Proctor and Gamble Faculty Fellowship at Princeton (1963), and the Guggenheim Fellowship (1980–81). He is Agate Brown and George L. Collard Professor of Religion at Princeton University.

Introduction

LEROY S. ROUNER

WHEN ASKED HOW I decide the themes for these volumes I regularly reply that God speaks to me in a dream. Truth to tell, however, colleagues speak to me at cocktail parties. The occasion which decided our current theme was a debate among Tom McCarthy, Jürgen Moltmann, and myself. During his years in the Philosophy Department at Boston University Tom was one of the Institute's major resources. He often served as lecturer, chair, or critic, and it was he who originally contacted Jim Langford at the University of Notre Dame Press suggesting the publication of this series. On this particular occasion he was serving as critic for Jürgen Moltmann's lecture in our program on Religious Pluralism, and during drinks before dinner preceding the lecture the talk turned to the question of civil religion. Jürgen was not only resolutely theological in seeing civil religion as false religion; he also recalled the tragic experience of his homeland under Hitler when German civil religion celebrated Nazism with a corrupted Christianity.

I was ready to admit all the bad things that could be said about civil religion but argued that some common values, held at a depth of commitment which can only be called religious, are a necessary binding ingredient for a pluralistic, democratic society. I recalled the American experience of giving people of varied ethnic backgrounds a common identity and purpose, therefore making it possible for them to be at home in the New World. Tom pointed out that Jürgen and I were using civil religion in different ways, that these ought to be clarified and their relation to political theologies of all sorts made clear, since both civil religion and political theology are means of making religious ideas and values operative in a secular society.

1

I promised to do a program on that theme if they would both participate. They agreed and I then set about inviting our other distinguished participants. The program included a panel discussion among Harvey Cox, Jürgen Moltmann, Richard Neuhaus, and Peter Berger, which gave evidence of what a lively and difficult topic this is. For all the literature on civil religion, the term is still difficult to define, and the term has been used both for certain sociologically specifiable practices and for the unspecific, vague ideas and values which inform those practices. Many, like Bellah, now abandon the term entirely. Political theology is likewise subject to varied definitions. It has sometimes meant the politicization of a religion and at other times meant the application of religious ideas and values to political life.

Our authors share the conviction that religion must be relevant to political life without being co-opted by it. This is the same fine line which Augustine sought to draw in *The City of God*. With the barbarians at the gates he defended Christianity from the charge that it had undermined the state, but he also sought to protect it from becoming only one more civil institution as it made common cause with the state on some issues. In our day the relation of religious communities to the *polis* is even more critical. The barbarians are at the gates once more, this time armed with world-destroying power, and too often religious people are among them. Since religious commitment may be the strongest of all human motivating forces, the common ground of the role of religion in social and political life is critical. The theme of this book is the role which Christianity does and should play in the life of the *polis*. Our first section deals with the ways philosophy, theology, and science help establish a common ground of values in a democratic society. Part 2 focuses on America as a test case for understanding the dangers and possibilities of Christian influence in political life. Our concluding section deals with the ways political theology is actually practiced, with essays on liberation theology, feminist theology, black theology, and a process theology of Christian economic values.

Political theology is readily identified with the Hegelian-Marxist tradition of social thought, but Tom McCarthy begins our section on philosophical foundations by examining the affinities between Kant's emphasis on practical reason and political theology, especially Helmut Peukert's *Science, Action, and Fundamental Theology*. The bridge from nontheistic Marxism to a theology of the world is often made by claiming that we cannot avoid moral-political despair without faith in a just God who will reconcile virtue and happiness by redeeming the victims of history. McCarthy traces this argument back to Kant's Second Critique where Kant argues that the moral law commands us to pursue actions which are rationally justified by their universality. Rational action is moral if its intent is to do what anyone in that situation ought to do. Kant notes, however, the antinomy of pure practical reason in the inherent conflict between virtue and happiness. The highest good, he argues, consists in a proper combination of both virtue and happiness. We are commanded by reason to pursue the highest good, but we know that it is not in our power to achieve it, since happiness is a matter not merely of will or inner intention but also of natural causes and effects. The only way to avoid moral despair, Kant continues, is to assume the possibility of the highest good. We are therefore morally required to postulate the existence of a God who has the power to produce the necessary harmony between virtue and happiness.

Having sketched Kant's approach to the matter McCarthy examines Peukert's views by way of the influence which Habermas's idea of communicative ethics had had on Peukert's theology. Kant's ethics is subjectivist in the tradition of Descartes. Kant therefore separates the intent of rational virtue from the ends of happiness, since these ends vary from person to person and are not universal. Habermas's theory does not ascribe moral validity to the actions of others just because I can will that action to be a universal law, as Kant does. Habermas establishes universality through a community of communication, in which the unforced power of the better argument prevails. My individual maxim must be submitted to all others for discursive confirmation of its universality. The ends of happiness are not eliminated, for it is a universal evaluation of human needs, interests, and desires — that is, happiness — which is sought. Habermas has socialized Kant's subjectivity but maintained Kant's notion of a universal moral law. In so doing he overcomes the gap between justice and happiness.

Peukert, however, finds an antinomy of Habermas's practical social reason in the unresolved injustice which remains in history even if a final human generation of happiness and solidarity could be achieved. It would rest on past injustice. The happiness of the living would consist in the expropriation of the dead. The dream of perfect justice turns out to be a nightmare because of the unresolvable evil of the historic past. Here Peukert returns to the fundamental Kantian argument that a rational morality demands the idea of a God who alone can right past wrongs. He does not present a complete or updated version of the argument, however, and McCarthy concludes by sketching the direction in which such an argument might run, noting that Peukert's argument does not establish the idea of God as an absolute necessity of practical reason. What it does show is that any view of history without God must finally be written as tragedy.

Jürgen Moltmann's approach to the relation between religious commitment and effective social action is theological, not sociological; ecclesiastical, not civil; and ecumenical, not nationalistic. His interest is in demythologizing all civil and political religions and in liberating people everywhere from them. His point is confessional. Theologically he begins with a confession of faith. Personally he confesses the influence of German historical experience on his point of view. Nazism so desecrated German nationalism that one imagines Moltmann now shrinking from any talk of "a good German." Is this a loss? (Even Americans on the political left still speak of "a good American.") He expresses ambivalence. "Perhaps," he says, "my generation is . . . a skeptical and disillusioned one." But if there is a lack of consensus and common identity among his generation of Germans, there is also a freedom from any government's attempt to legitimate itself by appeals to political transcendence. This may be the most critical danger for any nation, and Americans are not so well protected.

Moltmann clarifies his views in contrast to those of Carl Schmitt, the theoretician of the National Socialist dictatorship in Germany in the thirties. Schmitt argued that all major political concepts are secularized versions of theological notions: constitutional monarchy corresponds to the deistic conception of God, democracy is a version of pantheism, and so forth. He defended dictatorship through the existential category of being/nonbeing and propagated what Moltmann calls the "friend/foe thinking of a new political Manichaeism." Clearly Schmitt represents all that Moltmann abhors. But Christian faith must be relevant to social and political life. For this relevance Moltmann suggests a new political theology which begins with the existence of the church in society and a criticism of the privatization of theology and church life. "The new political theology is a theory of the public, critical, and liberative functions of the Christian church in modern society." This is in contrast to the celebration of secularization associated with Bonhoeffer's notion of a religionless Christianity and Harvey Cox's "secular city." Moltmann stands for a revitalization of religion with Johann B. Metz, Dorothee Sölle, Jan Lochman, and other European theologians. He discusses both the creative return of religion to politics and the dangerous return of politics to religion.

Under "the return of religion to politics" he notes movements for political peace and ecological renewal. But "the return of politics to religion" involves the rise of security politics, whereby national security becomes the unconditional, the world is divided into a Manichaean dualism of good and evil, and political life once again claims transcendent authority. Here is the religious philosophy of Carl Schmitt all over again. Moltmann does see important functions for civil or political religion, especially in legitimizing and integrating a society, but these functions are bound up with the friend/foe schema. "The external enemy and the internal enemy strengthen collective legitimation and integration." These political and civil religions never represent the whole life of a society but are used by certain social powers. Moltmann's new political theology is a politics of Christian discipleship, geared to the ideas of the crucified God, the triune God, the God of the poor, the God of ecumenism, and the God of hope. While he does not articulate a program for such Christian political action, he is clear about the dangerous possibilities for co-option which a valid Christian faith faces in effecting its legitimate political concern.

Yaron Ezrahi's essay is directly concerned not with the relation of religion to social and political life but rather with the conditions under which a secular democratic society can provide for freedom of religion. He is critical of those who regard science as a dehumanizing force in contemporary culture. He argues that science has provided for the public recognition of commonly held

values. He cites numerous religious critics of science who link science and technology to materialism and self-interest. These critics
— Robert Bellah in *The Broken Covenant* is his primary example —
set science over against renewed religious concern for the development of the inward person and the spiritual dimensions of the self.
Ezrahi in turn criticizes these critics for flirting with subjectivism. His point is relevant to Peukert's struggle with the subjectivism which has dogged political theologians in their appeals to
practical reason.

Ezrahi recalls the religious wars of the seventeenth century,
in which the epistemological status granted to the subjective religious imagination had led to factionalism, unresolvable conflicts,
and an overheated public temper. Here is a historical illustration
of the theoretical problem which McCarthy raised concerning the
conflict between virtue and happiness. Kant's emphasis on universalizing the moral values of the good will invoked subjectivism as
protection for rational universality. Subjective idealistic ethics are
often irrelevant, however, since subjective moral intentions do not
necessarily have any effect in the world of historical events. All
religions believe in loving others, yet no wars are bloodier than
religious ones. Ezrahi points out that such advocates of the new
science as Francis Bacon and Robert Boyle were enlisted in an effort to find new models of public speech and action which could
civilize and moderate political discourse through the discipline of
universal principles of rationality employed by an enlightened public. In helping to create the modern public as a political category
science was a major force in the rise of democracy.

Ezrahi's primary concern is the epistemology of liberal-
democratic politics and the contribution of science to those ideas
of reality which make objectivity possible. The cultural force of
science has declined in liberal democracies, and journalism now
becomes the chief advocate of epistemological realism. Ezrahi is
not persuaded that journalism is adequately committed to the
distinction between fact and opinion, however, and he sees a real
crisis of civil epistemology in the retreat to subjectivism. Ironically, the major voices here have come from within the scientific
enterprise itself. He notes, critically, the work of Kuhn, Feyerabend, Rorty, and Goodman, who have "given encouragement to
a very sophisticated epistemological anarchism according to which

the difficulties with the idea of knowledge as a mirror cannot be corrected by perfecting the mirror or educating the eye because the problem is with the very status of objects as constructs." He questions whether the epistemology of liberal-democratic discourse can survive this erosion of classical concepts of knowledge and reality.

With this introduction to some of the philosophical, theological, and scientific ground issues, we turn specifically to the American scene and the relation of Christianity to American political life. Robert Bellah's discussion of public philosophy and theology reviews the recent seminal literature on the topic, beginning with John Dewey, Walter Lippmann, and Reinhold Niebuhr, and making the issue current with comments on Richard Neuhaus, William Sullivan, and Bellah's own *Habits of the Heart*. Dewey, Niebuhr, and Lippmann were all fine practitioners of the jeremiad, a hallowed tradition in American public discourse, and they were agreed that Americans lack not only a common set of values but even a common conversation about the central issues of American public life. They differed, however, in prescribing the renewal of such a conversation. Dewey sought a new individualism which could escape the merely traditional, bound as it was by custom and inertia. Informed by the methods of natural science, he proposed a new collectivism in which individualism would be fulfilled through personal participation in the development of a shared culture. Walter Lippmann, on the other hand, equated public philosophy with the perennial philosophy of classical antiquity. It was precisely the recovery of tradition which, for Lippmann, would provide the content of common conversation in morals and politics. Lippmann's world of rational discourse presupposes a natural law which is close to neo-Thomism.

Bellah finds Reinhold Niebuhr refreshing in his concreteness after the abstract traditionalism of Lippmann and the equally abstract historicism of Dewey. Niebuhr knew that there will always be unresolved social and political conflict and sought enough common ground within the community so that it could be at least partly resolved. An example was Niebuhr's opposition both to those secular universalisms that are empty of meaning and to religious triumphalisms which provide too much meaning for too few. His context for public discourse was religious toleration inspired by

religious humility, recognizing the conditional character of all human enterprises. Bellah is appreciative of Niebuhr's influence on
Richard Neuhaus but criticizes Neuhaus's suggestion that all Americans should agree that "on balance, and considering the alternatives, the influence of the United States is a force for good in
the world." Bellah finds this virtually impossible to test as an empirical proposition and argues that even Neuhaus's "critical patriot" would be tied into "a kind of civil orthodoxy that would
irreparably rupture the Niebuhrian dialectic." Neuhaus warns of
the same danger which so concerns Ezrahi, the disintegration of
our public life into warring religious and political factions. Bellah
notes that William Sullivan warns us of the dangers in our intellectual life of allying technical reason and psychological individualism. Bellah stands with Sullivan in warning that academic specialization has turned many social and religious thinkers away from
public discourse to discussions with other experts.

Bellah concludes with observations on his and his colleagues'
intentions in their recent *Habits of the Heart*, which he presents
expressly as a contribution to both public philosophy and public
theology, and on the first draft of the Catholic Bishops' Pastoral
Letter on Catholic Social Teaching and the U.S. Economy. In both
he emphasizes the critique of American individualism and the im-
periled status of our public philosophy and theology.

Richard Neuhaus makes an extensive case against regarding
civil religion as a religion. He speaks appreciatively of Bellah's essay of some nineteen years ago which began the civil religion debate. There Bellah himself was ambivalent as to whether he was
speaking of a religion or a religious dimension. After this provi-
sional bow in the direction of the sociology of religion Neuhaus
turns to the fundamental Christian affirmation that God works
in history. Bellah had raised the question, "Why should the history of a people living two or three thousand years ago be religiously meaningful but the history of a people living in the last
two or three hundred years be religiously meaningless?" In other
words, why are Christians so clear about God's work in Israel's
history and so unclear about God's work in our own? Neuhaus
notes wryly that "to speak of American history as being religiously,
even theologically, meaningful makes many of our contemporaries
exceedingly nervous." This nervousness is both historical and theo-

logical. Jürgen Moltmann, for example, not only remembers Hitler's claim that God was on the side of the Third Reich; he also remembers his teacher Karl Barth's warning against the temptation to substitute any human program of thought for the biblical kerygma. So it is not incidental that Moltmann presents not a program for political theology but rather the theological principles on which varied programs must be based if they are to be authentically Christian. Moltmann's resolutely theological approach to political theology is clear in its theological principles and in the need for Christian political action, but Neuhaus is asking for something more. His recalling of Bellah's question asks for a theological interpretation of how God is at work in our present history, specifically American history. He admits that supporters of liberal democracy like himself are immediately reminded of manifest destiny and other models whereby Americans have committed nationalistic idolatry. He notes, however, that our skittishness has "left the task of articulating the religious meaning of America to those who do not understand the ambiguities of the American experience," and he calls for a "critical patriotism" which understands both vindication and judgment, righteousness and guilt.

Neuhaus defines public philosophy as "the intellectual task of saying what we believe to be true about ourselves and how we articulate that belief to ourselves and to the world." It is the lack of this conversation which led him to speak of "the naked public square." He looks for a public philosophy which would be democratic, pluralistic, religiously attuned, critically affirmative, and modest in its expectations — all principles Reinhold Niebuhr affirmed. Neuhaus appeals to a natural law, but unlike Lippmann, whose transcendental notion stood over against the instincts of "the people," Neuhaus is a populist. "I daresay there is more respect for something like natural law in the neighborhood bars of Brooklyn than in the philosophy seminars of Harvard." Like Niebuhr, pluralism for Neuhaus involves recognition of differences and engagement with them. He does not speak of *the people* but of their astonishingly diverse particularities. He sees this as a time of testing for American democracy. In domestic life the debate over abortion is critical: "the strong, the successful, and the healthy increasingly impose their idea of quality of life in order to exclude the marginal. . . . " If it sometimes seems too late

to restore a shared moral discourse, Neuhaus looks to the church
as the community of transcendent hope, which "can prevent our
just causes from turning into holy wars and our public philosophies from turning into civil religions."

John Wilson introduces the idea of common religion as distinct from both civil religion and political theology. He defines
civil religion as "specific social and cultural beliefs, behaviors, and
institutions [which] constitute a positive religion concerned with
civil order in the society." Political theology, on the other hand,
"is a specifically theological program concerned to place questions
of the political order in more universal perspectives." Common
religion is anchored in the notion emerging from the struggles of
the sixteenth and seventeenth centuries whereby each political
unit was presumed to have one official religion. In America this
claim to formal establishment of one religious group or another
lasted only into the early nineteenth century, but the informal assumption remained that there should be a religion common to the
society. Wilson's point is that we have had such a common religion until quite recently, and that the possibility of either a civil
religion or a political theology rests on the prior reality of common religion. He also argues that it was this common religion
which was the real binding ingredient of American society, rather
than either civil religion or political theology as such.

Wilson notes that American culture became "self-consciously
and ubiquitously Protestant" as set forth in Martin Marty's volume on *Righteous Empire* and Robert Handy's book *A Christian
America*. Wilson is not concerned to establish that point since he
regards the evidence as overwhelming. He is interested, rather, in
the extent to which observers concerned with American society
simply took that point for granted, and he refers to three of them:
Justice Joseph Story in his *Commentaries on the Constitution*; Philip
Schaff in his essay on "Church and State in the United States";
and James Bryce, the British student of *The American Commonwealth*. Wilson then turns to a second stage in which Protestantism was no longer the common religion. The common religion was "the Judeo-Christian tradition" as articulated especially
in Will Herberg's study of *Protestant-Catholic-Jew*, published some
thirty years ago. Herberg argued that in America the same people
were both increasingly religious and pervasively secular. Herberg

spoke of "the American way of life" as a celebration of American values, primarily consumption. But he insisted that an amalgam of Protestantism, Catholicism, and Judaism melded together to provide a common religion for this American way.

John Wilson is critical of much of Herberg's analysis, but his primary point is that "it is difficult to maintain that there is now a recognizable spiritual ethos in the culture that is the common religion of this society in anything like the way Protestantism, Catholicism, and Judaism in their presumed commonality were in the immediate postwar era." He argues that we may now have a departure from a very long-standing tradition in America. Wilson is bemused about its causes. America continues to be religious, in spite of being secular. The problem is that a common religion seems to have disappeared. Wilson turns to Dean M. Kelley's study of *Why Conservative Churches are Growing* and notes that this growth of conservative, demanding versions of religious life has characterized the last several decades of church life in the Protestant communities. The pattern of Jewish development has been toward increasing recovery of Jewish practices and beliefs and away from the general acculturation which Herberg saw. And Wilson notes Martin Marty's pleas for *The Public Church* in the hope that responsible Roman Catholics, sensitive evangelicals, and ecumenical Protestants may yet make common cause. Wilson regards this as a minimalist view of the significance of religion for common American life — all that remains of the old common religion. He suspects that this is, indeed, the end of an era in American life, and that the discussion of both civil religion and political theology must now take an entirely new turn because both were rooted in a common religion which now no longer exists.

My own contribution on civil religion as a home-making common bond is a philosophical counterbalance to Jürgen Moltmann's resolutely theological position. I am not interested in the academic arguments about whether civil religion is really a religion or not. My essay is an exploration of what we need to have in order to feel at home in a world that is initially alien to us. My thesis is that civil religion — as vague and visceral loyalty, rather than as the civic institution Neuhaus argues about — provides a binding ingredient which is necessary for people to be at home in a pluralistic, democratic society. We all have some touch with a traditional community, where the bonds are the natural associations of blood, region, language, caste/class, or religion. And we are all now thrown into a new social and political conglomerate where all that is stripped away, and we are expected to live by a creed instead of a culture. I make a distinction between traditional cultures, where the idea of the community is dominant, and modern cultures, where the idea of the individual is dominant.

I have engaged Moltmann indirectly on a theological issue, and that is whether or not we can say that God works in our history. I side with him initially in my critique of positive programists from the Moral Majority to the New Left, but Moltmann is not specific enough, and I agree with Bellah and especially Neuhaus that we should not claim religious realities we are not prepared to specify. If we believe that God works in history then we should be prepared to say why and how, in spite of all the dangers involved in such affirmations. I gingerly make the assertion that democracy is evidence of God's work among us. While I agree with Bellah that Neuhaus's test of orthodoxy for the critical patriot is too constraining, I think the burden of proof is on anyone who is against democracy to argue that a present, viable, and operative system of government is more closely attuned to the kind of political organization Christians can support. This is to say that democracy represents not the best of all possible political worlds but only the best of all presently actual ones.

My view is a variation on a theme by Carl Friedrich and Ernest Hocking. From Friedrich I learned the distinction between creedal nations (he uses the United States and the Soviet Union as examples) and cultural nations; and from Ernest Hocking I learned the significance of a binding ingredient for what he called *The Coming World Civilization*. We Americans are a creedal nation, held together not only or primarily by ties of economic interdependence, common history, or even what John Wilson calls common religion, but by a common sense of who we are and what we are to do. This is a vague notion, regularly distorted in the telling of it, and not readily available to sociological analysis. It is symbolized by the prestige which America has for its citizens and the fact that we are so troubled when we are not clear about our national purpose.

The significance of the American experience is that it is one of the early test cases for what is now happening even more dramatically in India, China, Africa, and Latin America. Conglomerates of traditional folk are increasingly being organized into modern nation-states, seeking to indigenize themselves through identification with a new and wider community. I do not say that America is a model for the world's future. We are too rich for that. I suspect that India or China will be the dominant model for future global nation building. But American civil religion is still the most carefully studied, and probably the most vivid, example of the way this necessary binding ingredient actually works to bring disparate folk together in a potentially alienating conglomerate where they might well have been lost.

Our final section is concerned with the practice of political theology, and we begin with Johann Metz's essay on the structure of political theology which he proposes as a paradigm for all theological reflection. He takes the notions of paradigm and paradigm shift from Thomas Kuhn's theories of science, which have also been adapted to theological interpretation by his Roman Catholic colleague Hans Küng. The criteria for this new paradigm include the capacity for perceiving crises which stem from theology's intimate contact with historical events; a capacity for reduction/concentration in which dogmatic issues are reduced to life issues and a hermeneutic of crisis or danger refines theology to its root concepts; and a capacity for recovering suppressed elements in the tradition, relating them to the actual historic life of the ecumenical church.

Within contemporary Roman Catholic theology Metz finds three competing paradigms: neo-Scholastic, transcendental-idealist, and post-idealist. He identifies his own political theology, which is also a theology of liberation, as an emerging post-idealist view. He notes that the neo-Scholastic model is still the dominant one in Roman Catholicism, although he regards it as defensive and nonproductive, in spite of its popularity in the church's present neoconservative mood. The transcendental-idealist paradigm seems to him more creative, involving a productive confrontation of theology with modernity. The major figure in this movement is Karl Rahner, and the influence of this paradigm in the life of the Roman Catholic church can be seen in those social and ecclesial changes which have resulted from Vatican II. Post-idealist theology has been called forth by three crises: the Marxist challenge, the Auschwitz challenge, and the Third World challenge.

The Marxist challenge is initially epistemological. Marx argued that knowledge is bound by interest. Post-idealist theology has tried to face this assumption, recognizing that the political implications of theology are now inescapable. Like Moltmann, Metz rejects Carl Schmitt's view that politics represents the totality of life. He shares with Moltmann the view that theology has been rightly suspect because of its failure to engage the political realities of its historic context. Like Moltmann he is also wary of a civil religion as a means whereby politically enlightened societies seek to legitimize and stabilize themselves. Political theology of the post-idealist type criticizes this politicization of religion in two ways: first because the myth of legitimation makes religion suspend its truth claim; and second because its theology then becomes the theology of a political religion. For the new political theology, as for Marxism, the world is a historical project, human beings are the agents of their history, and God is specifically the Lord of this historical situation. The new political theology contradicts the Marxist anthropology, however, by saying that guilt is not derivative from social context but an authentic phenomenon within the historical process of liberation.

The Auschwitz challenge represents not only a crisis of modernity but a crisis of Christian theology. It directs theology to those histories of suffering which cannot be rationalized in any idealistic theologies of evil but can only be remembered with practical intention. Here Metz is close to Peukert and his sense of the antinomy within Habermas's philosophy of communication. Critical to Metz's political theology is the *memoria passionis*, the memory of suffering. However, Metz does not directly answer McCarthy's challenge that political theologians have not yet shown that the idea of a saving God is more coherent than the acceptance of a tragic history.

His concern for liberation brings Metz finally to the Third World challenge, wherein the church finds itself in transition from a cultural Eurocentrism to a polycentric universal church. He sees this historically as a major event in the present epoch of the church's life. Following Rahner he divides theological history into three periods: the foundational epoch of Judeo-Christianity; a long epoch of Hellenistic influence on European culture; and the current epoch of worldwide cultural polycentrism. He stresses the guilt which European theology must confront, as well as its responsibility for the world's poor, and he calls for a rejection of the bourgeois religion which has characterized much of the church's history.

Matthew Lamb is a student of Metz and an American interpreter of European political theology. He turns to the issue of domination which has been critical for political theology, since liberation is always from some sort of domination. He notes that Metz's first articulation of a political theology came at the same time that Robert Bellah, in America, was beginning to explore civil religion. Lamb is somewhat more appreciative of civil religion than either Metz or Moltmann, arguing that both civil religion and political theology can be either liberating or repressive. He approaches the dialectic between civil religion and political theology as domination versus liberation and argues that there is this same dialectic within each, as well as between them. For Lamb, as for other political theologians, the intelligibility of history is now to be found only in solidarity with the victims. He argues that both civil religion and political theology can help move history away from the impending atomic holocaust through the recovery of subversive memories and the practice of reason as communicative action, rather than by the exercise of domination by one group over another. Here he sounds themes from Metz and Peukert and makes the same connection with Habermas's theory which McCarthy outlined in analyzing Peukert's political theology. On this issue he quotes McCarthy's view that the discontents of modernity are grounded not in rationalization as such but in the failure of modernity to institutionalize and balance the different dimensions of reason. Whereas Metz and Moltmann focus on specifically theological issues, Lamb is also concerned for the renewal of contemporary philosophy. He notes five major pathologies in contemporary culture: sexism, racism, economic oppression or classism, environmental pollution, and militarism. Political and liberation theologies seek a social transformation of these pathologies in order to avert the mounting probabilities of ecological and/or nuclear devastation.

Margaret Miles's essay is a study in historical theology which illuminates present issues of patriarchalism in the life of the church.

Metz, Lamb, Peukert, and others have spoken of the need to recover subversive memory in the life of the church and to identify
with the victims of history. Miles's essay is a case study in such
a recovery. The context is the concern for martyrdom and the activity of the Holy Spirit within North African Christianity during
the two-hundred-year period after the establishment of the church.
The significance of these two issues for Miles's research is that the
relevant documents give evidence of women's participation in both
these aspects of church life. The Holy Spirit was thought of as providing both the training and the discipline which made martyrdom possible. Initially there was a sense of equality among men
and women, and martyrs were known to have a great deal of ecclesiastical and personal power. Miles quotes Tertullian, however,
in opposition to the leadership roles of women and through these
writings discovers conflict over gender in the churches.

One of these conflicts concerned dress. To what extent should
Christians distinguish themselves from the culture around them?
Tertullian wrote two books on women's dress which Miles suggests
were probably not representative of a majority opinion in the Carthaginian Christian community but which nevertheless give considerable information about the attitudes and practices prevalent
in the life of the church regarding the participation of women.
Some women were apparently arguing that women's dress need
not be distinguishingly drab and that the redemption of the non-
Christian community ought properly to take place as a "salt of
the earth" model of renewal from within secular society. Tertullian, on the other hand, proposed a Christian separatism. There
is also evidence that many Christian women were relieved of the
concern for reputation and male approval now that "God is the
inspector of the heart." From Tertullian's point of view, however,
the natural beauty of women was to be feared.

Even after the death of Tertullian the "woman question" remained unresolved in North Africa. Miles argues that it was in the
process of resolution through the establishment of patriarchal order.
By the beginning of the fifth century Augustine was responding
to the sack of Rome by arguing that there is a hierarchy of values
and relations, centered in four hierarchical pairs: spirit and flesh,
husband and wife, Christ and the church, ruler and people. Augustine noted that "the former cares for the latter in each case,

and the latter waits upon the former. All are good when among them, some, excellently as superiors, and others, fittingly as subjects, preserve the beauty of order." Miles argues that this Augustinian formula became a major influence in Western Christian society.

Miles concludes by noting the importance of reinterpreting these early struggles over the role of women in the church. In the light of our present peril she notes the need within the church for the service and talents of all Christians equally. "Recognizing and acknowledging the extent to which the political essence of Christianity has been patriarchal order, we must reappropriate the struggle, begun so long ago, for gender equality and we must give this struggle a different outcome in our perilous world."

James Cone's social and political focus is on oppressive racism. His is a political theology of the black church and the aspirations of black people. His essay deals with two warring ideals in black religion, its African elements and its Christian ones. Black religion is not identifiable with the Christian theology of white Americans any more than it is identifiable with the traditional beliefs of African religion. "It is both — but reinterpreted for and adapted to the life situation of black people's struggle for justice in a nation whose social, political, and economic structures are dominated by a white racist ideology." Cone is concerned with common ground in American life, but he seeks to recover the authentic history of black religious thought in America, so that black religion can take its rightful place on that common ground without fear of losing its own distinctive identity. He notes that black theology has been challenged by other liberation theologies to address issues of sexism and classism and has challenged them in turn to face racism. He argues that this confrontation has deepened and reinforced theologies of liberation and helped bring about a theological revolution comparable to those inspired by Luther in the sixteenth century, Schleiermacher in the nineteenth, and Barth in the twentieth.

The major part of his paper is devoted to a history of black theology in America. (We have included his extensive footnotes, in contrast to our common practice, since many readers will find this an important resource.) He begins with the roots of black thought in the history of slavery and outlines a theology of that experience with generous quotations from the poetry of black spirituals. He turns then to the civil rights movement and the influence of Martin Luther King, Jr. This movement stood over against the accommodation philosophy of black leaders like Booker T. Washington, although Cone credits Washington with creating the conditions which gave rise to the civil rights movement.

The early years of the civil rights movement were influenced by Adam Clayton Powell and his son, Adam, Jr., whose *Marching Blacks* accused white churches of distorting the message of Christianity, which is equality and brotherhood. He notes also the influence of Benjamin Mays and of Howard Thurman, who was Dean of Marsh Chapel at Boston University during Martin Luther King, Jr.'s student days there. King was, of course, the most influential single figure in the contemporary struggle for civil rights by black people, and Cone stresses the influence of the black church on his basic theology. While King was a sophisticated student of the history of European white theology, "he did not arrive at his convictions about God by reading white theologians. On the contrary, he derived his religious beliefs from his acceptance of black faith and his application of it to the civil rights struggle." Cone concludes with reflections on black religious thought, black power, and black theology. Here he makes common cause with Metz especially in insisting that black theology is a theology of praxis. He differs from Metz and others in his specific focus on the content of black religious experience as the basis for his understanding of liberation.

Our concluding essay is by John Cobb on the possibility of a Christian economics. He outlines general principles of interpretation where it seems to him that Christian theology and economic theory meet. His paper is not a defense of either socialism or capitalism. It is, rather, a dialectical examination of both, and the proposal that the legitimate Christian concern for economic theory should move beyond both socialism and capitalism. Cobb thus identifies himself with political theologians such as Moltmann and Metz, and he states his indebtedness to feminist theology as well as black theology and Latin American liberation theology for renewing his awareness that the salvation which Christians seek is, in Dorothee Sölle's words, the indivisible salvation of the whole world. In calling political theologians to concern for economics Cobb strikes a note which Robert Bellah urged as a crucial issue for public theology and philosophy.

Cobb begins with an appreciation of current forms of political theology but also notes appreciatively the criticism which neoconservative writers such as Michael Novak and Peter Berger have made of a political theology which maintains its distance from policy formation. For Cobb this is a crucial element in any theological emphasis on praxis. Novak argues that a political economy concerned for the poor should be productive at the same time that it defends the freedom of individuals. For Novak this points to a capitalist political economy. Cobb, for his part, sorts out what seem to him to be both strengths and weaknesses in capitalist and socialist understandings of political economy.

Cobb proposes five assumptions for Christian economic theory. Of special interest is his comparison of socialist and capitalist anthropologies. He finds capitalist thinking grounded in a view of human nature that corresponds to the Christian understanding of sin. This he finds to be a strength of the capitalist position. However, it turns out that when this natural human greed is recognized and acted upon, the result is the welfare of all. "Universal selfishness turns out to be the principle of salvation!" Socialist theory is also criticized, however, in its assumption that human self-centeredness is the product of certain social structures, and that this problem will also be eliminated when the social structures are changed. For socialism, sin is the result of social evil, not its source.

Cobb's paper is a call for new theories and a suggestion of some of the criteria which should be considered. He is quick to note that he has not presented an economic theory, and he calls for help from various disciplines in shaping a point of view. He notes that economists should not try to pursue this task alone. Here Cobb strikes a note that Neuhaus, Bellah, and others have already sounded concerning the specialization of academic disciplines and the resulting difficulty in shaping a genuinely public theology and philosophy. Like most of our authors Cobb is in sympathy with the principles which Lamb and McCarthy refer to from Habermas's theory of communication and communicative action. "The kind of thinking that is needed cannot be done without the full cooperation of economists, but it requires also political theorists, sociologists, anthropologists, ecologists, and representatives of many other disciplines."

Our authors remain divided on the matter of civil religion, but they are of a mind in regard to political theology. If Matthew Lamb is right the two are interrelated. John Wilson warns that without a common religion in America both civil religion and political theology may be jeopardized. Lamb seems to imply that without civil religion, in America at least, the viability of political theologies may be limited. I would note only that there can be neither public theology nor public philosophy without common ground. This book is a celebration of that common ground and an expression of the current commitment of Christian thought to engagement with those historical issues which concern the entire human family.

PART I

Philosophy, Theology, and Science: Foundations of a Common Ground

1

Philosophical Foundations of Political Theology: Kant, Peukert, and the Frankfurt School

THOMAS A. McCARTHY

IN ANSWERING THE THIRD of his three basic questions of philosophy—For what may I hope?—Kant gave a historically important twist to the philosophical foundations of religious belief. He made the answer to that question depend directly on the answer to the second of his basic questions—What ought I to do?—and only indirectly on the answer to the first—What can I know? In contradistinction to the mainstream of traditional philosophical theology, Kant regarded speculative proofs of the freedom of the will, the immortality of the soul, and the existence of God as one and all spurious. The attempt to establish such propositions on theoretical, that is, cosmological-metaphysical, grounds was hopeless, for knowledge of these things lay beyond the bounds of theoretical reason, as he established to his satisfaction in the *Critique of Pure Reason*. At the same time, these limits ensured that speculative disproofs of such propositions were ruled out of court as well. In fact, through confining our knowledge to the phenomenal realm, the realm of appearances, while insisting on the necessity of thinking—not knowing—a noumenal realm, a realm of things-in-themselves, Kant's *Critique of Pure Reason* had left open a space that might be occupied by other means. As you know, he filled this space in the Second Critique, by means not of theoretical but of practical reason. There Kant presents us with moral arguments for religious belief to replace the now disqualified cosmological and ontological arguments. They provide a justification for a moral faith in a moral religion, which he distinguished sharply and consistently from any metaphysically or historically based faith. In contrast to speculative theology, which Kant regarded as shot through with error and confusion, a moral theology he thought to be quite possible. To put it in a nutshell: for him, to adopt the religious attitude was to regard moral duties as if they were divine commands.

I am not concerned here with the thorny exegetical debates about just how to interpret Kant's idea of a moral religion and the arguments he presents on its behalf. I want to give only a brief account of these arguments as a prelude to my principal topic, which can be summarized as follows: a number of contemporary political theologians have approached the tasks of fundamental theology in a way reminiscent of Kant; that is, they have discussed the philosophical foundations of religious belief from the point of view of practical rather than theoretical reason, and have conceptualized its essential content from the same point of view. There is, to be sure, one very important difference from Kant: whereas he starts from the experience and practice of individual morality, they start from the experience and practice of social-political morality. In one case we get a moral theology; in the other, a political theology. Yet the structure of at least some of the central philosophical arguments exhibits striking similarities to that of Kant. What I would like to do here is to examine one such argument, the original of which is to be found in Kant's discussion of the postulates of pure practical reason in the Dialectic of the Second Critique. Of the several variations on this theme in contemporary political theology, I shall consider that developed by Helmut Peukert in *Science, Action, and Fundamental Theology*,[1] for it is one of the more philosophically self-conscious versions of the argument for what might be called a political faith in God. My remarks will fall into three parts: first, an account of the general structure of Kant's postulate arguments; second, a brief look at the general perspective of political theology for the purpose of comprehending why and how this sort of argument might prove attractive to it;

third, a reconstruction and assessment of Peukert's version of the argument.

I

First, a rough summary: Kant's postulate arguments seek to establish that morality makes no sense unless we postulate the immortality of the soul and the existence of God. The relation of freedom to morality is somewhat different, for it is a direct presupposition of moral agency. By comparison, the arguments for God and immortality are indirect. Their form is something like the following: we are commanded by the moral law to pursue certain ends which would be impossible to achieve if God did not exist and the soul were not immortal. The inherent tension between our rational-moral duties and aspirations, on the one hand, and our finite limitations, on the other, would lead to moral despair without God and immortality. Thus it is a practical necessity that we postulate them; not to do so would be to commit moral suicide. Moral faith is thus a practically rational response by finite rational beings to their inability to fulfill the moral demands of their nature on their own. Its mode of conviction is not logical but moral certainty. Kant warns us to say not even "*It is* certain that there is a God, etc.," but only "*I am* morally certain, etc."[2] This faith is not, however, irrational. The postulate arguments justify a certain religious conviction as, in Kant's terms, "the most reasonable opinion for us men" to hold.[3] Allen Wood sums up their status as follows: "On the basis of practical considerations holding for each man personally as a moral agent, Kant proposes to justify and even rationally to require of each man the personal conviction that there exist a God and a future life."[4] Let us turn now briefly to the argument for the existence of God.[5]

Kant locates the moral worth of an action in its intention and not in its results. Since one of the distinguishing marks of rationality is universality, I act rationally, and hence morally, only if the maxim of my action exhibits that property. As Kant puts it: I only have to ask myself the single question whether I could will that my maxim become a universal law, governing not merely this particular action of mine, but the action of anyone in similar circumstances. In other words, as moral judgments must — in order to be universal — hold without distinction of persons, an action can be morally right for me only if it would be right for anyone in my situation. The moral law is impartial. Accordingly, Kant distinguishes the concern of morality not only from the egoistic pursuit of narrow self-interest but also from the prudential consideration of overall happiness or well-being. Questions of duty are strictly separated from questions of happiness, whether in the short run or the long run, whether for an individual or for a community.

On the other hand, we are finite creatures of need, who naturally seek happiness. What Kant calls the antinomy of pure practical reason has its roots in this situation: we are, as it were, inhabitants of two worlds at once, rational beings who are commanded to act universally, without regard to our own self-interest, and natural beings who are urged by nature to seek happiness, the fulfillment of our own purposes. For such beings, the highest good is neither virtue by itself nor happiness by itself; it consists rather in a proper combination of the two: happiness conditioned by or in proportion to virtue, the happiness we morally deserve. This, writes Kant, would be the only reasonable state of affairs:

> Virtue (is not) the entire and perfect good as the object of the faculty of desire of rational finite beings. For this, happiness is also required, and indeed not merely in the partial eyes of a person who makes himself his end but even in the judgment of an impartial reason, which impartially regards persons in the world as ends-in-themselves. For to be in need of happiness and also worthy of it and yet not partake of it could not be in accordance with the complete volition of an omnipotent rational being. . . .[6]

And yet, as we know only too well, this is the way things are in this vale of tears we inhabit. Because nature and morality are distinct orders, there is no necessary connection, let alone just proportion, between moral virtue and earthly happiness. As rational beings we are commanded to do our moral duty, regardless of whether it conflicts with our own happiness or that of others; on the other hand, as rational beings we could not choose a state of affairs in which those in need of happiness and deserving of it fail to achieve it. Thus our object as rational beings must be a combination in which happiness is proportioned to virtue. This Kant calls the highest good. We are then commanded by reason to pursue the highest good — and yet it is not in our power to achieve it, for happiness is a matter not merely of the intention of the will but of natural causes and effects. Hence, even the most meticulous observance of the moral law cannot be expected to produce happiness. So we have a problem, which Kant puts this way:

> Since, now, the furthering of the highest good . . . is an a priori necessary object of our will and is inseparably related to the moral law . . . if the highest good is impossible . . . then the moral law which commands that it be furthered must be fantastic, directed to empty, imaginary ends, and consequently inherently false.[7]

The only way to avoid moral despair — which we have a moral duty to avoid — is to assume the possibility of the highest good. As it is beyond the power of finite moral beings to bend nature to the demands of morality, we have to postulate the existence of an infinite moral being who has the power to produce the necessary harmony between the two orders. In Kant's words:

> Now it is our duty to promote the highest good; and it is not merely our privilege but a necessity connected with duty to presuppose the possibility of this highest good. This presupposition is made only under the condition of the existence of God. . . . Therefore, it is morally necessary to assume the existence of God. It is well to notice here that this moral necessity is subjective, i.e., a need, and not objective, i.e., duty itself . . . as a practical need it can be called *faith*, and even pure *rational faith*, because pure reason alone is the source from which it springs.[8]

So here we have it: there is a pure practical need to assume the existence of God, for without it the moral life to which we are called as rational beings is threatened by moral despair in the face of nature's indifference.

II

The central objection to Kant's argument was formulated already in his lifetime by a certain Thomas Wizenmann, who disputed, simply, the right to argue from a need to the objective reality of what meets that need.[9] Kant tried to get around this objection by stressing the difference between particular, natural needs and a need of pure practical reason as such. But we do not have to determine the pros and cons of this debate, since the political theologians with whom we are concerned do not hold to these Kantian dualisms — in this sense they are post-Hegelians. In fact, if one were to classify them philosophically, they are probably closest to the left-Hegelians. And this, in a curious way, brings them back to Kant in one respect: the primacy of practical over theoretical reason. Just as Marx castigated the philosophers for trying to understand the world rather than to change it, political theologians typically give short shrift to traditional speculative theology. They are after a theology of the world which engages and transforms its orders rather than contemplating or withdrawing from them, a theology done politically, a theology articulated in terms of political practice. Let me recall briefly a few of the general features of this reorientation.[10]

1. It involves a new relationship to the Old Testament and a rehabilitation within Christian theology of the Jewish sense for history and narrative as against the long-dominant Hellenistic tendencies to cosmologies and logocentrism; and it involves a reading of revelation as a history of God's promises, a past which announces a future that calls for a present practice.

2. As this future is essentially open, it cannot be captured in the categories of a philosophy of history or a theology of universal history. In fact it escapes the grasp of pure theory altogether; for what the future will hold is essentially dependent on our practice in the present. Correspondingly, the task of a political theology is not merely to interpret the world but to change it. It must become a type of practical and critical thinking that informs and is informed by practice. The traditional primacy of doctrinal theory thus gives way to a primacy of practice, or at least to a constant mediation of theory and practice.

3. The sort of patience in question is indicated by the gospel of love, by its fundamental identification with the poor and the oppressed of this world. As Jürgen Moltmann has put it, the Bible is a revolutionary and subversive book; the hope it holds out is for the hopeless, the weak, the downtrodden, the destitute and de-

prived. We must, he says in the words of Theodor Adorno, learn to see the "messianic light" that shines from the eyes of the victim onto the "faults and fissures" of our own situation.[11] Thus political theology is not a sacralizing legitimation of the status quo, a domesticated civil religion, but a theology of emancipation and liberation.

4. As this liberation is essentially social in nature, political theology reverses the traditional individualism of Christian eschatological symbolism. It attempts to recover the social and political meanings of such symbols as covenant, kingdom, peace, reconciliation. In a world in which the conditions of individual existence and the character of interpersonal relations are largely determined by legal, political, and economic structures, the religious practice of alleviating human misery can be effective only by addressing the social causes of that misery, that is, by becoming politically engaged. For political theologians, the meaning and validity of religious faith proves itself not through doctrinal assertion but through the social practice of uplifting the downtrodden and liberating the oppressed.[12]

Even from this brief sketch it is not difficult to see the general affinity of political theology to the Hegelian-Marxist tradition of social thought. What I am especially interested in, however, is a more specific affinity to Kant's moral view of religion. To put the matter crudely, the bridge from a usually atheistic — or at least a-theistic — Marxism to a theology of the world is often framed in terms reminiscent of Kant's postulate arguments: roughly, without religious faith we cannot avoid moral-political despair; solidarity with the victims of history makes sense only on the assumption of a just God who reconciles virtue and happiness.

There are numerous versions of this argument, some looser and some stricter. I want to focus here on one of the more clearly spelled out versions, that advanced by Helmut Peukert in chapter 10 of his *Science, Action, and Fundamental Theology*. There he attempts to apply this type of argument to an influential stream of Western Marxism, namely, the critical social theory of the Frankfurt School. His point of departure is a discussion between Max Horkheimer and Walter Benjamin, which began with an exchange of letters and continued, implicitly, in their subsequent works.[13] Reacting to Benjamin's idea that the historical materialist cannot regard the past as *abgeschlossen* ("finished, closed, over and done with"), Horkheimer wrote to Benjamin:

> The supposition of an unfinished or unclosed past is idealistic if you don't incorporate a certain closedness into it. Past injustice has happened and is over and done with. Those who were slain were really slain.[14]

And he adds in a published work from the same period:

> What happened to those human beings who have perished cannot be made good in the future. They will never be called forth to be blessed in eternity. Nature and society have done their work on them and the idea of a Last Judgment, which the infinite yearning of the oppressed and the dying has produced, is only a remnant from primitive thought, which denies the negligible role of the human species in natural history and humanizes the universe.[15]

In the same vein he writes elsewhere that

> while the religious thinker is comforted by the thought that our desires [for eternity and for the advent of universal goodness and justice] are fulfilled all the same, the materialist is suffused with the feeling of the limitless abandonment of humanity, which is the only true answer to the hope for the impossible.[16]

Benjamin of course continued to be concerned with the redemption of the past. And to Horkheimer's charge that this was, in the end, theology, he responded that history is not merely a science but a form of remembrance, of empathetic memory (*Eingedenken*), which can transform what is closed, finished, over and done with — for example, past suffering — into something that is open and unfinished. "In empathetic memory," he writes, "we have an experience that prohibits us from conceiving history completely nontheologically, which is not at all to say that we can write history in directly theological concepts."[17] It is clear as well from Benjamin's "Theses on the Philosophy of History" that he resists any approach to universal history that has as its implicit principle empathy with its victors rather than its victims, and which thus becomes incapable of grasping "history as the history of the suffering or passion of the world."[18] He wants instead to develop an approach to history based on an "anamnestic solidarity" with its countless generations of oppressed and downtrodden. Horkheimer acknowledges the roots of this impulse, but regards the approach to history it entails as unjustified:

> The thought that the prayers of those persecuted in their hour of direst need, that the prayers of the innocents who die without comprehending their situation, that the last hopes for a supernatural court of appeals are all to no avail, and that the night in which no human light shines is also devoid of any divine light — this thought is monstrous. Without God, eternal truth has just as little footing as infinite love — indeed they become unthinkable concepts. But is monstrousness ever a cogent argument against the assertion or denial of a state of affairs? Does logic contain a law to the effect that a judgment is false when its consequence is despair?[19]

This last phrase recalls the drift of Kant's postulate arguments; but Horkheimer, like Wizenmann 150 years before him, stoically (or pessimistically) notes that need and despair are not forms of logical validity.

Though this debate serves as a point of departure for Peukert's fundamental-theological reflections on critical social theory, he mounts his central argument in terms of another, later, development in this tradition: Habermas's theory of communicative action. The reasons for his choice are not hard to see: the theory of communicative action is an attempt to reconceptualize the ideas of reason and rationality so that they might serve as foundations for political and social theory.[20] Thus Peukert can plumb the depths of Habermas's notion of practical reason and try to discover in its deep structure a foothold for his reconstituted version of the postulate arguments. Following Kant, he will argue that practical reason, even in the form of communicative rationality, requires a background of hope if it is to make moral-political sense. And this background of hope cannot simply be projected into the future, as it is in the Marxist tradition. A just society that might be established by human beings themselves in the indefinite future is no substitute, he will argue, for a reconciliation with the past grounded in religious belief. In the political sphere, as in the moral sphere, the answer to the question, For what may I hope? has to be a religious answer.

There is no need to go into Habermas's theory of communicative rationality in any great detail to catch the point of Peukert's argument. Speaking generally, the theory shifts the center of gravity of the concept of reason from the Cartesian point of subjectivity to communicative forms of intersubjectivity.[21] Kant, who still operated within the horizon of individual consciousness, could capture the universality of reason only in terms of the structures of transcendental subjectivity. For Habermas, universality takes the form of communicatively achieved agreement with others concerning disputed validity claims. Claims to the truth of a statement or the rightness of an action can be contested and criticized, defended and revised. There are any number of ways of settling disputed claims — for example, appeals to authority, to tradition, or to brute force. One way, the giving of reasons for and against, has traditionally been regarded as fundamental to the idea of rationality. And it is precisely to the experience of achieving mutual understanding in discussion which is free from coercion that Habermas looks in developing his idea of communicative reason. The key to this type of agreement is the possibility of using reason and grounds — the unforced force of the better argument — to gain recognition for contested validity claims.

Habermas is by no means the first to attempt to desubjectivize Kant's notion of reason while retaining the regulative idea of strict universality. In the heyday of American philosophy this line of thought reached a high point: Peirce tied truth to agreement in the unlimited, that is, potentially infinite, "community of investigators"; Royce, to the "community of interpretation" of all human beings; Mead, to the "community of universal discourse." The underlying idea is simple: *true* means true for everyone; *right* means right for everyone. Truth and rightness, insofar as they are dealt with on a rational basis, entail the idea of universal agreement.

Habermas's idea of a communicative ethics can be viewed as a corresponding revision of Kantian ethics. From this perspective, his discourse model represents a procedural reinterpretation of Kant's categorical imperative. Rather than ascribing as valid to all others any maxim that I can will to be a universal law, I must submit my maxim to all others for purposes of discursively testing its claim to universality. The emphasis shifts from what each can will without contradiction to be a general law, to what all can will in agreement to be a universal norm. A rational will is not something that can be secured and certified *privatim*; it is inextricably bound to communication processes in which a common will is both discovered and formed.

For Kant the autonomy of the will requires the exclusion of all "pathological" interests from the choice of maxims of action. If the particular ends of action (which can be summed up as happiness) are not excluded from its determining grounds, its maxim will be *ipso facto* unsuitable for universal legislation; for if a maxim can be universal, valid for all rational beings, then it must be independent of my particular inclinations. This constellation alters perceptibly when we shift to Habermas's intersubjective framework. The aim of practical discourse is to come to a consensus about which interests are generalizable. Individual wants, needs, desires, interests need not — indeed cannot — be excluded, for it is precisely concerning them that agreement is sought; they belong to the content of practical discourse. What that content is, concretely, depends of course on the historical conditions and potentials of social existence at a given time and place.

III

This abandonment of the Cartesian paradigm in ethics, in favor of a proceduralism which does not set reason against inclination in the way that Kant did, clearly narrows the gap between justice and happiness — happiness now belongs to the content of justice. It might seem, then, that we have no foothold here for renewing Kant's postulate arguments in relation to communicative ethics. Peukert thinks otherwise. Even if we put to one side for the moment the pain and suffering, loneliness and guilt, sickness and death that seem to be inevitably associated with the contingencies of human life in any society, there is, he argues, an antinomy built into the deep structure of communicative practical reason, an antinomy that points irresistibly to a background of hope that must be postulated if our moral-practical lives are to make sense. He locates the antinomy in the tension between the universalism of communicative ethics and "the annihilation of the innocent other" in history. The ideal of communicative rationality entails that discussions in which validity claims are decided upon cannot be arbitrarily restricted. It implies a community of discourse that is in principle unlimited. If, now, from the standpoint of some anticipated future state of perfect justice, we submit human history to discursive examination, the results are unsettling. Peukert puts the problem of any hypothetical, blessed generation in this future as follows:

> It has achieved the end state of happiness; its members can live with one another in perfect solidarity. But how is their relation to previous generations to be determined? They must live with the consciousness that they owe everything to the oppressed, the downtrodden, the victims of the whole historical process of human emancipation. This generation has inherited everything from past generations and lives on what *they* paid for. . . . The happiness of the living consists in the expropriation of the dead. Is happiness at all conceivable under these presuppositions? Is it not a presupposition of their happiness that the unhappiness of those who went before them be simply forgotten? Is amnesia, the utter loss of historical memory, the presupposition for their happy consciousness? But then is not the life of these future human beings inhuman? . . . How can one hold on to the memory of the conclusive, irretrievable loss of the victims of history — to whom one owes one's entire happiness — and still be happy? . . . The dream of "perfect justice" can, then, be only a nightmare. . . . Here we reach the extreme point of despair and, if despair does not kill, the point of inconsolable grief.[22]

We have come back to the exchange between Benjamin and Horkheimer; but now there is a third voice, more univocally religious than Benjamin's. And it speaks in terms reminiscent of Kant. Without a rational faith in God and immortality to supply a background of hope to practical reason, moral-political practice in solidarity with the victims of history makes no sense; it can only lead to despair. How convincing is this argument? If it is to succeed, Peukert will have to deal with Horkheimer's version of

Wizenmann's objection to Kant: the monstrousness of a state of affairs is no argument against its obtaining; there is no law of logic which says that a judgment that leads to despair is false. Kant tried to deal with the original objection — that need cannot establish existence — in terms of a strict distinction between the pure needs of reason and the empirical needs of nature. This avenue is not open to Peukert, since the theory of communicative rationality makes no such strict separation. How then can he defend himself against Horkheimer's Schopenhauerian pessimism? He does not attempt to do so in any detail, but rests content, more or less, with having exhibited the worm at the heart of the apple of progress, and with developing its theological implications. But we can imagine how the argument might proceed from here.

For one thing, Peukert might resist Horkheimer's framing of the question in terms of the laws of logic. Recall that for Kant the dialectic that gave rise to the postulates was a dialectic of practical reason. And the postulates themselves were not claims to knowledge but justifications of faith. In the *Critique of Judgment*, published two years after the *Critique of Practical Reason*, he puts the matter thus:[23] the moral law unconditionally prescribes to rational beings such as we a final end which we ourselves are incapable of attaining, indeed which — in light of the moral indifference of nature and the self-interestedness of human beings[24] — we must despair of attaining by our own efforts. To be rationally called to strive for an end which we rationally take to be impossible of realization places us in a dialectical perplexity from which we can escape only by assuming the possibility of the *summum bonum* and the reality of the conditions of its possibility. Thus there is a "pure moral ground" for postulating a moral world cause. This is not an "objectively valid proof" of God's existence, but a "subjective argument sufficient for moral beings."[25] It establishes not the "objective theoretical reality" of a moral world order but its "subjective practical reality."[26] As Allen Wood puts it, pure rational faith is not primarily an assent to certain speculative propositions, but a "belief about the situation of moral action," an "outlook" or "attitude," in virtue of which we may continue rationally to pursue a goal marked out for us by reason: the establishment of a just world order.[27] If all efforts toward this goal are doomed to failure, then the rationality of moral action

comes into question. Moral faith, as a trust in God to supply our
deficiencies if we do all that is in our power, is then a condition
of our continuing to act as rational moral beings. Thus it is not
an irrational leap in the sense of Pascal or Kierkegaard but a rationally justified hope that is required if we are not to abandon
rationality. In Kant's own terms: "We have to assume (God's) existence in order merely to furnish practical reality to a purpose
which pure reason . . . enjoins us a priori to bring about with all
our powers."[28] This type of proof yields not theoretical knowledge
but "a conviction adequate from a purely practical point of view."[29]
God, as a *res fidei*, has objective reality for us only "in a practical reference."[30] The postulate argument "proves the Being of God
as a thing of faith for the practical pure reason."[31]

Though Peukert cannot appeal to the Kantian notion of pure
practical reason, his argument bears unmistakable affinities to the
postulate argument. Practical reason, conceived now as communicative rationality, also has an inherent universal telos, for it refers moral-practical questions to agreement within a potentially
unlimited community of discourse. In this sense, it remains a
command of reason to pursue the goals of universal freedom, justice, and happiness. But history has not cooperated in this pursuit; it has been, as Hegel put it, a slaughter bench. Consequently,
no matter what happens in the future, the highest good of universal peace is unattainable, for the countless victims of history
can never participate in it. They are dead and gone. Their suffering is irredeemable. Thus the command of practical reason to seek
perfect justice must be, to use Kant's terms, "fantastic," "directed
to imaginary ends," or, in Horkheimer's words, "a nightmare."
Communicative action in universal solidarity with the innocent
victims of history makes sense only if this end is attainable, and
it is attainable only on the assumption of a Lord of History who
will somehow redeem past suffering. Peukert puts it this way: political theology articulates "the experience of a definite reality
corresponding to a certain way of acting," a reality that is asserted,
assumed, anticipated in this way of acting.[32] On his reading the
Judeo-Christian tradition is concerned precisely with the reality
experienced and disclosed in such limit situations of communicative action, and with modes of communication possible in response
to them.[33] Through faith communicative action anticipates the
salvation of annihilated innocents. Faith then opens up a "possi-

bility of existence"—the possibility of reciprocity and solidarity with the innocent other, of the redemption of his or her suffering —which is definitively closed without it. In the absence of this hope, anamnestic solidarity gives way to amnesiac self-interest. To act in solidarity with history's victims is to "affirm a reality that prevents them from being merely superseded facts of the past";[34] it is "to assert a reality that saves these others from annihilation."[35] This experience and disclosure of a saving reality, which is presupposed by communicative action in universal solidarity, is the point of access to possible discourse about God. It is the starting point for a political theology.

The analogies to Kant are clear: God's reality is said to be a presupposition of sensibly pursuing the dictates of practical reason. To affirm it is not an irrational leap of faith but a rationally justified assumption of the condition of possibility of continuing to act rationally. As an argument, however, this seems to be less than airtight. The antinomy of communicative reason might elicit a number of different "subjective practical" outlooks compatible, or at least not *per se* incompatible, with communicative action in universal solidarity—from Horkheimer's pessimism, through Stoic resignation or existential commitment, to Benjamin's empathetic solidarity or the compassionate solidarity that Habermas models after it.[36] It is difficult to see how these attitudes could be ruled out on intersubjectively valid grounds. Of course, Peukert might argue that it is only with the background of hope supplied by religious faith that the idea of perfect justice makes any sense at all, that the other attitudes are so many different ways of keeping a stiff upper lip—or biting one's lower lip—in the face of the monstrous realities of injustice. But that might be the best we can do, or at least the best that some people can do, while others might embrace the religious option on the strength of just such practical considerations. The point is that the justification of faith in question does not appear to have the force of a "proof"—neither in objective terms nor in terms of a universal subjective need. We are no longer dealing with the absolute dictates of a pure reason; and the practice of striving for universal peace and justice, at least in the future, might reasonably be defended on other, non-religious, grounds—for instance, on the type of grounds that Horkheimer or Habermas offers.

Peukert implicitly acknowledges this when he turns his argument in the end to "the dimension of *experience* indicated in the analysis of the paradox of anamnestic solidarity"[37] and proposes an interpretation of the Judeo-Christian tradition as "concerned with the reality experienced in the fundamental limit experiences of communicative action."[38] Religious experience and religious tradition remain key ingredients in his discussion of faith, which is not then presented as a matter of purely argumentative justification.

Peukert's deliberations do have the merit of reminding us once again that any account of history which does not appeal to religious premises — whether Marxist or not, whether in terms of progress or not — will have to be written as a tragedy. There can be no question of pursuing perfect justice; all that remains now is to combat injustice in the present and to seek to reduce it in the future, and to do so in compassionate solidarity with the victims of the past.

NOTES

1. Helmut Peukert, *Science, Action, and Fundamental Theology*, trans. James Bohman (Cambridge, Mass.: MIT Press, 1984); hereafter cited as SAF.

2. Immanuel Kant, *Critique of Pure Reason*, trans. Norman Kemp Smith (New York: St. Martin Press, 1961), p. 650; cited in Allen Wood, *Kant's Moral Religion* (Ithaca, N.Y.: Cornell University Press, 1970), p. 17. Wood's study will henceforth be cited as KMR.

3. Immanuel Kant, *Critique of Practical Reason*, trans. Lewis White Beck (Indianapolis, Ind.: Bobbs-Merrill Educational Publishing, 1956), p. 147; hereafter cited as CPR.

4. Wood, KMR, p. 17.

5. I shall not be directly concerned with the argument for immortality, which has a rather different structure.

6. Kant, CPR, pp. 114–15.

7. Ibid., p. 118.

8. Ibid., p. 130.

9. Cited in Kant, CPR, p. 149, n. 6.

10. I am thinking here chiefly of the work of Johann Baptist Metz and Jürgen Moltmann. See for instance Johann B. Metz, *Faith in History and Society*, trans. David Smith (New York: Seabury Press, 1980); and Jürgen Moltmann, *Theology of Hope*, trans. James W. Leitch (New York: Harper & Row, 1967).

11. Moltmann, *Theology of Hope*, pp. 290–91. Cf. Jürgen Moltmann, "The Cross and Civil Religion," in *Religion and Political Society*, ed. Jürgen Moltmann (New York: Harper & Row, 1974), pp. 9–47, especially pp. 41ff.

12. This is particularly stressed by Latin American liberation theologians such as Gustavo Gutierrez and Juan Segundo. See Matthew Lamb, *Solidarity with Victims* (New York: Crossroads Press, 1982).

13. Peukert, SAF, pp. 206ff. Peukert builds on earlier treatments by Rüdiger Tiedemann, "Historische Materialismus oder politische Messianismus?" in *Materialien zu Benjamins Thesen "Über den Begriff der Geschichte,"* ed. Peter Bulthaup (Frankfurt: Suhrkamp, 1975), pp. 77–121; and Christian Lenhardt, "Anamnestic Solidarity: The Proletariat and its *Manes,"* *Telos* 25 (1975): 133–53.

14. Max Horkheimer, letter to Walter Benjamin, March 16, 1937.

15. Max Horkheimer, *Kritische Theorie*, 2 vols. (Frankfurt: S. Fischer, 1968), 1: 198.

16. Ibid., p. 372.

17. Walter Benjamin, *Passagen*, cited in Tiedemann, "Historische Materialismus oder politischer Messianismus?" p. 88.

18. Walter Benjamin, *Illuminations*, ed. Hannah Arendt, trans. Harry Zohn (New York: Schocken Books, 1969), pp. 253–64. The phrase quoted appears in Walter Benjamin, *The Origin of German Tragic Drama*, trans. John Osborne (London: New Left Books, 1977), p. 166.

19. Horkheimer, *Kritische Theorie*, 1: 372.

20. See Jürgen Habermas, *The Theory of Communicative Action*, vol. 1, *Reason and the Rationalization of Society*, trans. Thomas A. McCarthy (Boston: Beacon Press, 1984).

21. On what follows see Thomas A. McCarthy, *The Critical Theory of Jürgen Habermas* (Cambridge, Mass.: MIT Press, 1978), pp. 310–33, especially pp. 325ff.

22. Peukert, SAF, pp. 209–10.

23. Immanuel Kant, *Critique of Judgment*, trans. J. H. Bernard (New York: Hafner Press, 1951), secs. 86–91, pp. 292ff.; henceforth cited as CJ.

24. In CJ, p. 303, Kant says of the righteous man: "Deceit, violence, and envy will always surround him . . . and the righteous men with whom he meets will, notwithstanding all their worthiness of happiness, be yet subjected by nature, which regards not this, to all the evils of want, disease, and untimely death . . . until one wide grave engulfs them together (honest or not, it makes no difference) and throws them back . . . into the abyss of the purposeless chaos of matter from which they were drawn."

25. Kant, CJ, p. 301, n. 15 (added in second edition).

26. Ibid., p. 304.

27. Wood, KMR, p. 154.

28. Kant, CJ, p. 308.

29. Ibid., p. 314.

30. Ibid., p. 322.

31. Ibid., p. 327.

32. Peukert, SAF, pp. 212ff.

33. Ibid., p. 315.

34. Ibid., p. 234.

35. Ibid., p. 235.

36. Jürgen Habermas, "A Reply to My Critics," in *Habermas: Critical Debates*, ed. John B. Thompson and David Held (Cambridge, Mass.: MIT Press, 1982), pp. 219–83.

37. Peukert, SAF, p. 213 (my emphasis).

38. Ibid., p. 215.

2

Christian Theology and
Political Religion

JÜRGEN MOLTMANN

I. THE BEGINNING OF A NEW CONFLICT

I AM A CHRISTIAN theologian and not a sociologist of religion. For me political religion is not a neutral scientific phenomenon which I research and want to describe but a power I have to deal with. Political religion challenges me not only to sound knowledge but also to a confession of faith. Following our experiences in Germany, every militant political religion unavoidably leads to a struggle between church and state (*Kirchenkampf*).

As a Christian theologian, I am also a church theologian. The church of Christ in all countries and in different societies and nations is the community to which I belong, out of which I come, and for which I work. I am not a theologian of the civil religion of my society, nor am I a theologian of the political religion of any nation. The ecumenical solidarity of the Christian church is for me higher than national loyalty or cultural, class, or racial associations. Along these lines, I agree with the early Christian writer Diognet that to Christians every home is foreign and every foreign place is home.

When I view the phenomenon and vicissitudes of civil religions and political religions in light of these Christian presuppositions, then my interests lie only in their demythologizing and in liberating from these religious powers the church, Christians, and especially the people. The critical disengagement of the church

41

from the civil religions of the societies in which it lives and the prophetic liberation of the Christian faith from the forces of political religion which captivate it are for me the points of departure for a free, peaceful, and more humane world.[1]

It is, however, not only the confession of the Christian faith which leads me to this starting point, but probably also a bit of personal and collective German biography. In World War I, in the name of the political religion of the German nation, "for God, King, and Fatherland" our fathers were driven to their deaths in Langemark and Verdun. In the Second World War, in the name of the political messianism of the Third Reich, "for Führer, People, and Fatherland" my generation was marked by the crimes of the concentration camps and hounded into the mass graves of Stalingrad. Since then, political religion is dead for us and we are dead to its claims. Politics will never again become our religion, neither political nor civil. Without the deadly horror and the unbearable guilt of such a political religion we would probably not be so critical. Without Auschwitz the national flag would perhaps still hang in the Christian churches in Germany.[2]

Perhaps my generation is a marked generation, therefore a skeptical and disillusioned one, at times a generation prone to cynicism. The succeeding generations in both German states live in societies without revered flags, national holidays, national hymns, and state symbols. Indeed, they are there, but they no longer awaken any enthusiasm. They lack any political sacredness. The God who is named in the preamble of our Constitution is purely decorative; no one calls upon that God. Perhaps our country and our government have their lamentable legitimation deficit because of this. Perhaps for this reason we lack a consensus of citizens and a collective identity, which in times of crisis unify people against internal and external enemies. Our governments must legitimate themselves only through the fulfillment of their promises, and the consensus of the citizens exists in the mutual bond of the Constitution and not in any supplementary political transcendence. My purpose here is not to glorify the Federal Republic of Germany as a state without a civil religion. Rather, I would like to reveal openly to you the historical context within which I attempt to develop a Christian political theology.

About fifteen years ago first Johann B. Metz and then I, followed by Dorothee Sölle, Jan Lochman, Helmut Gollwitzer, George Casalis, Giulio Girardi, and other European theologians began to develop a new political theology.[3] It had to be called *new* because a political theology already existed. This earlier work was written by the influential constitutional lawyer Carl Schmitt and was published in 1922 and again in 1934.[4]

Carl Schmitt, the theoretician of the National Socialist dictatorship, started from the historical observation that all influential political concepts are in reality secularized theological concepts. He recognized the correspondence between the fundamental political and theological concepts in various periods of European history. For example, political sovereignty restricted by natural law corresponds to the God of the cosmos; the sovereign of the absolutist period corresponds to the nominalist concept of the almighty God; constitutional monarchy corresponds to the deistic concept of God; and the democratic doctrine of the sovereignty of the people corresponds to pantheism. Schmitt himself defended political dictatorship through the existentialist category of being/nonbeing and propagated the dualistic friend/foe thinking of a new political Manichaeism. What Carl Schmitt named political theology was nothing more than the theory of a political religion necessary for the support of the state. It had nothing to do with any specific Christian theology.

The new political theology, on the other hand, began with the existence of the Christian church in society and with a criticism of the captivity of the church in a modern society which claimed that religion is a private matter. The new political theology is a theory of the public, critical, and liberative functions of the Christian church in modern society. It is not the theory of a political religion of this society. In light of the religious legitimation and self-justification of society, the new political theology is therefore not affirmative but critical. That is what distinguishes it from Carl Schmitt. Schmitt understood only states, revolutions, and counterrevolutions as historical subjects. The new political theology, however, wants to make the Christian church into an "institution of socio-critical freedom" (Metz).

Fifteen years ago many in Germany and also in the United States believed in the "era of secularization," in Bonhoeffer's "religionless era," and in Harvey Cox's "secular city."[5] The critique of religion by Feuerbach, Marx, and Freud was the beginning of all theology which claimed to be modern. Today the challenge throughout the modern secular world has yielded to the challenge of Christianity through the revitalization of religion. Those who in 1970 had anticipated the Marxist "withering away of religion" had miscalculated, at least in Poland. Those who at that time had declared God dead were taught fear again by the Ayatollah Khomeini with the Iranian revolution. The modernist underestimation of religion has led to catastrophic political misjudgments. Be it capitalist, Marxist, or positivist, the more the secular belief in progress rules in those crises which it itself produces, the more strongly the religious passions of the people are awakened, even in public life.

Religious experiences, however, are through and through two-sided. They can be just as dangerous as they can be liberative. Berdyaev meant much the same thing with his famous statement: "Mankind is incurably religious." If I understand that correctly, then we who today live in the First World experience a double religious movement: the return of religion to politics and the return of politics to religion.

The return of religion to politics is recognizable in the critical movements inside and outside the church: in the peace movement, the Third World movement, and the ecological movement. With the growing rejection of the use, threat, and acquisition of the means for nuclear mass destruction, Christians and churches step into the political arena and enter into confrontation on religious grounds. With the increasing criticism of the unjust world economic system which each year causes the deaths of more than forty million people in the Third World, Christians and churches step into the economic arena and enter into confrontation with the economic powers of the world. Finally, with their increasing criticism of the industrial destruction of the natural environment and of wildlife, Christians and churches step into the cultural arena and with their new lifestyle attack the lifestyle of extravagant waste.

The return of politics to religion is recognizable in the restoration of political religion. We find it only superficially in the new patriotism. That movement is grounded in the politics of national security. Security politics in the First World takes on religious dimensions because it addresses and exploits people's deepest anxieties. Our security becomes more and more threatened from both outside and inside. In the name of national security constitutions are rescinded, illegal acts justified, human rights suppressed, and political opponents liquidated. Politically this means that national security has assumed the characteristics of the unconditional (Tillich) and of transcendence over and against law and Constitution. This security ideology leads to apocalyptic Manichaeism. Total security is unattainable; therefore it is nothing but a utopia. Because it requires tremendous sacrifice and is built on the threat of world destruction, it is a deadly utopia. In this manner the politics of national security becomes modern political religion and indeed becomes the political apocalyptic of the approaching final battle (Armageddon). If religion returns to politics in the way described above and if politics again becomes religion, then confrontation is inevitable. The *status confessionis* is then present for the Christian churches.

II. THE POLITICAL THEOLOGY OF POLITICAL RELIGION

Political religion and its formulation in political theology are no inventions of Christianity but the essence of ancient religions.[6] The expression *genus politikon* developed out of the philosophy of the Stoics. "Panaitios delineated three classes of god-forms: natural powers thought of as persons, the gods of the state religion, and the gods of myth (*genus physikon, genus politikon*, and *genus mythikon*)."[7] The god-images of the poets are mythic, the concepts of the philosophers are metaphysical, and the cult of the *polis* is political. Therefore mythic theology belongs in the theater, metaphysical theology belongs in academia, and political theology belongs in government. Augustine perceived only a two-part division because political theology was simultaneously mythic theology and would otherwise remain unintelligible to the people.[8]

For the Roman Stoics political theology was most important, because in a commonwealth the citizens and the priests must know which state gods are recognized and which holy rituals should be performed to honor them. According to ancient state doctrines, honoring the gods of one's own land is the highest purpose of the state (*finis principalis*) because these gods secure the welfare and peace of the state. The public practice of religion is therefore the primary civic duty. In Rome the *crimen laesae religionis* was given not yet through theoretical denial of the state religion but only through the practical neglect of the requisite observance of the cultus. *Godless* was only used to blame those who refused publicly to honor the state gods. Behind this stood the idea of *do ut des:* the state gods care for the welfare and peace of the state only if the citizens correctly practice their cults. When famine, war, and plague come, it is because the gods are angry on account of defective cultic practices. Religious dissidents, the godless, must then be sacrificed to placate the gods. This is what occurred again and again to the Jews and Christians in the Roman Empire. As Tertullian said, "When the Tiber overflows its banks, when the Nile does not overflow its banks, the people cry: the Christians to the lions."[9]

Has political religion disappeared from modern pluralistic and secularized society? Or has it only adopted new forms? Robert Bellah's 1967 studies in "Civil Religion in America" have, in spite of the American division between church and state, drawn renewed attention to the phenomenon of an American civil religion.[10] He employed the expression *religion civile*, coined by Rousseau, but he could not clarify the distinction between civil religion and political religion. This distinction is indeed difficult to find because a civil religion as a religion of the republic can include many different political religions by emphasizing their commonality and linkage. However, it can, of course, at any time become a uniform political religion as is seen, for example, in the new patriotism.

The peculiarity of modern civil or political religion lies in the fact that the gods of "the Fatherland" fade away and are replaced for the most part by vague and generally acceptable concepts of transcendence. No one knows who the God in the preamble of our German Constitution really is. And the God "in whom we trust" when we pay with dollars is equally unknown. What is probably meant is the summary of all that which people like to think of as a highest religious authority.

Obviously, the functions of civil or political religions in modern societies are still important. I perceive five functions.

1. The correspondence with the gods or, as the case may be, transcendence, provides self-esteem, self-justification, and a collective public feeling of dignity, thus legitimation of one's own power in the wider sense of the word.
2. The harmony of citizens in the cultus of political religion creates the symbolic integration of society. This harmony is especially important in the United States, a nation of immigrants: *E pluribus unum*. It is also important in the multinational Soviet Union: Soviet ideology produces a new Soviet people out of many nationalities.
3. Both functions are bound up with the friend/foe schema: no social consensus without identifying dissent. The external enemy and the internal enemy strengthen collective legitimation and integration. Every insecure identity probably needs enemy images in order to project self-anxiety onto others. The enemy of the state is always also the enemy of the state gods, that is, an enemy of that which is most highly valued by one's own political religion.
4. This political religion can be, but must not be, totalitarian. It functions best when it leaves open the private sphere and only deals with proper public behavior and prescribed public expression.
5. This political religion of modern society cannot dominate other spheres because it sanctions only the political system. This political system, however, is not in a position to control the economic system. Based on this powerlessness of politics against multinational corporations, modern political religion remains in the grip of ideology and is only a pseudoreligiosity. It does not move others but is itself moved. It determines nothing but is itself determined by others. It does not represent the whole life of society but is used by certain social powers.

III. CHRISTIAN POLITICS OF THE MILLENNIUM

At this point we once again return to a historical perspective. The Constantinian turn changed Christianity from a community persecuted in the name of the political religion of Rome into a politically organized religion (*religio licita*). Then, under the Emperors Theodosius and Justinian, it became the dominant state religion (*religio publica*) of the Roman Empire. Christianity took over the existing functions of Roman state religion and Christianized the Roman Empire. At the same time, however, for reasons of state it was itself politicized. The Christianity which was previously persecuted for being godless and an enemy of the state began persecuting Jews, heretics, and pagans for being godless people and enemies of the state. Christianity had to do this because it had been changed into an imperial political religion. Otherwise it could not achieve the self-esteem and integration of the Empire.

This Constantinian turn heralded the Constantinian era, whose end has often been declared but has in no way yet arrived in Europe, the United States, or Latin America. The main idea is that since the Christianization of the Roman Empire the subject of the salvation history of God is no longer the Christian church but has become the Christian state, be it named the Holy Empire[11] or the Christian nation.[12] The following conceptions are fundamental:

1. *Theocracy*. Erik Peterson, in his important essay "Monotheismus als politisches Problem" (1935), which was written against Carl Schmitt's *Politische Theologie* (1934), explored and described the history of this first Christian political theology. The early Christian apologists did not accept the particular political religions of the pagan people and the cities. Instead they adopted the universal metaphysical theology of Aristotle in order to show that the God of the Bible is the one and only omnipotent power. The universe has a monarchical structure: one God, one logos, one cosmos. The divinity is the world-transcendent point of conjunction of the many. In political theology this monotheistic-monarchistic cosmology corresponds to the imperialism of the one emperor: one emperor, one law, one empire.

The Constantinian turn, then, gave the imperial theologians the opportunity to interpret the natural theology of the philosophers politically. The one church formed out of many peoples into the one people who worship the one God is superior to polytheism, and the one empire with the one emperor brings political peace among many nations. If both unite, then the Christian idea of the one God and the unity of the one church determine the unity of the political empire.

Constantine's model was Augustus. Thus his court theologian, Eusebius, declared: "When the Savior appeared on earth and concurrent with his arrival Augustus as first Roman became lord over the nations, the rule of many on earth was dissolved and peace embraced the whole earth."[13]

The legitimation model for the Christian emperors was the correspondence to the divine-world monarchy: one God, one Christ, one emperor, one religion, one empire. This was the accepted theological doctrine of sovereignty until the time of European absolutism. That this did not have anything essentially in common with the Christian faith was demonstrated, for example, by the Mongol lord Ghengis Khan who in 1254 sent a message to the pope in Rome: "In heaven there is no other than the one, eternal God; on earth there is no one other than the single lord, Ghengis Khan, the Son of God. That is the word that is being said to you."[14]

2. *The millennium*. With the triumph of the Emperor Constantine, the fulfillment of the biblical promise that those who now suffer with Christ will later rule with him seemed to have come to pass. When? In the thousand-year reign of Christ. On account of this, those who were persecuted greeted the Christian empire as the thousand-year reign of Christ on earth and interpreted this epoch in a chiliastic way. Christ's reign of peace was realized through the Pax Romana. The Christian expectation of the imminent parousia of Christ was politically fulfilled. The ideas inherent to the millennium must be made clear in order to understand this Christian imperial politics.[15] In the millennium Satan is trussed up for a thousand years so that he can no longer lead the pagans astray. Evil no longer has any power against God in this reign. In the millennium the martyrs are resurrected; they sit in judgment with Christ and rule with God for a thousand years. It is the rule of the good, against which evil has no power. If, together with Christ, they rule the world, then they cannot tolerate dissidents, pagans, or Jews, because they have been given the power of judgment.

Only after the thousand-year reign has run its course will Satan again be turned loose, and the final battle of Gog and Magog will come to the holy city of Jerusalem — a battle in which God, with fire from heaven, will triumph victoriously. Thus, those who believe themselves to be living in the thousand-year reign of Christ live in fulfilled hope and can only see before them the apocalyptic final battle of Gog and Magog (or, as others say, Armageddon).

Those, however, who consider the kingdom of evil, like Satan, incapable of being politically conquered must expect the final battle of Gog and Magog or Armageddon in our generation. The conservative apocalypticism which today may possibly ignite a nuclear inferno is a sign of millennium politics. Not to be biased, I can also point out that the Communist Internationale has sung for over one hundred years, "People hear the signal, unto the Last Battle," and by that has revealed its Marxist apocalypticism. Russian Marxism is in theory and praxis the secularized orthodox chiliasm of the old belief in a Russian world-salvation: Moscow the Third Rome and the Last Rome.[16]

3. *Apocalyptic Manichaeism*. Out of the Persian Zarathustra religion was developed the religious dualism which Mani and the so-called Manichaeans disseminated: it is the idea of an ongoing struggle between good and evil, between the children of light and the children of darkness. Yet only with the adoption of biblical thought forms did this become an apocalyptic dualism, and only when it was combined with Christian millennium politics did the political Manichaeism, which later intensified the friend/foe thinking into apocalyptic dimensions, arise. It is not the Christian belief in the triumph of God over Satan in the cross and resurrection of Christ which lies behind this, but the pagan expectation of a judgment of God that in the final battle must be compelled.

The image world of the Book of Revelation has stimulated the apocalyptic interpretation of politics even more strongly. Since the Puritan Revolution in England, the last book of the Bible has been made into the secret revelation of the history of the world. The red dragon which pursues the woman with child has today been interpreted by both the Protestant and the Catholic underground as a reference to those places where the flags are already red. When such religious apocalypticism is transformed into anti-Communist ideology, then politicians also begin to see only "red" and become blind to the multifaceted problems of reality. They reduce all problems of the world to pro- and anti-Communism. Everything is drawn into this one conflict.

4. *Imperial mission*. Any theology bound through its Con-

stantinianism to the Imperium Romanum had to limit severely the universality of the Christian proclamation. In fact, it was precisely for this reason that early Christianity had already become a religion of the West. Many churches outside the Roman Empire were forsaken and lost. On the other hand, the Christian mission was changed into a state mission involving the expansion of the Imperium Romanum. This is shown by Charlemagne's mission to the Saxons, Otto I's mission to the Slavs, and the missionary work of the Order of German Knights in Eastern Europe. Even that is a millennial mission: the pagans are brought under the judgment and government of the Christian ruler.

The great missionary movements of the eighteenth and nineteenth centuries, in a different but still recognizable way, were bound to Western colonialism, the expansion of the so-called superior European civilization, and the opening up of all nations for the European world market. Thus European-American Christianity either came to power through this form of mission or shed its European and Western characteristics in order to become truly open to the world. The first is Christian cultural mission, which today through anti-Communism becomes the religious propaganda of the "Free World"; the second is the mission of the Gospels and of faith. The first is continued millennium politics; the second is church proclamation of the gospel.

5. *The dissolution of the church into a political religion of the empire.* With this we come to the price of the lauded Constantinian era. The church existed up till then in visible, voluntary communities. Since the time of Constantine it was made into the religion system of the Christian empire. These congregations were correspondingly replaced by the residences of the national diocese and parishes. The church administrations were part of the public order, and participation in them was a civic duty. The separation between clergy and laity was decisive. Association in a Christian community was replaced by association with the church, that is, with the hierarchy. The hierarchy was part of the political rule. The leader of the church was the consecrated emperor. In Protestant Constantinianism the Protestant prince was the *sum episcopus*, the archbishop. The dissolution of the particular existence of the church into the religion of the empire was not looked on as a sacrifice but was greeted as part of the fulfilled millennium

hope. In the reign of Christ there is no longer any church, because its responsibility is fulfilled.

In the nineteenth century Richard Rothe, whom Ernst Troeltsch and the present-day German theologians of the organized churches followed in their own work, praised both the dissolution of the church into the state and the transformation of faith into good patriotic ethics as the transition of the Christian spirit from its church period to its political period. "Christianity in its deepest essence wants to go beyond its *church* form; it wants nothing less than to have the entire organism of human life in one organism, i.e., the state."[17]

Rothe thought that the secularization of the church is at the same time the Christianizing of nations and cultures, and vice versa. With this, not only was the return of religion to politics edified, but also the return of politics to religion. The state became the body of Christ, and the church became the soul of this Christian state.[18]

IV. THE POLITICS OF CHRISTIAN DISCIPLESHIP

Together with the dissolution of the church into a Christian state religion, millennium politics led even more to the dissolution of Christian memory and to the repression of biblical traditions of hope. However, wherever the Christian memory was alive and the biblical traditions were present, criticism became louder, Christian opposition developed, and the untenability of millennium politics was revealed. From its true source the reformation of Christianity led to a critical disengagement from the onerous functions of civil and political religion in the Christian empire and in the Christian nation.

1. *The crucified God.* No apologetic, no matter how obliging or skillful, can deny the fact that Christ was judged in the name of the Pax Romana as a Jewish Messiah-pretender and died on a Roman cross. The event of the cross and its enduring memory in the Eucharist and in the discipleship and martyrdom of Christians stands at the center of the Christian political conflict. The legendary harmony of the birth of Christ with that of the Roman peace emperor Augustus can never crowd out the memory of the fatal

disharmony between Christ and the Roman procurator Pontius Pilate. It is true that the Christian tradition of the trial of Jesus has accented the Jewish guilt and allowed Pilate to wash his hands in innocence. The disciples of the crucified man from Nazareth could otherwise hardly have survived in the Roman Empire. Even some present-day apologist exegetes interpret the execution of Christ by the Roman occupational forces as what Bultman calls an unfortunate "miscarriage of justice."[19]

Nevertheless, these are nothing more than allegations trumped up by theologians in order to obscure the historical conflict and to remove their own conflict with the gods and powers of their contemporary political religions. It remains a fact that Christ was murdered for political reasons in the name of the political religion of the Roman Empire. It remains a fact that the Christian faith was originated by God in the resurrection of this Crucified One. The alternative for Christians still remains clear: either Christ or Caesar, that is, either the freedom of the Christian faith or subjugation under the gods of the state religion and the power of political religion. Christian theology which is derived from the cross of Christ can only come into conflict with that political theology which is derived from reasons of state and political metaphysics. This means no retreat of theology from politics but, on the contrary, the critical dissolution of self-justification and political foe images, integrations, and oppressions which are produced by political religions.

The criticism based on the cross naturally always first aligns itself against the falsification in the Christian churches of the Christian faith as a religion of success. Peter Berger was correct when he wrote in 1961:

> We suspect that it is a theological task in our situation to elaborate the eschatological character of the Christian faith against the this-worldliness of American religiosity, to set justification by faith against our pervasive legalism, to explain the meaning of the cross in a culture that glorifies success and happiness."[20]

He is still correct in 1986, at least in Germany.

2. *The triune God.* In 1935 Erik Peterson declared that through the doctrine of the Trinity and its conception of God the

early church had freed itself from that religious monotheism which had legitimated political monarchism. Historically this thesis is not entirely correct, because the anti-Arian theologians combined the Trinity with the world monarchy of God and saw in the Trinity itself a monarchy of the Father.[21] Theologically, however, this is true because the doctrine of the Trinity names God the Father of Jesus and binds the God-concept to the fate of the crucified and resurrected Jesus. In principle this makes it impossible to use this concept of God for the legitimation of political dominance. The renunciation of the doctrine of the Trinity led, and still leads today, to the dissolution of the Christian faith into the political religion of a theocratically understood empire, be it Islamic or Western imperialistic.

The Christian doctrine of the Trinity, therefore, forces one to speak of God in light of the crucified Christ, and this view toward the crucified Christ makes the distinction between God and the idols, between belief and superstition.

3. *The God of the poor.* The crucified Christ was never a good identification figure for rulers and the powerful. He also at no time allows himself to be used as a symbolic model for a nation. The poor, the sick, the oppressed, however, understand him through their own suffering: "You are a God of the poor, the refuge of the oppressed, the support for the weak, the protector of the lost, the rescuer of the desperate" (Judg. 9:11).

Jesus proclaimed the coming reign of God to the poor, he beatified those who suffered, he healed the sick, he took to himself disenfranchised sinners and publicans, and he "had mercy on the people." The people of Jesus are the beatified people. If the kingdom of God belongs to the poor, the suffering, the oppressed, and the helpless, then the coming God is already represented through them in the present. From this developed the mission, the evangelization, and a certain messianism of the poor for the Christian faith. The poor are a "sacrament of Christ" (Luke 16). They are the humblest brothers and sisters of the coming world judgment (Matthew 25). On them — in general — the fate of the world rests.[22]

According to this, the Christian community cannot follow the homogeneity principle of civil religion: "Like attracts like." Nor can it consent to the symbolic integration of society because through Christ himself it is referred to every Other, to the disenfranchised and oppressed. The true Christian community establishes itself on the edges of society, as a community of Jews and Greeks, men and women, rulers and slaves (see Gal. 3:28; Rom. 10:12; 1 Cor. 12:13).

Precisely because Christians believe in justification through grace alone, they no longer need personal and collective self-justification and therefore cast off these mechanisms of self-glorification. They no longer need to have a society of people just like themselves who mutually confirm each other, but desire community with the Other, in order to live in acceptance of others.[23]

4. *The God of ecumenism.* Civil religions are limited to certain societies and must serve to delimit these societies from others. Political religions are limited to certain states and must serve the friend/foe schema of these states. The Christian church, however, is in this regard universal. For the sake of its universal mission it cannot bind itself to any society or nation. Here we find a remarkable asymmetry. Civil religion represents the commonality in a society, while the church is only one religious community among others. The church, however, is present in all societies and therefore represents something universal within individual societies. This produces the conflict between ecumenical solidarity in Christianity and political loyalty in a nation.

All political religions create enemy images and barriers against others through the legitimation of their own dominance and the symbolic integration of their own people. In particular, the modern, messianically conditioned political religions exaggerate this hostility into an apocalyptic drama. Modern political messianisms teach fear and hatred of the national enemy or the class enemy. If Christians themselves do not want to abandon and deny all that they have learned from Christ, then they must — for the sake of their own souls — resist the apocalyptic fear and hatred of the enemy and proclaim and practice love of the enemy not only in their personal lives, but also in their public lives. The love of the enemy which Jesus preached and lived presupposes inner sovereignty over and against the fear of enemies, and is the creative transformation of a situation conditioned by enmity to one conditioned by reconciliation in friendship. Love of the enemy does not allow the rules of the game to be stipulated by the opponent but is derived from the demand of God who lets the sun rise over evil and good (Matt. 5:45; Rom. 12:20–21).

5. *The God of hope.* The world-historical mistake and the theological heresy of Christian millennium politics lie in the equating of the political empire with the kingdom of God and in the equating of the Christian nation with the people of God. From this equation results the unchristian persecution of Jews, pagans, and atheists. The Pax Romana was not Christ's reign of peace, and it was not Christ but often enough the anti-Christ in the alleged "Thousand-Year Reichs" in history.

The peace of God is higher, broader, and also other than the peace of the political religions. That millennium in which Christians rule and judge and in which Satan is bound is the object of pure hope, not a possible political praxis. It is future, not present. Thus it can only be a reality, following the visions found in the Book of Revelation, when the crucified Christ comes in glory and power. He has not yet come, neither in the glory and power of the Christian rulers and kingdoms nor in the glory and power of the church. The kingdom of Christ is neither politically present nor present in the church. It is pure messianic future. The lordship of Christ, however, is present. It reaches historically as far as people become obedient and follow Christ so that they may take their cross upon themselves. Those who confuse the lordship of Christ with the thousand-year kingdom of Christ destroy the church. Chiliasm in the present is therefore a Christian heresy, for true Christian chiliasm, since it is simultaneously a hope for Israel and its redemption, belongs only in the future.[24]

The politics of Christian discipleship, whose fundamental theological idea we have set over and against Christian millennium politics, has been since the beginning of the Constantinian era not only taught but also lived. The Constantinian turn led not only to the dissolution of the church into the political religion of the empire but also to the unheard-of blossoming of Christian religious orders, that is, those resistant Christian groups who lived in the spirit of the Christian martyrs of the times of persecution. This Christian resistance has occurred throughout the whole history of Christian empires and nations.

Today—I believe—these persistent groups of disciples are returning to the church-at-large and to politics. Today, in the questions of peace, economic justice, and the life of creation, they represent the Christian alternative to the apocalypticism of the political religions of the great powers.

NOTES

1. Jürgen Moltmann, *Politische Theologie — Politische Ethik* (Munich: Kaiser, 1984). Translated as *On Human Dignity: Political Theology and Ethics*, trans. M. Douglas Meeks (Philadelphia: Fortress Press, 1984).

2. Jürgen Habermas, ed., *Stichworte zur "Geistigen Situation der Zeit"* (Frankfurt: Suhrkamp, 1979). Translated as *Observations on the Spiritual Situation of the Age*, trans. Andrew Buchwalter (Cambridge, Mass.: MIT Press, 1984).

3. See the overviews of Siegfried Wiedenhofer, *Politische Theologie* (Stuttgart: Kohlhammer, 1976); and Alfredo Fierro, *The Militant Gospel* (London: SCM Press, 1977).

4. Carl Schmitt, *Politische Theologie* (Leipzig: Duncker & Humblot, 1934); *Politische Theologie II* (Berlin: Duncker & Humblot, 1970).

5. This was recognizable in Harvey G. Cox, *The Secular City* (New York: Macmillan Co., 1965); and *Religion in the Secular City* (New York: Simon & Schuster, 1984).

6. Here I am following the presentations of Erik Peterson, "Monotheismus als politisches Problem," in *Theologische Traktate* (Munich: Kösel Verlag, 1951); and Arnold Ehrhardt, *Politische Metaphysik von Solon bis Augustin*, 3 vols. (Tübingen: Mohr, 1959–69), vol. 1.

7. Max Pohlenz, *Die Stoa*, 3 vols. (Göttingen: Vandenhoeck & Ruprecht, 1964), 1: 198.

8. Augustine *City of God* (trans. Healey-Tasker) 6.5.

9. This was comprehensively treated in Hendrikus Berkhof, *Kirche und Kaiser* (Zürich: Evangelischer Verlag, 1947).

10. Robert N. Bellah, "Civil Religion in America," *Daedalus* 4 (1967); and *The Broken Covenant* (New York: Seabury Press, 1975). See also Sidney E. Mead, *The Nation with the Soul of a Church* (New York: Harper & Row, 1975). After a long delay a German discussion of civil religion has finally appeared. See Niklas Luhmann, "Grundwerte als Zivilreligion," in *Soziologische Aufklarung*, 2 vols. (Cologne: Westdeutscher Verlag, 1974–75), 2: 293–308; H. Lübbe, "Staat und Zivilreligion," in *Legitimation des modernen Staates*, ed. H. Lübbe et al. (Wiesbaden: Steiner, 1981), pp. 40–64. For a challenge to both, see Jürgen Moltmann, "Das Gespenst einer neuen Zivilreligion," in Moltmann, *Politische Theologie — Politische Ethik*, pp. 70–78.

11. Alois Dempf, *Sacrum Imperium* (Munich: Oldenberg, 1962).

12. Norman Cohn, *Das Ringen um das tausendjärige Reich* (Bern: Francke, 1961); Ernest L. Tuveson, *Redeemer Nation* (Chicago: University of Chicago Press, 1968).

13. Peterson, "Monotheismus als politisches Problem," p. 91.

14. Miguel de Ferdinandy, *Tschingis Khan* (Hamburg: Rowohlt, 1958), p. 153.

15. See M. Darrol Bryant and Donald W. Dayton, *The Coming Kingdom* (New York: International Religious Foundation, 1983); and Joseph Bettis and S. K. Johannesen, *The Return of the Millennium* (New York: International Religious Foundation, 1984).

16. This has been convincingly presented by Emmanuel Sarkisyanz, "Russischer Chiliasmus als Ausgangsatmosphäre des Bolschewismus," in Emmanuel Sarkisyanz, *Russland und der Messianismus des Orients* (Tübingen: Mohr, 1955), pp. 95ff.

17. Richard Rothe, *Theologische Ethik* (Wittenberg: Zimmermann, 1867), p. 477.

18. I must remark that Wolfhart Pannenberg seemingly holds this to be historically and theologically positive. See Wolfhart Pannenberg, "Das christliche Imperium und das Phanom einer politischen Religion," in Wolfhart Pannenberg, *Die Bestimmung des Menschens* (Göttingen: Vandenhoeck & Ruprecht, 1978), pp. 61–84.

19. Rudolf Bultmann, *Das Verhaltnis der urchristlichen Christusbotschaft zum historischen Jesus* (Heidelberg: C. Winter, 1960), p. 13: "Sie (scil. seine Hinrichtung) geschah vielmehr auf Grund eines Missverstandnis seines Wirkens als eines politischen." Against this view see Jürgen Moltmann, *The Crucified God*, trans. R. A. Wilson and John Bowden (New York: Harper & Row, 1974).

20. Peter L. Berger, *The Noise of Solemn Assemblies* (Garden City, N.Y.: Doubleday & Co., 1961), p. 133.

21. For the historical viewpoint, see Alfred Schindler, *Monotheismus als politisches Problem?* (Gütersloh: Verlagshaus Mohn, 1978). For the theological point of view, see Jürgen Moltmann, *Trinität und Reich Gottes* (Munich: Kaiser, 1980); translated as *The Trinity and the Kingdom of God*, trans. Margaret Kohl (New York: Harper & Row, 1981).

22. Gustavo Gutierrez, *The Power of the Poor in History*, trans. Robert R. Barr (Maryknoll, N.Y.: Orbis Books, 1983).

23. I have presented this principle in Jürgen Moltmann, *The Church in the Power of the Spirit*, trans. Margaret Kohl (New York: Harper & Row, 1976).

24. Pinchas Lapide and Jürgen Moltmann, *Israel und Kirche: ein gemeinsamer weg?* (Munich: Kaiser, 1980).

3

Science and the Civic
Spirit of Liberal Democracy

YARON EZRAHI

IN HIS BOOK *The Broken Covenant: American Civil Religion in Time of Trial*,[1] Robert Bellah has noted the central place of science in the political culture of American democracy. For him science is an essential ingredient of the culture of materialism and self-interest. He traces some of the trouble to the fact that Bacon, Newton, and Locke were the intellectual heroes of early American leaders like Jefferson; that their scientific outlook helped to repress in American politics an alternative poetic-imaginative vision which, as in the case of William Blake, assumes that "there is always more than what appears, and [that] behind every evident literal fact is an unfathomable depth of implication and meaning."[2] In his *Reconstructing Public Philosophy*,[3] political theorist William M. Sullivan expresses similar concern about the loss of civic spirit and republican virtues in modern America. Again science and technology are among the villains held guilty by association with competitive utilitarian individualism and with the values of this-worldly effectiveness and efficiency.

Such attacks on the role of science in the erosion of the civic spirit in America have become widespread. In the search for new ways to reconstruct American civic life such writers tend to see in the recent criticism of science and its influence in the larger society a hopeful sign.[4] They welcome it as indicating renewed concern for the development of the inward person and the spiritual dimension of the self.

The idea of science as undermining virtues is, of course, not new. For Thomas Carlyle, the spread of technical values seemed to be leading toward the deterioration of the inward self. For Marx it was part of a grand strategy of enslaving the soul and subjugating the body of the weak. Insofar as science has come to symbolize the decay of spirit, virtue, autonomy, and dignity, both rightist and leftist ideologues have associated a critique of science and technology with calls for cultural and political reform. In the last few decades this position has spread to widening social circles and has gathered new cultural and political forces within the liberal-democratic state. It is, however, a position which is based on a gross distortion of the historical record and an untenably biased reading of political theory and ideology.

The spread of materialistic and instrumental values in political life has not resulted simply from the spontaneous erosion of religious, spiritual, and moral values in public affairs. The combined influence of science, technology, materialism, and instrumentalism has also been part of a powerful cultural strategy to redefine political authority following the crisis of the religious wars of the seventeenth century. It sought to limit the disruptive political effects of religious enthusiasm. Advocates of the new science such as Francis Bacon, John Wilkins, and Robert Boyle were enlisted in the effort to "diminish the epistemological status of the imagination" and generate new models of public speech and public action which would lower the temper of public life and check the dangers of unresolvable conflicts and factionalism.[5] The rising cultural influence of science was associated with aspirations to civilize and moderate political discourse and action by discipline imposed by the gaze of an enlightened public.[6] It was linked with the evolution of the modern public as a political category and with the need to generate new modes of discipline independent of hierarchy and transcendence.

As part of this process, science was closely involved with the movement to secure universal understanding by discovering or constructing a perfect universal language, the attempts to compose and publish a definitive encyclopedia which would serve as an authoritative referent for resolving disputes, and the rise of the public science museum as an instrument for disciplining perception by knowledge.[7] Underlying all such efforts was the commitment to an idea of reality as a public observable object and the concomitant idea of knowledge as a mirror of reality.[8] These interdependent ideas furnished the foundation of a liberal-democratic epistemology of political discourse and action. As a cultural institution, science has articulated the possibility of speech regimented by referents in the "external" sphere of observable facts rather than in the "internal" sphere of unobservable moral and spiritual qualities.

The cultural impact of the industrial revolution and the rise of science-based technologies have further reinforced the attitude that actions are not primarily expressions of personality, character, or conscience but calculated measures for producing at least partly predictable effects in a public, observable world of facts. The authority of science in the cultural and social spheres of the modern state was associated with the relevance of these new views of speech and action to the attempts to redefine political authority and accountability. The association of science with the redistribution of social trust among alternative modes of discourse and action, a shift reflected partly in the decline of religious paradigms of discourse and action in public affairs, has therefore had moral significance for its advocates.[9] To view the relation of science and politics only in terms of the conflict between materialistic and spiritual-moral orientations in the sphere of public affairs is, therefore, to miss an important point.

Misconstruing the historical and ideological role of science in supporting the underpinning of liberal-democratic civic culture leads to a misdiagnosis of the significance of recent indications for the decline in the cultural authority of science. The changing status of science may be part of a more general challenge to the very idea of a public sphere and its liberal-democratic values as a cultural possibility. To focus on the tensions between utilitarianism-instrumentalism and civic morality is to miss the crucial role of science in supporting the social credibility of the epistemology of liberal-democratic politics. Without these beliefs about reality, knowledge, and reliable communication, liberal-democratic principles of political life cannot become norms of political practice. Ironically, the spread of capitalism and utilitarian individualism gave science its role as a source of discipline for checking the anarchistic implications of self-interest. In social epistemology science provided a public dimension for private actions by enabling private individuals to generate public discourse. As cultural models, science and technology institutionalized the practice of judging speech independently of the character of the speaker. Actions could thus be evaluated in relation to their consequences rather than to their source.

This separation of private persons from public speech and action was necessary for realizing the liberal-democratic political idea of public order as a condition which is continually produced and transformed by free individuals. The commitment to both a private and a public realm is, of course, bound to remain continually vulnerable to imbalances. The public realm can extend far enough to undermine the integrity of individuals. The private realm can extend far enough to threaten the integrity of the public order. Science as a cultural institution has clearly been associated with upholding the integrity of the public realm rather than that of the individual. It confirms the value of objectivity rather than subjectivity. As an expression of public values, science has had a different cultural and political import than the fine arts, which have come to represent the value of individual freedom to engage the imaginative and emotional faculties without the strictures of cooperative discipline or peer control. The scientific enterprise rejects both transcendental and personal authorities. Nevertheless, the deep antagonism of the scientific tradition toward dogmatism[10] has constituted an important check upon the uses of science to support public authority where it denies the integrity of individuals. As Karl Popper pointed out, perhaps the most important aspect of science as a cultural foundation of the open society is that scientific knowledge gains authority only through an ongoing critical dialogue which never reaches an end.[11]

Particularly relevant to the functions of science in supporting a liberal-democratic concept of the public realm is the essentially unresolvable tension within the scientific subculture. Mathematical versus empirical traditions balance an urge for certainty and perfect rational discipline with the residue of inconclusiveness and indeterminism inherent in empirical evidence. The relatively conclusive language of proofs struggles with the open-ended discourse which rests on testimonies.[12] The coexistence of these two traditions in a delicate balance has provided an enormously rich and flexible cultural and institutional model of discourse and action. This model has exemplified the possibility of generating discipline without denying uncertainty. As such, norms of public speech and public action supported by science could not be extended to deny the legitimacy of individual testimonies and criticisms without appearing to support dogmatism and violating the very ethics and ethos of science. On the other hand, radical interpretations of empirical uncertainties could not be upheld without denying the intellectual discipline which individuals require in order to generate science.

Although this need to balance certainty and uncertainty, discipline and freedom, determinism and creativity, has been central to both the scientific and the liberal-democratic political enterprises, the points at which each has struck a balance have often been far apart. Edward Purcell has shown, for example, how during the thirties and forties, precisely when Western democracies, challenged by modern totalitarian states, urged that freedom and criticism not jeopardize agreement and technical effectiveness, the scientific subculture began to question well-established presuppositions and to doubt that science could mirror the universe.[13] In the twentieth century the so-called crisis of physics — the acceptance of certain degrees of indeterminism as inherent in the scientific knowledge of the universe — has weakened the cultural force of science in supporting the naive realism of liberal-democratic epistemology.[14]

No wonder that other cultural institutions have moved to fill the gap and become custodians of the epistemological codes of liberal-democratic political discourse and action. Among these the most prominent has been mass media news reporting. News reporters have been claiming that facts are determinate and that "reality" can be objectively represented and reported precisely when such ideas are coming into question among scientific intellectuals and philosophers of science.[15] In contemporary liberal democracies, journalists play a central role in criticizing and challenging political authority by juxtaposing its assertions and actions against the "facts" and discrediting decisions and objectives as unwarranted in light of observable "realities." While leading members of the late twentieth-century Western intelligentsia are ready to take for granted the notion that, as Nelson Goodman once observed, "facts are small theories,"[16] such ideas still appear subversive when stated in the political context of liberal-democratic discourse.

The idea of an autonomous professional press as a neutral and reliable mirror of the political process has, of course, been subject to powerful attacks since the beginning of this century.[17] However, a political universe which accepts only perspectives and interpretations but recognizes no "facts" is a most problematic context for the practice of liberal-democratic citizenship and for the accountability of political leaders. "Factual reality" has become a necessary cultural artifact for supporting a free press and myriad other democratic institutions. Recognizing that the idea of factual reality is a dogma or a myth does not require, of course, that it be discarded. W. V. Quine observed in his "Two Dogmas of Empiricism" that the "myth of physical objects is epistemologically superior to most in that it has proved more efficacious than other myths as a device for working a manageable structure into the flux of experience."[18] This observation can be enlarged to encompass an equally pertinent political observation. The myth of factual reality has proved effective in supporting political institutions whose leaders are subject to external public tests of adequacy. The special affinity between democratic politics and optimistic epistemological realism in America was already noted by Tocqueville. In a society where citizens are placed on equal footing, he observed,

> they readily conclude that everything in the world may be explained, and that nothing in it transcends the limits of understanding. Thus they fall to denying what they cannot comprehend, which leaves them but little faith for what is extraordinary, and almost insurmountable distaste for whatever is supernatural.[19]

Denying the reality of that which is incomprehensible is, perhaps, the most powerful imperative of civic epistemology in democracy. This principle has often lent popular notions of reality a greater force than scholarly ones, and has often given the popular press an edge over science. Tocqueville observed:

> Democratic citizens like to discern the object which engages their attention with extreme clearness; they, therefore, strip off as much as possible all that covers it, they rid themselves

of whatever separates them from it, in order to view it more closely and in the broad light of day. This disposition of mind soon leads them to condemn forms which they regard as useless or inconvenient veils placed between them and the truth.[20]

Such an attitude can also support anti-intellectual dispositions and render abstract scientific theories suspect in the eyes of common citizens. Despite the recurrent incongruities between scientific and common-sense constructions of reality, however, the spectacular cognitive success and technological fruitfulness of scientific conceptions of reality have persistently supported the position of science as the ultimate cultural anchor of the myth of reality. Science is the gold standard which has upheld the currency of realism even in its more vulgar popular forms. The historical success of the scientific enterprise has served the social credibility of the myth of reality in much the same way that miracles once served the social credibility of the myth of supernatural agents.

The significance of factual reality for liberal-democratic politics becomes more evident if we recall Walter Benjamin's observation that "fascism aestheticizes politics."[21] The liberal-democratic theory of political knowledge tends to regard art in politics as a veil. It is suspicious of aestheticization of political speech or action as a way to corrupt liberal-democratic accountabilities. From the liberal-democratic perspective, the aestheticization of politics is a potent tool with which the necessary yet precarious duality between individual and society, private and public can be undermined. An attitude which does not lend facts and observations an authority to check claims and actions is not congenial, as students of German democracy have pointed out, for the evolution of liberal-democratic civic culture.[22] John Dewey was well aware of this point when he insisted on the political relevance of what he called the "scientific attitude" to the realization of liberal-democratic political principles. He saw science as "a working model for the union of freedom and authority which is applicable to the political as well as other spheres."[23] Against the background of art in the service of fascism, Dewey insisted that "the spread of the scientific attitude is the only defense against deception by propaganda."[24]

This association of the scientific attitude and liberal-democratic political values feeds on a tradition that goes back as far as John Locke. For Locke, politics is the domain of outward things whereas the inward domain of faith and morality is beyond the legitimate reach of political authority. The insistence on the need to limit political authority to the domain of external observable referents — like the attack on "innate ideas"— was part of a wide cultural strategy to redefine the nature of authority. In politics this strategy was designed to serve the causes of stability and peace. Locke advocated naturalism to support the epistemology of liberal politics. He warned the philosophers that their paradoxes might corrupt language and "destroy the instruments and means of discourse." "Settled standards of nature" according to Locke can serve both science and politics. They "advance not only knowledge but also peace."[25] This early and most influential formulation of the liberal-democratic theory of knowledge was consistent with the epistemological commitments of early members of the Royal Society.[26] Their approach was largely inspired by the view that the religious and civil wars of the seventeenth century relied on transcendental notions of authority. Influential thinkers like Bacon, Newton, and Locke made important contributions to instrumental materialism as a cultural strategy to limit politics to this-worldly questions which are manageable in public forums. It is this fundamental commitment to despiritualize and demystify politics which encouraged liberal thinkers such as Bentham to suspect fiction and poetry, and which led many others to view utilitarianism and materialism not so much as means for the despiritualization of politics as for promoting disciplined public discourse and action.

Today, the cultural force of science declines and the journalistic profession becomes chief advocate of epistemological realism in liberal-democratic culture, especially those parts of it which are now committed to the language of documentation over and above the languages of fiction and entertainment. The journalistic imperative of separating facts from opinion has not led mass media news reporters in modern democracies to deny the legitimacy of opinion and interpretation entirely. Daily newspapers print personal stories and poems as expressions of personalized speech. The ethos of journalism insists, however, on separation between the reporting of facts and personal responses to the facts. This dualism is consistent with the liberal-democratic rejection of radical personalism and radical objectivism as positions which leave no cultural space for democratic discourse.

The liberal-democratic commitment to preserving both personal and public discourse reflects the idea of political order as immanent neither in nature nor in history nor in society, but as a structure continually negotiated by individuals. Liberal-democratic epistemology has had, therefore, to support a commitment to the private sphere of individuals which at the same time is compatible with a commitment to the possibility of a public sphere generated and upheld by individuals. Key features of liberal-democratic politics such as public debate, voting, free press, decisions by majorities, and the citizen's right to know are inseparable from the liberal-democratic civic epistemology which sustains the idea of a public sphere constituted by individuals. The duality in the liberal-democratic individual between a socially invisible inwardness and a visible outward existence as a citizen has exposed liberal-democratic strategy to attacks by both humanistic and deterministic monists who would cancel the dualism by allowing one of the parts to encompass the other. Fascism and Communism illustrate in the twentieth century two ways of undermining liberal-democratic politics by canceling the essential dualism between the subjective world of the self and the public world of the citizen. In totalitarian states where the public sphere is not limited by commitment to the integrity of the private sphere, science and technology are used to build up authority but not to secure accountability. While the liberal-democratic polity has engaged science both in order to generate discipline and to expose claims of authority to public tests, in the totalitarian state this latter function of science has not been realized. While in the controlled public sphere of the totalitarian state science has been enlisted to the politics of justification, in the liberal-democratic polity it is heavily engaged also in the politics of search and criticism.

In each case a particular political culture adopts and edits the impact of science to fit its particular needs. This process goes on, of course, at many levels of the modern state. As professors Hart and Honoré have shown, in the legal context of modern democracies the validating of scientific constructs of causality has been tempered by an underlying policy of defending certain vital norms of criminal responsibility.[27] Similarly, at the popular level of liberal-democratic politics, the commitment to what Tocqueville called a denial of "that which cannot be comprehended" has often led the public to be suspicious not only of miracles and angels but also of genes and electrons. The failure of particular scientific concepts or theories to acquire credibility in the common sense context of social and civil discourse should not obscure, however, the fundamental affinities between the images of knowledge and reality projected by science in the wider society and the epistemological presuppositions of liberal-democratic politics.

Calls for restoring the moral, spiritual, and aesthetic dimensions of politics have all too often neglected to consider the implications of such moves for the epistemological foundations of political discourse and action.[28] If there is a crisis of republican civic virtues in late twentieth-century liberal democracy, it is a minor crisis by comparison with the emerging crisis of liberal-democratic epistemology. The corrosive influences of materialism, egotism, and narrow utilitarianism on civic morality are not what is new in the life of late twentieth-century liberal democracy. Tensions between individualism, utilitarianism, and public values were salient already during the seventeenth century.[29] What is novel and increasingly threatening to many is, rather, a growing social distrust of a liberal-democratic theory of knowledge. This crisis of civil epistemology goes further than the skepticism voiced in earlier decades by people such as Walter Lippmann and Harold Laswell about the capacity of democratic citizens to pass rational judgments on matters concerning public affairs.[30] Such distrust still permitted some critics to seek a remedy in the rationality and expertise of administrative and technical elites. The urge to enhance the role of experts in government often represented disenchantment with the hope of fusing knowledge and democratic political participation. The anti-democratic connotations of intellectual and technical elitism were supposed to be mitigated by the assumption that knowledge, expertise, and internal professional codes can persist as constraints on the arbitrary use of power or the unrestrained pursuit of self-interest.

American liberal-democrats who in earlier decades were critical of Russian technocratic centralism still believed, with people such as Herbert Croly and Charles Meriam, that there is also a democratic variant of politics as technique, although this variant does not presuppose mass political participation. Today the crisis in the epistemology of liberal-democratic politics has gone much beyond questioning the competence or the equipment of democratic citizens. In its radical forms it questions the very notion that political discourse and action have a public dimension, and challenges the very feasibility of using facts and certified notions of causality to judge utterances and actions or relations between impersonal referents. If Dewey's claim that science displays the "possible union of freedom and authority" sounds anachronistic today, this is not due to some recent upsurge of a romantic reaction to scientific rationalism. The main impact has not come from the disciples of William Blake, Coleridge, or Ruskin, although they have been active among us. It has come from the heart of science itself.

Such voices, to be sure, have always been heard. James Conant, for instance, insisted in 1953 that science should not be expected to mirror or map reality. But the temper of the postwar years was not hospitable to cognitive pessimism. The atmosphere was rather of optimistic instrumental meliorism. A decade or two later, mounting internal criticism of optimistic epistemological realism was already evolving against a background of social attacks upon science and its role in liberal-democratic politics. As illustrated in the work of Theodore Roszak, the massive use of drugs in the 1960s was partially directed against the epistemology of liberal democracy, a way of dispensing with the cultural artifact of reality as a source of disciplined and responsible conduct.

As we near the end of the present century, the scientific intelligentsia has lost much of its earlier confidence in defending the lines between facts and fictions. Such ideas as that facts are theory-laden, that reality is largely unobservable, and that the world we live in is a world which lends itself to infinite interpretations are not being spread by anti-intellectuals or representatives of a counterculture. They are being expounded by philosophers like Kuhn, Feyerabend, Rorty, and Goodman, who work within the centers of scientific culture.[31] They have given encouragement to a very sophisticated epistemological anarchism according to which the difficulties with the idea of knowledge as a mirror cannot be corrected by perfecting the mirror or educating the eye because the problem is with the very status of objects as con-

structs. At the popular level of political epistemology, such attitudes imply that the gap between what is really happening and
what democratic citizens perceive cannot be bridged by education. The very idea of a gap is conceived as a result of thinking
in terms of the discarded mirror metaphor. When James Reston
observes that in Washington "theater has replaced government"
he touches one of the most important political consequences of
the declining authority of "reality" as a norm in political discourse
and action.[32] Liberal political observers like James David Barber
watch with increasing anxiety this detachment of politics from reality, this "drift towards fiction, [this phenomenon of] politics as
theater."[33] Perhaps the most significant political manifestation of
the change is discernable again in the field of mass media news
reporting. Mass media professionals who know that news consists
not of purely unedited pictures of reality but of largely selective
constructs of experience have nevertheless tended to defend the
ethos of news reporting as mirroring objective facts.[34] Such a commitment to the notion of reality as a world of objective facts is
probably guided by the need to protect journalistic credibility.[35]
But since the mid-1960s a series of trials and exposures which revealed to the public the process of constructing the news has gradually narrowed the gap between what journalists do and what they
are believed to be doing. In earlier times there was some guilt because of the pretended innocence of news reporting. It has been
recently replaced by a more self-conscious, less defensive employ-
ment of the freedom which comes with the realization that even
mirrors select. This realization remains, however, a major source
of anxiety. A *New York Times* reviewer of Strobe Talbott's book
*Deadly Gambits: The Reagan Administration and the Stalemate
in Nuclear Arms Control*[36] showed concern over signs that "the
line between journalism and fiction has become blurred." "We are
not accustomed," he complained, "to giving journalists the same
leeway we give novelists."[37]

Such developments indicate the extent to which the classical
epistemology of liberal-democratic politics is undermined by current cultural and intellectual trends. Michael Schudson, a historian of American journalism, has recently shown concern over the
gap between the idea of democratic journalism and its practice.
Once it is realized that this gap is due not to a moral failure but

to changing sensibilities, the willingness to recognize liberal-democratic epistemology as a cultural artifact, as a myth, increases. Schudson is ready, therefore, to recommend that "the news media should be self-consciously schizophrenic in their efforts to perform a democratic political function."[38] He implies that faith in the feasibility of democratic persuasion is too important to be conceded in the face of merciless recognition of the elusive nature of political facts and realities. In the end, however, Schudson underestimates the magnitude of the cultural break in liberal-democratic epistemology. He suggests, very much as the skeptics of the 1920s and the 1930s did, that "if the press cannot communicate about government to the people at large, it can nevertheless hold the governors accountable to a relatively small number of informed and powerful people."[39]

The problem is that the very factual-documentary language of reporting and accountability loses its grip and credibility at all levels. This process is accompanied by signs of change in the nature of the issues which constitute the agenda of late twentieth-century democratic politics. Several students of democratic politics like Samuel Barnes, Max Kasse, Kendall Baker, and others already noted a few years ago a shift from old to new political styles of action paralleled by what they interpreted as a movement from instrumentalist-materialist to postmaterialist political orientations. Whereas the dominant style is still materialistic and the primary concerns are still with economic policies and their effects, they note the rising saliency of postmaterialist concerns with issues of principle and identity, like abortion and women's rights, which do not lend themselves to being settled by the politics of compromise and regular democratic procedures. These authors link the rise of such postmaterialist issues in Western democracies with the rise in political protest and direct action. Such styles of political action are attributed partly to the constraints on handling postmaterialist issues by usual democratic political procedures. "New politics issues," observed one political analyst, "are difficult to negotiate. [They] tend to polarize the electorate because they focus on values."[40] Another writer pointed out that the new politics "creates severe dilemmas for political parties and the process of representation."[41] If postmaterialist politics is indeed what such authors describe, it might signify a trend which counters Locke's strategy of materializing politics in order to secure stability and peace. Postmaterialism in politics may be just another aspect of the crisis in the epistemological premises of liberal-democratic civic life. Without a believable and knowable world of facts, political speech and political action cannot be depersonalized as elements of the public order.

In a world where neither science nor journalism nor the nature of public issues supports the civil epistemology of liberal-democratic politics, canons of liberal-democratic political speech and action cannot remain unalterable. Where a concept of reality external to all persons is not a culturally acknowledged given prior to all perceptions and interpretations but a continually changing and hence epistemologically elusive product of interaction, it is much harder to sustain a liberal democratic commitment to the duality of the private and the public realms.

The power of anarchistic epistemology in modern liberal democracies is boosted, of course, by its harmony with radical interpretations of individual freedom. In democracies solipsism is a powerful rationale for attacking authority and for radical decentralization. The freedom to construct and interpret reality is perhaps the ultimate challenge to all authorities. Anarchistic epistemological starting points from which any particular claims of authority are exposed tend to deny the basis of all alternative claims. Hence, in the late twentieth century, liberal-democratic epistemology can no longer draw strength from positivist contempt for metaphysics, myth, or fiction. The combination of the two words *science fiction* may have a deeper meaning in this context than we might have realized. The difficulties in grounding the civil epistemology of democracy in natural science or in common sense informed by vulgar realism have exposed the inseparable relations between epistemology and ideology.

In the end we cannot follow people like Robert Bellah and choose our favorite ethics separately from our favorite epistemology. A choice between alternative epistemologies or alternative myths of reality is also a choice of the kind of issues and ideas which are permitted to dominate the political agenda. A choice between alternative political issues and ideas is in turn also an implicit choice among respectively alternative epistemologies within which such issues and ideas can be conceived and handled.

The late twentieth-century democratic state is caught up in a dilemma of having to choose between a realistic epistemology whose complementary materialism and instrumentalism have been repugnant to the public spirit of civic morality, and a postmaterialist ethics which, like the ethics of religious politics in earlier times, entails an epistemology which is at best a fragile basis for a democratic political order. This dilemma has recast the question concerning the place of science in the modern democratic state. In the earlier phase the main issue was how science could inform and limit democratic politics without becoming politicized. Today the issue is increasingly whether the epistemology of liberal-democratic political discourse and action can survive the erosion of classical concepts of knowledge and reality.

NOTES

1. Robert N. Bellah, *The Broken Covenant: American Civil Religion in Time of Trial* (New York: Seabury Press, 1975).

2. Ibid., p. 72.

3. William M. Sullivan, *Reconstructing Public Philosophy* (Berkeley, Calif.: University of California Press, 1982).

4. Perhaps the most articulate criticism of science to have come from the student protest during the 1960s is Theodore Roszak, *The Making of a Counterculture* (Garden City, N.Y.: Doubleday & Co., 1968). For a discussion of the critics of science see John Passmore, *Science and Its Critics* (London: Duckworth, 1978).

5. See, for example, Michael Heyd, "The Reaction to Enthusiasm in the Seventeenth Century: Towards an Integrative Approach," *Journal of Modern History* 53 (June 1981): 258–80.

6. See Keith Thomas, *Religion and the Decline of Magic* (Harmondsworth: Penguin Books, 1971); and Charles Gillispie, *The Edge of Objectivity* (Princeton, N.J.: Princeton University Press, 1966).

7. On ideals of discourse see, for example, Hans Aarsleff, *From Locke to Saussure* (Minneapolis: University of Minnesota Press, 1982), especially the chapter on John Wilkins, pp. 239–77. On the role of the encyclopedia see Charles C. Gillispie, "Introduction," in *A Diderot Pictorial Encyclopedia of Trades and Industry* (New York: Dover, 1959). On science museums see Alma S. Wittlin, *The Museum: Its History and Its Tasks in Education* (London: Routledge & Kegan Paul, 1949).

8. See Richard Rorty, *Philosophy and the Mirror of Nature* (Princeton, N.J.: Princeton University Press, 1979).

9. Edward L. Youmans, ed., *The Culture Demanded by Modern Life* (New York: Appleton & Co., 1867).

10. On the concept of "organized skepticism" see Robert K. Merton, "The Normative Structure of Science," in Robert K. Merton, *The Sociology of Science*, ed. Norman W. Storer (Chicago: University of Chicago Press, 1973), p. 270.

11. Karl Popper, *The Logic of Scientific Discovery* (New York: Basic Books, 1959); and *The Open Society and Its Enemies* (London: Routledge & Kegan Paul, 1945).

12. Yaron Ezrahi, "Science and the Problem of Authority in Democracy," in *Science and Social Structure: A Festschrift for Robert K. Merton*, ed. Thomas F. Gieryn, Transactions of the New York Academy of Sciences, series 2, vol. 39 (April 1980): 43–60.

13. Edward A. Purcell, Jr., *The Crisis of Democratic Theory* (Lexington, Ky.: University Press of Kentucky, 1973), especially pp. 117–59.

14. See on this issue Yaron Ezrahi, "Einstein and the Light of Reason," in *Albert Einstein: Historical and Cultural Perspectives*, ed. Gerald Holton and Yehuda Elkana (Princeton: Princeton University Press, 1982).

15. On the use of the mirror metaphor to describe news reporting see Edward J. Epstein, *News from Nowhere* (New York: Random House, 1973). On the philosophical decline of the mirror metaphor as a description of scientific knowledge see Rorty, *Philosophy and the Mirror of Nature*.

16. Nelson Goodman, *Ways of World Making* (Sussex: Harvester Press, 1978).

17. See, for example, Walter Lippmann, *The Phantom Public* (New York: Harcourt & Brace, 1925).

18. W. V. Quine, "Two Dogmas of Empiricism," in W. V. Quine, *From a Logical Point of View*, 2nd ed. (Cambridge, Mass.: Harvard University Press, 1961), p. 44.

19. Alexis de Tocqueville, *Democracy in America*, 2 vols. (New York: Vintage Books, 1955), 2: 4.

20. Ibid., pp. 4–5.

21. Walter Benjamin, *Illuminations*, ed. Hannah Arendt, trans. Harry Zohn (New York: Schocken Books, 1969), p. 242.

22. Rolf Darendorf, *Society and Democracy in Germany* (Garden City, N.Y.: Anchor, 1969), pp. 142–55.

23. John Dewey, *Intelligence in the Modern World: John Dewey's Philosophy*, ed. Joseph Ratner (New York: Modern Library, 1939), p. 360.

24. John Dewey, *Freedom and Culture* (New York: Putnam, 1939), pp. 148–49.

25. John Locke, *An Essay concerning Human Understanding*, 2 vols. (New York: Dover, 1959), 2: 106–20.

26. Thomas Sprat, *History of the Royal Society*, ed. Jackson I. Cope and Howard W. Jones (St. Louis, Mo.: Washington University Press, 1958).

27. H. L. A. Hart and Anthony M. Honoré, *Causation and the Law* (Oxford: Clarendon Press, 1959).

28. Sullivan, *Reconstructing Public Philosophy*.

29. See, for instance, J. A. W. Gunn, *Politics and the Public Interest in the Seventeenth Century* (London: Routledge & Kegan Paul, 1969).

30. Purcell, *The Crisis of Democratic Theory*, pp. 95–114.

31. See Thomas Kuhn, *Structure of Scientific Revolutions* (Chicago: University of Chicago Press, 1970); Paul Feyerabend, *Against Method* (London: New Left Books, 1975); Goodman, *Ways of World Making*; and Rorty, *Philosophy and the Mirror of Nature*.

32. *New York Times*, 20 January 1985, p. 23.

33. James David Barber, *The Pulse of Politics* (New York: Norton, 1980), p. 320.

34. Epstein, *News from Nowhere*.

35. Herbert J. Gans, *Deciding What's News* (New York: Vintage Books, 1980), p. 186.

36. Strobe Talbott, *Deadly Gambits: The Reagan Administration and the Stalemate in Nuclear Arms Control* (New York: Alfred A. Knopf, 1984).

37. Theodore Draper, "Journalism History and Journalistic History," review of *Deadly Gambits* by Strobe Talbott, *New York Times Review of Books*, 9 December 1984, pp. 3, 32–34.

38. Michael Schudson, "News Media and Democratic Processing," *Society*, January–February 1984, p. 48.

39. Ibid., p. 51.

40. Kendall L. Baker, Russell J. Dolton, and Kai Hildebrandt, *Germany Transformed* (Cambridge, Mass.: Harvard University Press, 1981), p. 290.

41. Samuel H. Barnes and Max Kasse, *Political Action* (Beverly Hills, Calif.: Sage Publications, 1979), p. 531.

PART II

Civil Religion and Political Theology in America

4

Public Philosophy and Public Theology in America Today

ROBERT N. BELLAH

HAVING BEEN INVOLVED for almost seven years in a project that is in part a contribution to both public philosophy and public theology, and which has just been published,[1] this seemed a good occasion to step back and look at the larger issues of the place of public philosophy and public theology in America today. I will consider first some recent predecessors: John Dewey, Reinhold Niebuhr, and Walter Lippmann. I will then look at two books that clearly pose the terms of the current discussion: William M. Sullivan's *Reconstructing Public Philosophy* and Richard John Neuhaus's text *The Naked Public Square*.[2] Finally I will relate the discussion to my own most recent work, to the Catholic Bishops' draft Pastoral Letter on Catholic Social Teachings and the U.S. Economy, and to some other recent developments. Throughout I will be concerned with the following issues: the necessity of public philosophy and public theology; the content of public philosophy and public theology; and the difficulties which the present state of our intellectual life and of our public life poses for these undertakings.

Alexis de Tocqueville's classic *Democracy in America* posed the problem starkly and in terms quite different from any of our twentieth-century authors. For Tocqueville Christianity was simultaneously our public philosophy and our public theology. It provided the secure basis of our freedom and our capacity to experiment and innovate in the economic and political fields. He went so far as to say that religion should be considered "as the first of their political institutions," not because it is established by law or intervenes directly in government, but because it provides the secure principles of our public life. "Christianity," he wrote, "reigns without obstacles, by universal consent; consequently, everything in the moral field is certain and fixed, although the world of politics is given over to argument and experiment."[3]

Our twentieth-century authors differ from Tocqueville in two important respects. The first is that they do not expect or hope for a consensus quite so "universal" as Tocqueville described (we will have to consider what they do hope for as we go along) and which was probably not quite accurate even for the America of the 1830s. The second is that they are dismayed by the lack of even a minimal and nuanced consensus such as they feel is necessary for the survival of free institutions. Instead they describe an individualism, a privatism, a liberalism, a secularism, or a utilitarianism that has all but destroyed the basis of our common life. The images are quite striking and reinforce each other. I have already noted Neuhaus's image of "the naked public square." Walter Lippmann, writing in 1955, spoke of "the hollow shell of freedom." He said that "the citadel is vacant because the public philosophy is gone, and all that the defenders of freedom have to defend in common is a public neutrality and a public agnosticism."[4]

William Sullivan spoke of "the exhaustion of political imagination." He found that the philosophical liberalism which is common to both liberals and conservatives in contemporary American politics is "deeply anti-public in its fundamental premises" and "denies meaning and value to even the notion of common purpose, or politics in its classic sense."[5] Reinhold Niebuhr found in 1944 that modern secularism "creates a spiritual vacuum" and that "it stands on the abyss of moral nihilism and threatens the whole of life with a sense of meaninglessness."[6] John Dewey in 1930 said that "the loyalties that once held individuals, which gave them support, direction, and unity of outlook on life, have well-nigh disappeared." In consequence such individuals are "lost, confused, and bewildered."[7] Indeed the litany of woes stretches back far enough that we might well ask how come the game has not been lost long before this.

We must note that the jeremiad, which continues, as it has since the seventeenth century, to be a common form of American public discourse, is always admonitory. The overt message is that things have come to a sad pass but the real message is that *if* things go on as they are *then* indeed all will be lost. John Courtney Murray offered a consummate example of the genre, precisely apt for our present concern, when he wrote in 1962:

> And if this country is to be overthrown from within or from without, I would suggest that it will not be overthrown by Communism. It will be overthrown because it will have made an impossible experiment. It will have undertaken to establish a technological order of most marvelous intricacy, which will have been constructed and will operate without relations to true political ends; and this technological order will hang, as it were, suspended over a moral confusion; and this moral confusion will itself be suspended over a spiritual vacuum. This would be the real danger resulting from a type of fallacious, fictitious, fragile unity that could be created among us.[8]

If our three older authors, Dewey, Niebuhr, and Lippmann, share a common diagnosis, they differ, and differ instructively, in the directions they would turn to for a cure. In the very title of the book I am using as a key to Dewey's position, *Individualism Old and New*, we can discern his key contrast. The old individualism is rooted in an outmoded form of society in which a *laissez faire* economy went hand in hand with a rugged individualism that virtually ignores society. The new individualism of which Dewey speaks is that not-yet-realized individual flowering that would develop in a genuinely cooperative corporate society toward which we are moving. For Dewey the "merely traditional," the "beliefs and institutions that dominate merely because of custom and inertia,"[9] are precisely the things that are holding us back from the creation of a new, more satisfying society. For Dewey natural intelligence, which is never merely technical, but is also moral and even emotional, can show us the way to the future by sloughing off the past and building on the methods of natural science, so that we can consciously create a new society in conformity with the possibilities of the modern world. In that new more collective and corporate society American individualism will be fulfilled: "equality and freedom expressed not merely externally and politically but through personal participation in the development of a shared culture."[10]

Walter Lippmann looks in precisely the opposite direction from John Dewey for a cure to our lack of public coherence: he looks to the old, not to the new. For Lippmann the very meaning of the term *public philosophy* is close to the perennial philosophy of classical antiquity which was the common sense of the educated throughout the history of the West, at least until the end of the eighteenth century. At the core of his project Lippmann wants to resurrect the idea of natural law and the reason that instructs all persons of good will as to its teachings. For Lippmann, even more than for Dewey, this reason is far from a merely technical rationality. It is not so much Dewey's natural intelligence that actively intervenes in the world to bring about a desired result as it is a moral reason that instructs us about our rights and our duties. Far from seeing modernity creating the conditions for a new sociality, as Dewey does, Lippmann tends to blame modernity for the radical subjectivism and relativism that has almost destroyed our ability to understand the teachings of the public philosophy.

It is interesting that neither Dewey nor Lippmann can do public philosophy without doing public theology. They are thus both characteristically American, as Bruce Kuklick argues in his *Churchmen and Philosophers: From Jonathan Edwards to John Dewey*.[11] But the way in which they do theology is characteristically opposed.

In *Individualism Old and New* Dewey merely derides the impotence of contemporary American religion, but in *A Common Faith*, published in 1934, Dewey offers a constructive alternative. He differentiates between religion and the religious. Religion is tied to the dogmas and superstitions of the past, chief of which is the idea of the supernatural. Dewey sees the idea of the supernatural as inevitably belittling the natural intelligence, as reinforcing the status quo, and, even against the intention of believers, taking an essentially *laissez faire* attitude toward the problems of this world. In place of the old static religion Dewey sees the religious attitude carried into all the spheres of life, an open-ended quest to realize the highest ideal values of our common humanity, which would make explicit what "has always been the common faith of mankind."[12]

If the originally Protestant John Dewey ends up with a faith in naturalistic historicism the originally Jewish Walter Lippmann could hardly have taken a more opposed route. In *The Public Philosophy* Lippmann is clearly flirting with a Catholic Neo-Thomism to give religious depth to his perennial philosophy. Lippmann affirms what Dewey denies: a "realm of the spirit," a vision that "is not of this world but of another and radically different one."[13] For Lippmann it is just such a sensitivity to the spiritual realm that supports morally serious men and women in their search for the good life. And far from calling for the end of the traditional religions and their replacement by a generalized religious faith in the ideals of humanity, Lippmann would strengthen the traditional church as a critical balance to the state:

> But while the separation of the powers of the churches and of the state is essential to a right relationship between them, the negative rule is not the principle of their right relationship. Church and state need to be separate, autonomous, and secure. But they must also meet in all the issues of good and evil.[14]

For all of these contrasts it will not do to characterize Dewey simply as a liberal and Lippmann as a conservative. There are Puritan and even Aristotelian aspects of Dewey's thought that prevent him from being classified as a liberal. As Daniel Bell has recently pointed out, neither conservatives nor liberals really understood Lippmann's book *The Public Philosophy*. The first thought he agreed with their ideas more than in fact he did. The second were merely charmed by his style. In their views of property and of the relation between the economy and society both men transcend the dichotomy between neocapitalists and welfare liberals that has characterized our political spectrum for some decades.

Dewey in 1930 decried a number of weaknesses of American economic life that the New Deal and the Great Society would greatly mitigate. In particular he called for unemployment insurance, old age insurance, and medical insurance, none of which existed in Hoover's America. But moving beyond those immediate needs Dewey raised issues that are still not resolved, indeed still barely discussed in American political life: democratic participation in economic decisions and whether our economy is to be or-

ganized for private profit or for public use. He was certainly not
a state socialist but he did favor a number of experiments and in-
novations that today we might classify under the rubric of economic democracy.

When we turn to Lippmann we discover that the very first
example that he gives of the process of "the renewal of the public
philosophy" is to call into question the absolute sanctity of private property that has developed in recent times. He sees many
of our current social and economic problems as arising from a system of private property in which the rights of ownership do not
have concomitant duties to the public good. In place of the "sole
and despotic dominion" that Blackstone would give the individual property owner, Lippmann takes the Thomist position that
"the ultimate title does not lie in the owner. The title is in 'mankind,' in *The People* as a corporate community." He goes on to say:

> Because the legal owner enjoys the use of a limited necessity
> belonging to all men, he cannot be the sovereign lord of his
> possessions. He is not entitled to exercise his absolute and
> therefore arbitrary will. He owes duties that correspond with
> his rights. His ownership is a grant made by the laws to achieve
> not his private purposes but the common social purpose. And,
> therefore, the laws of property may and should be judged,
> reviewed, and, when necessary, amended, so as to define the
> specific system of rights and duties that will promote the ends
> of society.[15]

On still another point Dewey and Lippmann seem to be op-
posites but in the end may not be so far apart. Dewey seems at
first glance to be as resolutely historicist as Lippmann is ahistorical. For Dewey everything changes according to the historical context. For Lippmann the public philosophy would seem to be true
at all times and all places. Yet it is hard to reconcile Dewey's stal-
wart commitment to specific moral virtues — compassion, justice,
equality — with a radical historicism from which they could never
be derived. And Lippmann's insistent use of the qualifier *Western*
seems to give his ahistorical reason a local habitation. At one point
Lippmann seems to be moving toward a more specifically historical understanding when he speaks of tradition:

But traditions are more than the culture of the arts and sciences. They are the public world to which our private worlds are joined. This continuum of public and private memories transcends all persons in their immediate and natural lives and it ties them all together. In it there is performed the mystery by which individuals are adopted and initiated into membership in the community.

The body which carries this mystery is the history of the community, and its central theme is the great deeds and the high purposes of the great predecessors. From them the new men descend and prove themselves by becoming participants in the unfinished story.[16]

Yet even here it is tradition and history in general that are being celebrated. Throughout the book we get little sense of a concrete history of which we might be a part. Both Dewey's historicism and Lippmann's ahistoricism are equally abstract. Neither situate us in a specific history or tie us to traditions that actually operate in our society. In this regard turning to Reinhold Niebuhr is a refreshing change.

Our exemplar of Niebuhr's public philosophy and public theology is *The Children of Light and the Children of Darkness* of 1944. The problem with which Niebuhr is concerned is similar to that of Dewey and Lippmann. He too wishes to offer a defense of free institutions more adequate than those currently available:

The thesis of this volume grew out of my conviction that democracy has a more compelling justification and requires a more realistic vindication than is given by the liberal culture with which it has been associated in modern history.[17]

And like the others he mixes philosophy and theology. He offers up the book as "political philosophy," whose religious and theological basis he does not seek to elaborate. Nevertheless he concludes the foreword by saying,

It will be apparent, however, that [these pages] are informed by the belief that a Christian view of human nature is more adequate for the development of a democratic society than either the optimism with which democracy has become historically associated or the moral cynicism which inclines human communities to tyrannical strategies.[18]

Related to Niebuhr's greater historical specificity is his greater willingness to deal in his Christian political philosophy with the reality of conflict and difference, compared to Dewey's common faith or Lippmann's public philosophy. Dewey, of course, believed in discussion and experiment as essential to the public process. Yet he saw the implicit historical direction that he discerned as inevitably winning out. Lippmann specifically disavows the idea that the public philosophy of a free society could be restored "by fiat and by force." Instead he sees the necessity of a form of moral education:

> To come to grips with the unbelief which underlies the condition of anomy, we must find a way to reestablish confidence in the validity of public standards. We must renew the convictions from which our political morality springs.[19]

But the inevitable antinomies of social life are as obscured by the notion of socialization into a common culture as they are by the idea of the progressive triumph of a single historical tendency. For Niebuhr on the other hand there is always the yes and the no, the light and the dark, the contending forces. Christian political philosophy does not offer any perfect resolution of these struggles but only the hope of enough common ground and enough perspective so that the conflict does not become self-destructive.

Central to Niebuhr's discussion of the conflicts between the individual and the community and between the community and property is his conviction that the bourgeois liberal alternative on these questions has run its course but that the Marxist collectivist alternative is, in any absolute sense, intolerable. He thus sees our common life as moving back and forth, upholding individual rights but also the common good of the community, defending economic decentralization but intervening firmly where private economic forces lead to grave injustice.

In his discussion of the conflict between secular universalism and religious particularity Niebuhr's observations are profound and especially relevant to our present situation in America. He is equally negative toward a secular universalism that ends in the emptying out of all meaning and a religious triumphalism that would assert something like a "Christian America." His own position is what he calls a "religious solution of the problem of religious diversity":

> This solution makes religious and cultural diversity possible within the presuppositions of a free society, without destroying the religious depth of culture. The solution requires a very high form of religious commitment. It demands that each religion, or each version of a single faith, seek to proclaim its highest insights while yet preserving an humble and contrite recognition of the fact that all actual expressions of religious faith are subject to historical contingency and relativity. Such a recognition creates a spirit of tolerance and makes any religious or cultural movement hesitant to claim official validity for its form of religion or to demand an official monopoly for its cult.
>
> Religious humility is in perfect accord with the presuppositions of a democratic society. Profound religion must recognize the difference between the unconditioned character of the divine and the conditioned character of all human enterprise. . . .
>
> Religious toleration through religiously inspired humility and charity is always a difficult achievement. It requires that religious convictions be sincerely and devoutly held while yet the sinful and finite corruptions of these convictions be humbly acknowledged; and the actual fruits of other faiths be generously estimated. Whenever the religious groups of a community are incapable of such humility and charity the national community will be forced to save its unity through either secularism or authoritarianism.[20]

Richard John Neuhaus and William M. Sullivan have quite recently published books which sharply pose the issue for public philosophy and public theology today and which draw in interesting ways on the writers and positions I have already discussed. Richard Neuhaus in *The Naked Public Square* clearly stands in the tradition of Reinhold Niebuhr in trying to recover a public discussion of fundamental religious and political truths even when we do not expect complete agreement. He calls to task both the liberal mainline churches and the conservative evangelicals for undermining this essential common task.

Particularly impressive is the sharpness with which Neuhaus criticizes the Christian right, in view of his own growing identification with political and religious conservatism in recent years:

> Fundamentalist leaders rail against secular humanists for creating what I have called the naked public square. In fact, fundamentalism is an indispensable collaborator in that creation. By separating public argument from private belief, by building a wall of strict separationism between faith and reason, fundamentalist religion ratifies and reinforces the conclusions of militant secularism.[21]

In this tendency Neuhaus finds that religious conservatives are ironically following the lead of religious liberals who for some time have abandoned the effort to relate Christian truths to current reality in favor of embracing uncritically some current version of liberal or radical ideology. Neuhaus attempts to recall both sides to faithfulness to their traditions and the public relevance of those traditions, but in the spirit of humility and contrition of which Niebuhr wrote. Neuhaus fears that in their various sectarian fervors the religious left and the religious right will withdraw so totally from the public square that it will be invaded by some form of authoritarianism or totalitarianism. It is this eventuality to which Niebuhr also warned a triumphant secularism would lead.

In an important chapter entitled "Critical Patriotism and Civil Community" Neuhaus makes a move in his fervent criticism of the religious left that I think is in serious need of rebuttal. He quite rightly suggests that when elements of the religious left reject the United States as totally corrupt, and perhaps also idolatrously praise some doubtful foreign regime, they have removed themselves from the public discussion and have undermined the possibility of our recovering a viable public philosophy. He correctly suggests that a critical patriotism is a necessary condition for a fruitful public discussion. But he makes a most un-Niebuhrian move when he offers a kind of loyalty test for admission into the public discourse.

The proposition to which he would have us all agree is one he calls "carefully nuanced." It reads: "On balance and considering the alternatives, the influence of the United States is a force for good in the world."[22] Yet, I would argue, adherence to such an empirical proposition, one almost impossible to test, would tie the critical patriot into a kind of civil orthodoxy that would irreparably rupture the Niebuhrian dialectic. I would agree that the critical patriot must *hope* that the United States will be an influence for good in the world. If there is no hope then one must withdraw into apolitical sectarianism or revolutionary mania. But Neuhaus misses the Niebuhrian irony of history that it may be precisely the best nation in history that does the worst thing that humans have ever done. It is as though Neuhaus has suddenly forgotten about sin. The critical patriot must hope that the United States will be a force for good in the world but must fear that it may be a force for evil. After all the United States is the only nation in the world to have used the atom bomb, and that against civilian populations in two large Japanese cities. It is certainly possible — it is a possibility toward which the critical patriot must exercise a salutary fear — that that same United States would set off a catastrophe which could destroy civilization if not life itself. For the critical patriot who is also a Niebuhrian Christian it is life lived in the tension between that hope and that fear that will make the greatest contribution to our recovery of a public morality, not some enforced patriotic orthodoxy, however "nuanced." Yet finally I want to emphasize the service that Neuhaus has done us in attempting to recall us from our sectarian enthusiasms of recent years to engage once again in a public discussion about the most important things.

If Neuhaus continues the Niebuhrian strand of the discussion, William M. Sullivan, in *Reconstructing Public Philosophy*, in interesting ways combines the traditions of Dewey and Lippmann. (Even the title suggests as much, for "reconstructing" is a Deweyan term while "public philosophy" recalls Lippmann.) Sullivan clearly agrees with Dewey that we are moving into an ever more interdependent world that demands greater corporate responsibility, not a return to atomistic individualism. He also raises the possibility that economic democracy should return to the agenda of our public discussion. But he does not believe that an ahistorical "natural intelligence" of the sort Dewey relied on is the appropriate vehicle to meet our present need. Indeed it is precisely Dewey's inability to differentiate such a natural intelligence from the purely technical or scientistic rationality that seems to be the cause of many of our problems that limits Dewey's relevance to our present discussion. Instead Sullivan turns to something much closer to what Lippmann describes, namely, the tradition of civic republicanism, which is rooted in Platonic and Aristotelian political philosophy but has been in subsequent centuries developed by Christian insights and the experience of republican and democratic societies. Sullivan's approach is more historically specific than Lippmann's, in that he seeks to trace the presence of civic republicanism in the formative phase of American history as well as in its survivals in the present day. Sullivan argues that only a rootedness in the classical tradition will help us avoid turning any effort at present reconstruction into one more experiment in disintegrative modernization.

Sullivan's contribution is critical as well as constructive. Neuhaus warned of the danger of the disintegration of our public life into warring religious and political sectarianisms. Sullivan warns us of the dangers in our intellectual life of an alliance of technical reason and psychological individualism that entirely precludes a serious consideration of public life. Increasing academic specialization has led philosophers and social scientists (and often theologians as well) to turn away from public discourse to the discussion of technical issues with fellow experts. It is partly for these reasons that we do not have today a journalist like Walter Lippmann, a theologian like Reinhold Niebuhr, or a philosopher like John Dewey, each combining the highest intellectual seriousness with full participation in public discussion.

It is only a step beyond Sullivan's book to recognize that recovering a notion of social science as public philosophy and even as public theology may be a part of our effort to reconstruct those enterprises. In fact Sullivan is one of my collaborators in the effort to do just that that I mentioned at the beginning of this essay. Before briefly summarizing our efforts and some related ones, let me discuss some of the obstacles to this task. There has been a great tradition of social science as public philosophy, without which our own efforts would have been impossible. Tocqueville is the classic exemplar, but he has been followed not unworthily in the twentieth century by such works as the Middletown studies of Robert and Helen Lynd and David Riesman's book *The Lonely*

Crowd.[23] Even as recently as 1976 we have the powerful example of Kai T. Erikson's *Everything in Its Path: Destruction of Community in the Buffalo Creek Flood*, which is a moving meditation on the inadequacies of an individualistic culture in the face of catastrophe.[24]

Yet throughout the twentieth century another notion of social science has been growing in prestige, one that sees social science not as a process of social self-understanding,[25] but as a quasi-natural science, one that produces purely factual "findings" that are value-neutral but can be "applied" by whoever can, or can afford to, apply them. Social scientists as public philosophers have always kept a critical distance between themselves and their society, in part because they are loyal not only to their own society but to traditions of social reflection that transcend their own society in time and space. But for technical social scientists the link is severed altogether. There is simply no relation between the scientist as scientist and the scientist as citizen. Not only do they not see social science as contributing to public discussion, they think of their profession as one more interest group in the competition for scarce resources.

This conception of social science was forcibly borne in on me when a colleague, with the best of intentions, sent me a copy of an article that had appeared in the January 1985 issue of *Footnotes*, the bulletin published by the American Sociological Association to carry news of the profession. The friend had seen a newspaper article about *Habits of the Heart* and commended me for doing what the article recommended. Upon looking at the article in *Footnotes* I discovered that it concerned the dissemination of sociological research findings in the media. It quoted a report of the ad hoc Task Force on Sociology and the Media as follows:

> On balance, we believe the arguments for informing the public outweigh those which argue against such action. The gains that can be produced by an active, sustained public relations program, in our judgment, will be greater than the losses that may be incurred. Moreover, the growing competition for students and research/training funds plus the continuing political attacks on social research dictate the development of an effective and ongoing public relations program that is aimed

at building support for sociology in special and general publics. In this effort, our presentation of self in the mass media is of maximum importance.[26]

In looking through the entire article, though there is much about the "profession's image in the eyes of the public," there is nothing at all to indicate that sociologists have anything to contribute to public discussion — or anything to learn from it either.

This is not the place to summarize the data or the argument of *Habits of the Heart.* All I can do is indicate briefly why the five of us who wrote it believe it is a modest contribution to public philosophy and even perhaps to public theology.[27] The focus of our study is on the classic problem of citizenship: why do some Americans become involved in civic life? what meaning does it have for them when they do? why do they sometimes withdraw from it? why do other Americans never become involved at all? We wanted to know whether Americans are still citizens because the answer to that question, if the traditions of social thought and political philosophy upon which we draw are at all right, will tell us something significant about the possibilities for the survival of free institutions in our society. In carrying out our study we used the oldest methods known to social science: participant observation and the interview. In short we spoke as citizens to other citizens about matters of mutual concern. We did not try to hide our own beliefs nor were we hesitant in probing the bases of theirs. And then we brought the public discussion which was the data of our study into the book itself, so that it could provide the basis of a still wider public discussion.

Our book drew on many of the writers discussed in this paper but our conclusions are somewhat different. We avoided, or I hope we avoided, the tone of the jeremiad. We did not find the public square naked or the citadel vacant, though we did find those occupying those places feeling more than a little beleaguered. We found many volunteers, some of whom know deeply what it is to be a citizen, but we also found many for whom the public sphere is baffling and alien. We saw not just one tradition in America but several, sometimes related in fruitful complementarity but sometimes related in destructive attrition. We took our stand that the biblical and the civic republican traditions are the ones most in need of nurturing today.

We did not hesitate to draw conclusions from our work, though we have no political program nor even any specific policy suggestions. One thing we noted repeatedly: the destructive consequences of the way our economic life is organized on all those commitments in private and public life that hold us together as a free people. We found the destructive forces of modern economic life everywhere at work and the challenge to democratic reconstruction in the face of those forces greater than ever.

Among a number of other recent works that deserve comment let me single out the just published *Varieties of Religious Presence* by David A. Roozen, William McKinney, and Jackson W. Carroll,[28] because it is an example of social science as public theology very congenial to the approach of *Habits of the Heart*. The authors studied ten congregations in Hartford, Connecticut, through participant observation and interviews, and came to understand and to bring into the larger public discussion the views of those to whom they spoke.

In conclusion I would like to turn to an example of another kind of public philosophy and public theology that helps us understand our present situation, and that also uses social science in doing so: the first draft of the Catholic Bishops' Pastoral Letter on Catholic Social Teaching and the U.S. Economy.[29] Again this is not the place to summarize a long and complex document. Let me merely indicate a few of the reasons I believe it is significant and admirable.

Needless to say the bishops in this document are going against the current of the times, as the great exemplars of public philosophy and public theology often do. This means they have gotten an exceptionally bad press and that unless you have read the document itself you are almost certain to have a very inadequate understanding of it. The first thing to note, in spite of some press commentary to the contrary, is the extraordinary humility and openness of the document. It brings to the discussion of matters of great public concern the resources of the Bible, the tradition of Catholic social teachings, a sensitivity to the Protestant dimension of American culture, and the arguments and data available to secular reason alone. The document is, wherever particular policy matters are concerned, tentative and open to further discussion. It is firm only in the assertion that morality is as applicable to our economic life as to any other aspect of our life together and that it is possible to discover criteria in the economic sphere that a good society should meet, even though actual societies are not likely to approximate them very closely.

In my view, and in the view of the drafters of the document itself, it is Part 1, Biblical and Theological Foundations, that is most important. The press has ignored Part 1 and concentrated on the policy suggestions of Part 2, on the assumption that Part 1 consists of platitudes in which we all believe. Part 1 is a clear critique of radical American individualism. It asserts that "the dignity of the human person, realized in community with others, is the criterion against which all aspects of economic life must be measured."[30] It balances an absolute commitment to the dignity of the person, based on the fact that we are created in the image and likeness of God, with the fact that that dignity is only realized in community. "Communal solidarity is at the heart of the biblical understanding of the human condition."[31] I would say on the basis of our research for *Habits of the Heart* that most Americans do not understand that and that the greatest service the bishops could render would be to help more of us to do so.

I think in Part 2, again in contrast to much opinion in the media, it is the sober and judicious use of social science to flesh out tentative policy suggestions that is most impressive. The call for a new experiment in economic democracy drew the greatest fire, though I believe it is well thought through and well argued, because it is most out of step with the popular mood of the moment. Here the bishops are indeed ahead of their time, but perhaps not as far ahead of their time as some suggest. The bishops are accused of serving up warmed-over Mondaleism, of advocating welfare liberal programs that have been tried and failed. But economic democracy has never been tried in America, at least not since the rural towns of Puritan Massachusetts. There is something reminiscent of the 1920s about the present moment in America. Untrammeled capitalism is offered as the answer to all our problems. Babbitt is again our national hero. One looks in vain to the White House for a seriousness to match that of the bishops (or to match that of earlier chief magistrates who were sometimes teachers of our public philosophy and sometimes, as in the case of Lincoln, of our public theology as well). Instead one finds an offhand and highly selective biblicism[32] on the one hand and an unrestrained confidence in science and technology as the solutions to all our problems, foreign and domestic,[33] that would have appalled every writer cited in this paper.

In short our public philosophy and public theology are in peril," as distinguished Americans have been pointing out for over fifty years. Yet in religious and civic organizations we have many among us who understand the truth of our traditions and of our present condition as well as Americans ever have. If that is not ground for optimism it is at least ground for hope.

NOTES

1. Robert N. Bellah, Richard Madsen, William M. Sullivan, Ann Swidler, and Steven M. Tipton, *Habits of the Heart: Individualism and Commitment in American Life* (Berkeley, Calif.: University of California Press, 1985).

2. William M. Sullivan, *Reconstructing Public Philosophy* (Berkeley, Calif.: University of California Press, 1982); Richard John Neuhaus, *The Naked Public Square: Religion and Democracy in America* (Grand Rapids, Mich.: Eerdmans, 1984).

3. Alexis de Tocqueville, *Democracy in America*, trans. George Lawrence, ed. J. P. Mayer (New York: Doubleday & Co., Anchor Books, 1969), p. 292, with omissions.

4. Walter Lippmann, *The Public Philosophy* (New York: Mentor, 1956), p. 88.

5. Sullivan, *Reconstructing Public Philosophy*, pp. xi, xii.

6. Reinhold Niebuhr, *The Children of Light and the Children of Darkness* (New York: Charles Scribner's Sons, 1944), p. 133.

7. John Dewey, *Individualism Old and New* (New York: Putnam, 1930), p. 52.

8. John Courtney Murray, "Return to Tribalism," *Catholic Mind*, January 1962, as cited in Neuhaus, *Naked Public Square*, p. 85.

9. Dewey, *Individualism Old and New*, pp. 70, 71.

10. Ibid., p. 34.

11. Bruce Kuklick, *Churchmen and Philosophers: From Jonathan Edwards to John Dewey* (New Haven, Conn.: Yale University Press, forthcoming).

12. John Dewey, *A Common Faith* (New Haven, Conn.: Yale University Press, 1934), p. 87.

13. Lippmann, *Public Philosophy*, p. 115.

14. Ibid., p. 119.

15. Ibid., p. 93.

16. Ibid., p. 105.

17. Niebuhr, *Children of Light and Children of Darkness*, p. xii.

18. Ibid., pp. xiv, xv.

19. Lippmann, *Public Philosophy*, p. 88.

20. Niebuhr, *Children of Light and Children of Darkness*, pp. 134–35, 137–38.

21. Neuhaus, *Naked Public Square*, p. 37.

22. Ibid., p. 73.

23. Robert S. Lynd and Helen Merrell Lynd, *Middletown: A Study of Contemporary American Culture* (New York: Harcourt, Brace, 1929); and *Middletown in Transition: A Study in Cultural Conflicts* (New York: Harcourt, Brace, 1973); David Riesman, with Nathan Glazer and Reuel Denney, *The Lonely Crowd: A Study of the Changing American Character* (New Haven, Conn.: Yale University Press, 1950). It is interesting that John Dewey draws on the Lynds' Middletown studies for data in support of his arguments in *Individualism Old and New*.

24. Kai T. Erikson, *Everything in Its Path: Destruction of Community in the Buffalo Creek Flood* (New York: Simon & Schuster, 1976).

25. On social science as social self-understanding see the title essay in Edward Shils, *The Calling of Sociology and Other Essays on the Pursuit of Learning* (Chicago: University of Chicago Press, 1980). See also Robert N. Bellah, "Social Science as Practical Reason," in *Ethics, the Social Sciences, and Policy Analysis*, ed. Daniel Callahan and Bruce Jennings (New York: Plenum Press, 1983); and Norma Haan, Robert N. Bellah, Paul Rabinow, and William M. Sullivan, *Social Science as Moral Inquiry* (New York: Columbia University Press, 1983).

26. Carla B. Howery, "Public Relations Program Features Multifaceted Efforts," *Footnotes* 13, no. 1 (January 1985): 1.

27. See the Appendix, "Social Science as Public Philosophy," in Bellah, *Habits of the Heart*.

28. David A. Roozen, William McKinney, Jackson W. Carroll, *Varieties of Religious Presence: Mission in Public Life* (New York: Pilgrim, 1984).

29. "Catholic Social Teaching and the U.S. Economy," *Origins, NC Documentary Service* 14, nos. 22–23 (November 15, 1984).

30. Ibid., par. 23.

31. Ibid., par. 69.

32. *San Francisco Chronicle*, 5 February 1985, reports that Reagan quoted Luke 14:31 in support of his call for a continuing military buildup. *San Francisco Chronicle*, 22 February 1985, reports Reagan as

saying that he found "that the Bible contains an answer to just about everything and every problem that confronts us, and I wonder sometimes why we won't recognize that one book could solve our problems for us."

33. *San Francisco Chronicle*, 22 January 1985, reports Reagan in his second inaugural address as saying: "There are no limits to growth and human progress when men and women are free to follow their dreams." *San Francisco Chronicle*, 7 February 1985, reports that in his State of the Union Address Reagan stated that "manned space stations" will provide "new opportunities for free enterprise" in manufacturing "crystals of exceptional purity to produce super computers, creating jobs, technologies, and medical breakthroughs beyond anything we ever dreamed possible."

5

From Civil Religion to
Public Philosophy

RICHARD JOHN NEUHAUS

I HAVE NOT ABANDONED my original title, "The Brief and Disap-
pointing Life of American Civil Religion." It has become the sub-
title or, more precisely, the preface to an expanded proposal. The
proposal is that it is past time for us to move on from the civil
religion discussion to the reconstruction of a public philosophy for
the American democratic experiment.

I come, then, both to praise and to bury civil religion. I praise
it because it has helped to fix our minds on the moral meanings
by which we might order our common life. And I would gladly
assist at the burial of the conceptual confusion created by the claim
that civil religion is in fact a religion.

We are told that professional historians chortled condescend-
ingly when Robert Bellah in 1967 thought he had discovered
American civil religion. They claimed it was old hat to them, and
there may be some justice in their claim. Such smug chortlings
aside, however, we are deeply indebted to Robert Bellah for his
synthetic achievement in framing the familiar in an unfamiliar
way. More than that, he has for nineteen years helped to sustain
and advance the discussion to its present point where it has out-
grown, I believe, the terms in which it was launched. In an early
response to his critics, Bellah asked a question which has been un-
happily neglected in the subsequent discussion. "What Christians
call the Old Testament," he wrote, "is precisely the religious interpretation of the history of Israel. Is it so clear that American analo-

98

gizing from the Old (or New) Testament is necessarily religiously illegitimate? Why should the history of a people living two or three thousand years ago be religiously meaningful but the history of a people living in the last two or three hundred years be religiously meaningless?"[1] In the subsequent debate, many have lost sight of Bellah's important question.

That question challenged us to address the American experiment in terms of God's purposes in history. Today that challenge has been taken up — in however unsophisticated a manner — by some of those associated with what is too easily dismissed as fundamentalism. It has not, for the most part, been taken up by those who have maintained the civil religion debate as a medium-sized academic industry — perhaps because they are not comfortable in talking about God, not to mention whether God has purposes in history. The civil religion debate has been, with few exceptions, a theologically sterilized controversy over conflicting social theories, conducted by appearing unbelievers who are nonetheless hung up on religion. As one wit observed in 1974:

> To the academic students of religion, civil religion was an "ideal" topic. Even more than secular cities and godless theology, civil religion made plausible the claim that religion ought to be studied by the nonreligious. Here, God be praised, was a religion that was nonreligious, to which the denominations had no claim and which ought properly to belong to departments of religion. Civil religion sent nonprofessing gurus into spasms of ecstasy (i.e., they began to write papers on the topic).[2]

That comment may be unfair, but I believe it contains a large measure of truth.

From the beginning, the debate has been distracted by the question whether civil religion is in fact a religion. Rousseau bit the bullet. He made clear that what he meant by civil religion was a religion and he was prepared to follow through on the totalitarian implications of that claim. Not so with Bellah and those who have joined him in inviting this latter-day revisitation of civil religion. They are, unlike Rousseau, not disposed toward the imposition of a statist orthodoxy regarding religious belief. And, even if they were, they recognize that such a project would be alien to the American experiment in democratic freedom, which is the context of their deliberations.

From the beginning — indeed in the next to the first sentence of his famed essay — Bellah admitted to his ambivalence about calling the phenomenon a civil *religion*. "This article," he wrote, "argues not only that there is such a thing, but also that this religion — or perhaps better, this religious dimension — has its own seriousness and integrity and requires the same care in understanding that any other religion does."[3] "Or perhaps better, this religious dimension"—yes, much better indeed. Almost two decades of the civil religion debate have, in my judgment, never overcome the caveat allowed in the second sentence of its initiating salvo. A religious dimension is quite different from a religion. Christianity, Islam, and Hinduism are not religious dimensions; they are religions. Our understanding of the American experiment is not a religion; it is possessed of a religious dimension.

It may be argued that when an understanding which is marked by a religious dimension is articulated with creedal confidence and is institutionally embodied, then it becomes a religion. That is an argument made by proponents of American civil religion, and I will return to it. It may also be argued that there is something suspiciously ethnocentric in the idea that a religion is to be so clearly distinguished from other identifiable enterprises. Even the idea of *homo religiosus*, it has been pointed out, is peculiar to people shaped by modern Western culture. Outside of our cultural context it is understood that there is only *homo sapiens*, with most people being sapient enough to recognize that their lives are part of a transcendent spiritual reality, and some people being less sapient.

What is called ethnocentricity in this connection is not a failing, however. It is the inescapable condition in which we consider all things, including ways to escape our ethnocentricity. We are, if we are to be deemed rational, centered in the language, ideas, and experience of the culture of which we are part. We cannot ignore what is meant by a *religion* in our culture. In this respect too we should have "a decent respect to the opinions of mankind," especially to the opinions of those who share the experience we would illuminate. I take it to be a fact of capital importance that, outside the relatively small community of those who write papers on the subject, nobody affirms an American civil religion. And some of us within that community do not affirm it, as is evident from the present paper.

Note that I say that nobody *affirms* an American civil religion. It is widely acknowledged that there may be a civil religion, or that one may come into being. Civil religion is not a fiction. Rousseau spelled it out in theory and, in our time, we have seen its practice in, for example, both Nazism and Marxist-Leninism. Civil religion is not a fiction, but *American* civil religion is not the past or the present or, I pray, the future fact.

Consider — and, again, with a decent respect for the way most people think — the characteristics that distinguish what we ordinarily mean by a religion.[4] A religion has certain cultic aspects. People get together, usually with periodic frequency, to celebrate certain events, persons, and beliefs crucial to the religion's construction of reality. Then there are recognized leadership offices invested, formally or otherwise, with sacred authority. Third, there is some explicitly defined means of participation, some initiation formula, some way of knowing who belongs and who does not. Then there is, at least implicitly, a statement of beliefs — and usually some way of proscribing or condemning wrong belief. Fifth, there is an express connection between belonging to the religion and individual and corporate behavior; that is, there is a moral code. Finally, and this is crucial — in a religion all five of these characteristics are institutionalized in a coherent way, or at least there is a conscious effort to knit these elements together to sustain the unique truth to which such a religion lays claim.

I have elsewhere employed these five criteria in a detailed dissection of the claim that civil religion is a religion, and will spare you that exercise here.[5] The proponents of the civil religion proposition strive mightily to find evidence to support the claim that, by these and similar criteria, civil religion is a religion. And let it be admitted that they meet with some modest success along the lines of Bellah's original essay. But their evidences are in almost all instances oblique, episodic, and anecdotal. To take an obvious example, in understanding the "sacred office" of the presidency, Abraham Lincoln is much more deviation than archetype. Yet some proponents of the civil religion leave one with the impression that Lincoln has been president for at least half the life of the republic. In other words, one can marshal bits and pieces of evidence to make civil religion match the standard criteria of what makes for a religion. But it is critically important that what is called civil religion is not coherently institutionalized in a belief system that presents itself as a religion. While they have regularly recognized the religious dimension of beliefs about the American experience, no president or court has ever called this a religion which, in Bellah's words, "exists alongside of and [is] rather clearly differentiated from"[6] what is called religion.

Of course it may be argued that, while civil religion does not call itself a religion, it nonetheless functions as a religion. In that case it is, so to speak, the religion that dare not speak its name. I have already suggested, however, that in fact it does not function in the ways that those enterprises which we call religion do function. Again, this is not to deny that civil religion could become a religion in the full sense of that term. But to say this is to speak of a threatening possibility, not of the present reality. It is noteworthy that religious leaderships in America today view civil religion as a threat to true religion. This is the case almost without exception across the religious spectrum. Civil religion is thought to be false religion. It is not seen as being complementary to and alongside of existing religion, but as a competitor which threatens to displace traditional religion. What is true of religious leaderships would, I suspect, be even more true of almost all religious believers in America, were they ever to hear about civil religion. They would, I suggest, say forcefully and with near unanimity that they already have a religion, thank you, and are not in the market for another, especially not for a religion sponsored by the state. Indeed the very idea of a civil religion would strike many, if not most of them, as both dangerous and blasphemous. In the literature of the religious right and of the religious left, civil religion is routinely condemned as idolatry. The condemnation may be unfair, but it says a great deal about the nonusable future of the proposition that civil religion is in fact a religion.

What I am saying in part, then, is that, outside a small community of academics who are intrigued by the prospect of dealing with religion nonreligiously, the idea of civil religion simply will not fly in America. Civil religion is not a religion. If it does not look like a duck, walk like a duck, or quack like a duck, the burden of proof rests with those who say it is a duck. After nineteen years of trying they have not made their case. And even to the extent that they do make their case, it is counterproductive; for most Americans view a civil religion that really is a religion as a threat to be resisted rather than as a benefit to be embraced. In short, only after we get past the question of whether civil religion is a religion can we address the important questions posed by the civil religion debate.

An important question posed by Robert Bellah in the beginning is the question of how we deal with what he called the "set of religious beliefs, symbols, and rituals growing out of the American historical experience interpreted in the dimension of transcendence."[7] Closely related is his question mentioned earlier, "Why should the history of a people living two or three thousand years ago be religiously meaningful but the history of a people living in the last two or three hundred years be religiously meaningless?"[8] To speak of American history as being religiously, even theologically, meaningful makes many of our contemporaries exceedingly nervous. This is especially true among those of us who embrace the proposition and the promise of liberal democracy. We are immediately reminded of talk about "manifest destiny, "the city upon the hill," and the "redeemer nation." All this, we have been miseducated to think, is the language of national hubris and chauvinism. Because we are so nervous about this language, we have left the task of articulating the religious meaning of America to those who do not understand the ambiguities of the American experience. The moral majoritarians do not hesitate to specify the place of America in God's cosmic purposes. Because we are so skittish about this subject, however, our mainstream culture is bereft of a critical patriotism that understands both vindication and judgment, both righteousness and guilt, both achievement and the way of pilgrims embarked upon an experiment of still uncertain result. Because of our nervousness, we have had for several decades now no public philosophy to guide our deliberations about what kind of people we are and are called to be.

We can, I believe, salvage the content of the civil religion debate from the distracting language in which it has been conducted. The content is to be discovered in the form of three discrete questions. The first has to do with operative values, the second with public piety, and the third with public philosophy. These are discrete questions, not separate questions. Operative values have to do with the behavioral side of our inquiry. By what values do we Americans actually order our lives? This is obviously an inquiry more descriptive than prescriptive and is to be pursued by the several disciplines pertinent to the analysis of social and cultural fact.

If the question of operative values is primarily behavioral, the closely related question of public piety is primarily affective. What are the emotional ties, the aspirations that are involved in being an American? By what symbols do we, as Americans, publicly represent ourselves to ourselves? The difference between operative values and public piety is that the accent in one case is behavioral and in the other affective. An additional difference is that one may be essentially private while the other is emphatically public. The third component of the confusedly undifferentiated civil religion debate I would call public philosophy. This is the cognitive dimension and entails the intellectual task of saying what we believe to be true about ourselves and how we articulate that belief to ourselves and to the world.

It is this third component that American life has been missing now for a very long time. Obviously, we have not been missing operative values. For better and for worse, people are making choices in accord with whatever they think the good life to be. And we have not been missing public piety, although among cultural and educational elites it has been frequently held in disrepute. Nonetheless, most of us know the strong sensation of being American as we view the Lincoln Memorial, or the Vietnam Memorial, or the raising of the flag at the Olympic Games. But we are stumbling and tongue-tied when it comes to saying what it means to be an American, and what America means—what it means to us, what it means for the world, what it means ultimately, if anything. Thus the expression of public piety looks more like a spasm than an affirmation, and the flag is waved more feverishly as the meaning of the flag becomes more elusive. What is missing is a public philosophy.

Public philosophy, the term, is not new; but public philosophy, the task, has been long neglected. Thirty years ago Walter Lippmann published his book titled *The Public Philosophy*. The name of John Dewey also springs readily to mind. In 1949 a much younger Arthur Schlesinger, Jr., published *The Vital Center*, a study in "the purposes and perils of American liberalism." More recently William M. Sullivan—not so incidentally a collaborator of Robert Bellah's—has given us *Reconstructing Public Philosophy*. So, as is not the case with civil religion, there is in the American experience a tradition of reflection on the public philosophy. I take that to be a strength. Unlike civil religion, public philosophy is not an eccentric concept but one that invites the participation of all who care about the future of liberal democracy.

I will attempt only to sketch some of the marks of a public philosophy that might sustain the American democratic experiment. I will then conclude with some remarks on the role of the churches in this enterprise. The public philosophy I envision will itself be democratic; it will be pluralistic; it will be religiously attuned; it will be critically affirmative; and it will be modest in its expectations. As we shall see, these characteristics are intertwined and interdependent.

In saying it should be democratic I mean that it should be unlike earlier efforts at public philosophy, such as Lippmann's. Lippmann believed that something like a natural law tradition must be asserted against the will of the people, for the people, he wrote, "had acquired power they are incapable of exercising, and the governments they elect have lost powers which they must recover if they are to govern."[9] A public philosophy for democratic governance cannot be premised upon such antidemocratic prejudices. Today this caution must be directed at the members of the new class, especially those in the academy, who habitually cultivate contempt for the values of the people whose lives they would more rationally order. A public philosophy that will take hold in America must be marked by popular, even populist, sympathies. Ironically—contra Lippmann and so many others—it is from the ordinary people of this society that there is likely to emerge the assertion of a normative ethic by which extreme propensities, including populist propensities, can be held in check. I daresay there is more respect for something like natural law in the neighborhood bars of Brooklyn than in the philosophy seminars of Harvard. In other words, the public philosophy I have in mind will be at least as attuned to Carl Sandburg as to John Rawls.

Second, such a public philosophy will be pluralistic. I do not mean the false pluralism of indifference to conflicting convictions. I mean the pluralism by which differences are engaged in civil contestation. This public philosophy will not be embarrassed by, nor will it try to override, the fact that we are a society of many societies, a community of many communities. It will not assert Rousseau's "general will" but will rather celebrate Burke's "little platoons." It will provide a sustaining philosophical rationale for what some of us have called the "mediating structures," the people-sized institutions in which people pursue their vision of the good for themselves and their children. Such a public philosophy will not speak of *the people* in the singular but of people in their astonishingly diverse particularities; it will speak less of *the public* than of the myriad publics which it is the obligation of the state to respect and to serve. In this public philosophy *society* will never be personified; it will never be written with a capital S. A public philosophy of pluralism will not seek final resolutions of questions that cannot be resolved short of the end time but will sustain an ever more open and honest debate within the rules of civility. That is to say, such a public philosophy will, by definition, always be unfinished. It will not apologize for—but will rather argue the virtue of—its incompleteness.

Third, such a public philosophy will be religiously attuned. Here we come, I believe, to the most fatal flaw in previous efforts to construct an American public philosophy. They were, almost without exception, premised upon the conceit of the secular Enlightenment that religion either is withering away or could be neatly confined to the private sphere of life. The notion that America is, or is becoming, a secular society has everything going for it except the empirical evidence. I have suggested that the three components of the civil religion debate are operative values, public piety, and public philosophy. None of these can be intelligently discussed apart from the religious reality of the American people. The attempt to exclude or ignore this reality results in what I have elsewhere described as the naked public square, which is, I believe, potentially lethal to the democratic experiment.[10]

The moral persuasiveness of the public philosophy we need depends upon its being historically and socially rooted, so to speak. It cannot rest upon the contrivance of an autonomous ethic, the pursuit of which has fevered the Western mind since Kant. This does not mean that public discourse must be subjected to authoritarian theological claims. That way lies religious warfare, a danger as great as its opposite, the naked public square. It does mean that particularist religion must be engaged in the development of a mediating language, a common moral vocabulary to be shared by those who are not of shared religious conviction. The resources for such a mediating language are to be found precisely in particularist religion, not least of all in the tradition of natural law. Those religious resources will let themselves be enlisted in this task because, unlike civil religion, a public philosophy poses no threat to the recognized religions.

Fourth, a public philosophy must be critically affirmative. This cannot be taken for granted, as witness the contempt for patriotism among many in our cultural elites. This contempt is not a new thing; it is a cultural corrosion that has long been at work among us. In 1948 Richard Weaver wrote:

> It is said that physicians sometimes ask patients, "Do you really wish to get well?" And, to be perfectly realistic in this matter, we must put the question of whether modern civilization wishes to survive. One can detect signs of suicidal impulse; one feels at times that the modern world is calling for madder music and for stronger wine, is craving some delirium which will take it completely away from reality. One is made to think of Kierkegaard's figure of spectators in the theater, who applaud the announcement and repeated announcements that the building is on fire.[11]

If we substitute *liberal democracy* for *modern civilization*, Weaver's observation is painfully pertinent to the subject at hand.

It is, I believe, a matter of great cultural moment that many in our society, including many in positions of religious leadership, believe that liberal democracy does not deserve to survive—indeed that justice demands its demise. Therefore, even if they do wish it to survive, they wish it with a bad conscience. They may be right in their judgment of liberal democracy and its expression in the American experiment, although I do not think so. But, whether they are right or wrong, it seems certain that those who have reached that conclusion will play no positive part in the construction of a public philosophy that can both affirm and criticize this experiment, prodding it ever so slowly and erratically toward the fulfillment of its promise.

Finally, the public philosophy that we need will be modest in the expectations that it raises. It will speak religiously of the American experience but it will not make the American experience a religion. Unlike the social gospelers of an earlier time and their heirs on both the right and the left today, it will not suggest that we are building the Kingdom of God on earth. It will not be surprised by times of testing but will rather recognize that testing is in the very nature of being an experiment. In 1967 Robert Bellah spoke of Vietnam as a time of testing. The global testing continues, exploring whether American democracy is a historical aberration or an instrument of freedom for humankind. And, of course, given the vagaries of history, it may turn out to be neither oppressive aberration nor instrument of freedom but something quite unimagined.

In our domestic life the time of testing is upon us in the debate over abortion. The question is not only abortion, of course, but, much more comprehensively, how do we define the community for which we accept common responsibility and provide legal protection? In a society where the strong, the successful, and the healthy increasingly impose their idea of quality of life in order to exclude the marginal, we do not have even a shared vocabulary for discussing these questions of such great moral moment. In pondering the question, "Who is my neighbor?" we have in two hundred years descended from speaking of providence to speaking of privacy, from affirming the obligations of community to embracing the technologies of convenience. In the face of such realities I readily admit that it may be too late to construct the kind of public philosophy that can restore a shared moral discourse about the meaning of the social experiment of which we are part.

But we are not permitted to surrender hope. And this is my last point: the church is the community of transcendent hope. Our churches—left, right, center, and unspecifiable—have largely forgotten this. Activists of all stripes, and theologians of an activist penchant, urge us to invest our ultimate hopes in temporal struggles, struggles which cannot bear and will inevitably betray those hopes. We are told that people will not give themselves religiously to the political task if that task is viewed as penultimate. And yet our duty is precisely to the penultimate, to work in faithfulness to the moment that is ours and in love toward the neighbor whom God has given us. And if we weary in that work, the answer is a renewal in transcendent faith and love, not the illusion that our work is coterminous with the workings of God. The only religion that will help construct the public philosophy that we need is the religion that knows that all of our politics and all of our philosophies are, at best, faint intuitions of the City of God to which we are called. Only such a lively hope as this can prevent our just causes from turning into holy wars and our public philosophies from turning into civil religions.

I end with a story. In an Eastern European shtetl one man had the job of going out and scouring the countryside several times a day to see if the Messiah was coming. This he did faithfully for some years but, with growing family responsibilities, he one day felt the need to approach the rabbis for an increase in salary. The community could not afford it, they said. Then they said to the man, "It's true the salary is not very good, the hours are long, and the working conditions are not satisfactory, but look at it this way: the work is steady." Those who care about the construction of a public philosophy that can illumine the meaning of America within the horizon of transcendent hope are assured of steady work.

NOTES

1. Robert N. Bellah, "Civil Religion in America," with commentary and response in *The Religious Situation 1968*, ed. Donald R. Cutler (Boston: Beacon Press, 1968), p. 391; reprinted from *Daedalus* 4 (1967). For a critique of the civil religion debate, see Richard John Neuhaus, *Time toward Home: The American Experiment as Revelation* (New York: Seabury Press, 1975), especially chap. 19, "The Public Piety of a Pilgrim People."

2. Russell Richey and Donald Jones, eds., *American Civil Religion* (New York: Harper & Row, 1974), p. 5.

3. Bellah, "Civil Religion in America," p. 331.

4. These chief characteristics of a religion are adapted from John F. Wilson, "The Status of 'Civil Religion' in America," in *The Religion of the Republic*, ed. Elwyn A. Smith (Philadelphia: Fortress Press, 1971).

5. See Neuhaus, *Time toward Home*, chap. 19.

6. Bellah, "Civil Religion in America," p. 331.

7. Ibid., p. 389.

8. Ibid., p. 391.

9. For a discussion of this aspect of Lippmann's thought, see Ronald Steel, *Walter Lippmann and the American Century* (Boston: Little, Brown, 1980), pp. 491ff.

10. Richard John Neuhaus, *The Naked Public Square: Religion and Democracy in America* (Grand Rapids, Mich.: Eerdmans, 1984).

11. Richard M. Weaver, *Ideas Have Consequences* (Chicago: University of Chicago Press, 1948), p. 185.

6

Common Religion in American Society

JOHN F. WILSON

BOTH CIVIL RELIGION and political theology take their significance from the place and role of common religion in our culture. On the one hand, civil religion as a subject concerns the possibility that specific social and cultural beliefs, behaviors, and institutions constitute a positive religion concerned with civil order in the society. On the other hand, political theology is a specifically theological program concerned to place questions of the political order in more universal perspectives. In seeking to relate the political order to more universal perspectives, political theology necessarily reflects the interests of particular religions, often those aspiring to be hegemonic. It seems to me an error to confuse civil religion with political theology, for the one concerns religious expression of particular social orders, while the other seeks to relate transcendent and universal perspectives to claims made about particular civil orders. But at least as important as this distinction is recognizing that both civil religion and political theology take on markedly different significance depending upon the social and cultural status of common religion.

My thesis is that for a century and a half, roughly until several decades ago, American society had a manifest common religion. The particular content of this common religion developed and broadened over time, but in general there was acknowledgment that common religious elements held together our sprawling social and cultural experiment. Within the last several decades,

111

by contrast, the status of common religion has come under question and, possibly, it may no longer operate. If that is the case, I will argue, very significant implications arise for what civil religion might be in this new context and also what the nature of political theology might be.

Common religion in our society is anchored in the territorial solution to the religious issue that emerged in early modern Europe after the exhausting struggles of the sixteenth and seventeenth centuries. Whether ruled by prince, king, parliament, or whomever, each political unit was presumed to have one official religion, its own version, if you will, of the older universal Christendom. Of course in seventeenth- and eighteenth-century European experience, no less than in contemporary colonial American experience, effective multiplication of religious communities and increasing toleration between them were the order of the day. In the colonies, for example, there were Roman Catholics and all British Protestant groups, as well as the variety of religious traditions emigrating from the continent. With the coming of the Revolution and the new nation there could not be an establishment of religion in any traditional sense. Of course, several of the New England states maintained the territorial premise for several decades, but it was out of the question that the new nation itself might have opted for a formal religious expression as counterpart to its political identity. First in the middle colonies, due to overwhelming religious diversity, then in Virginia and the associated southern colonies as a fruit of revolt against the British, the claims of a formal establishment were eroded and then simply ended. The shadow of the territorial church tradition was increasingly weak in New England, lasting until 1833 when it finally faded entirely. The presumption in favor of an establishment was simply the means of signaling in law that a particular religion was believed common and fundamental to the society.

Although the idea of a formal religious establishment eroded, the assumption that there should be a religion common to the society did not fade so easily. So even though the American colonies became states which formally disestablished any particular religious tradition, they did not exclude the possibility that some more general expression of Christianity would be presumed common to the social order. Of course, in the early years of the nineteenth century it was taken for granted that Christianity meant versions of Protestant Christianity, indeed perhaps even the British-derived versions of Protestant Christianity. So the denominational system that evolved in the new American nation presumed that each version was a specification of a broader dominant religion. This religion played something of the value-generating and order-ensuring role ascribed to establishments in the older territorial patterns. To be sure, in the early years of the new American nation there were intellectuals who would have dissented from this concern for religious commonality within the social order, but in general the critics of that premise lost ground as the nineteenth century developed.

This story of how American culture became self-consciously and ubiquitously Protestant in the course of the nineteenth century has been told with great effect and power in several books, notably Martin Marty's *Righteous Empire* and Robert T. Handy's book *A Christian America*.[1] Evidence that Protestant Christianity became the functional common religion of the society would overwhelm us if we sought it out. What is of more interest here is how observers concerned with American society simply took this phenomenon for granted.

The first of our witnesses to this point is Justice Joseph Story, a conservative pillar of the Supreme Court in the nineteenth century's early decades. His *Commentaries on the Constitution* gives a very different reading indeed to the religion clauses than is implied in Thomas Jefferson's metaphor describing a "wall of separation" between church and state.[2] Justice Story insisted upon "the right of a society or government to interfere in matters of religion"; indeed, he thought that "it is impossible for those, who believe in the truth of Christianity, as a divine revelation, to doubt, that it is the especial duty of government to foster and encourage it among all the citizens and subjects."[3] He thought that "there will probably be found few persons in this, or any other Christian country, who would deliberately contend, that it was unreasonable, or unjust to foster and encourage the Christian religion generally, as a matter of sound policy, as well as of revealed truth."[4] He also believed that "probably at the time of the adoption of the constitution, and of the amendment to it now under consideration [Amendment 1], the general, if not the universal, sentiment in

America was, that Christianity ought to receive encouragement from the state, so far as was not incompatible with the private rights of conscience and the freedom of religious worship."[5] Justice Story's testimony makes it clear how by the early decades of the nineteenth century it could be taken for granted that Protestant Christianity was thoroughly if informally woven into the fabric of American society as its common religion.

As a second witness to the presumptions current in American society during the nineteenth century about the place of Christianity as its common religion, let me turn to Philip Schaff. Justice Story was native-born and a jurist; Philip Schaff was a Swiss immigrant who became a distinguished church historian and participated in the development of the American historical profession in the latter decades of the nineteenth century. In a rather remarkable essay on "Church and State in the United States," Schaff echoed some of the themes that Alexis de Tocqueville had developed in his remarks on religion in American culture half a century earlier.[6] Philip Schaff noted:

> The American system grants freedom . . . to irreligion and infidelity, but only within the limits of the order and safety of society. The destruction of religion would be the destruction of morality and the ruin of the state. Civil liberty requires for its support religious liberty, and cannot prosper without it. Religious liberty is not an empty sound, but an orderly exercise of religious duty and enjoyment of all its privileges. It is freedom *in* religion, not freedom *from* religion; as true civil liberty is freedom *in* law and not freedom *from* law.[7]

He goes on in subsequent paragraphs to argue:

> Destroy our churches, close our Sunday-schools, abolish the Lord's day, and our republic would become an empty shell, and our people would tend to heathenism and barbarism. Christianity is the most powerful factor in our society and the pillar of our institutions. . . . Christianity is the only possible religion for the American people, and with Christianity are bound up all our hopes for the future.[8]

Our third witness is James Bryce, the British student of *The

American Commonwealth.[9] After distinguishing the American view of religious bodies from the European, Lord Bryce went on to detail the way in which Christianity was woven into the operation of the civil government as well as the more general society. He concluded with the following judgment:

> The matter may be summed up by saying that Christianity is in fact understood to be, though not the legally established religion, yet the national religion. So far from thinking their commonwealth godless, the Americans conceive that the religious character of a government consists in nothing but the religious belief of the individual citizens, and the conformity of their conduct to that belief. They deem the general acceptance of Christianity to be one of the main sources of their national prosperity, and their nation a special object of the Divine favour.[10]

Without tracing in any detail the stages, we should note that in the course of the early decades of the twentieth century a progressive broadening of the definition of Christianity as common religion occurred. Having begun in the early nineteenth century with the assumption that largely British Protestant denominations embodied Christianity in the American context, broader definitions of Protestantism gradually prevailed and by the end of the nineteenth century a similar extension to include Roman Catholic Christianity followed directly from them. Indeed, by the conclusion of World War II, which marked several basic realignments in American society following the Depression and the mobilization for war, a further effective broadening took place. In the 1950s the watchword became the "Judeo-Christian tradition" as expression of the common religion of the society. This particular new configuration was at once exemplified and analyzed in a book published thirty years ago that is worthy of note. The book is, of course, *Protestant-Catholic-Jew* by Will Herberg.[11]

For Herberg, post-World War II American society was marked by a paradox. It was simultaneously increasingly religious and pervasively secular. In his view no culture had ever been so thoroughly committed to progressively expanding consumption. But it was also an era that fostered a religious revival or at least a perception of one. Churches and synagogues were booming and involvement with religious activities shattered existing records. One might argue that ancient Rome offered a comparable contrast between simultaneous religiousness and secularism too, but there those committed to orgies and life at its most secular were not usually simultaneously searching for religious salvation. For Herberg, religion in his contemporary America was notable because the same people were both pervasively secular and increasingly religious and he saw both elements of this apparently paradoxical situation as deriving from the same sources. In short, what he observed was not a true paradox or logical contradiction but rather a very particular confluence of developments in American society.

Herberg thought that some deep-going changes, the culmination of long-term dynamics of American society, explained this apparent paradox. For one thing, he thought that American society, for the first time in three hundred years, was no longer being significantly affected by continuing immigration, which had been a given throughout three centuries of its social life. He thought that World War I, and restrictive legislative policies thereafter, had essentially terminated the flow of immigration that had so worked to transform American society repeatedly from its beginnings. He borrowed from Marcus Lee Hansen the three-generation hypothesis conveniently summarized in the aphorism "What the son wishes to forget the grandson wishes to remember." His point was that Americanization involved a selective adaptation of the cultures brought from the countries of origin and that the religious components of those cultures were what proved functional in American society. Thus the grandchildren of immigrants might be placed in America not in terms of their origins in a small Polish village or Sicilian port, but as Jews or Catholics. America transmuted the immigrants so that the means of determining their location in the society were the religious ingredients of ethnicity rather than others such as language or country of origin. That the third generation, descendants of the last group of immigrants, so to speak, came to maturity in the 1940s and 1950s was, for Herberg, one of the chains of social dynamics that explained why this most secular American society was simultaneously so very religious.

Herberg thought other patterns were also present in the dynamism of American society. Ethnic intermarriage had been frequent within each of the three great faith communities of his title, but not between them. Ethnic lines etched within the American Catholic community or the American Jewish community were clearly dissolving. So were the lines of tension between the American Protestant denominations, which so often reflected ethnic population pools. At the same time, loyalty to those expanded religious pools held selectively firm. This was also related, in Herberg's view, to the long-term trend toward other-directedness in the culture, the development of the peer group as reference point for personal and social values as well as for fashions in clothing and music. This other-directedness was replacing tradition that had functioned in the Middle Ages and the internalized conscience of the early modern world. So American society had become composed of only three great population pools, and they were defined in religious terms — Protestantism, Catholicism, and Judaism.

In fact Herberg did not like this development. He thought that each of these religions was but a different expression of a single social reality that was in fact the true religion of American culture. This he called "the American way of life" and saw its substance as celebration of particular American values, most prominent among them consumption. Just as when in the 1950s you stripped away the chrome from Chevrolets, Fords, or Plymouths and discovered that it was hard to tell the difference, so the distinctive notes of Judaism, Roman Catholicism, and Protestantism were, in Herberg's view, superficial, masking the real religion of Americans — the American way of life. For Herberg, insofar as true or authentic Jews, Catholics, or Protestants did exist, they were very much minority figures, virtual aliens in American society, prophets crying in the cultural wilderness. For from their tradition-informed viewpoints they saw that the real object of religious loyalty for most Americans was American society. Secularism was the explicit religious reality that so marked the era.

There is much to question in Herberg's analysis. Had the dynamics of immigration and assimilation in fact ceased as finally as he assumed? What was the place of minorities in American life? Herberg's book is essentially without reference to the black community; it lacks any sense that there would be a struggle for civil rights that would deeply affect social reality in the following decades. There is nothing to anticipate that counter-cultural protests against the grossness of American culture would become manifest within a few years, or that constructive political programs would arise to attempt to preserve the environment against the depredations of the greedy. None of these or other impending realities of the intervening decades was focused in Herberg's field of vision. What impressed him most about his contemporary America, however, was that a consensus Americanism, which he termed "the American way of life," provided the substance for the religious revival of the 1950s.

For Herberg the spiritual aspect of our society and culture was the American way of life that had become, if you will, the common religion of our society. He took as particular witness for this fusion Dwight D. Eisenhower. In a celebrated exchange with Marshal Zhukov, the then Supreme Commander had declared that the American form of government "has no sense unless it is founded in a deeply felt religious faith. . . . With us of course it is the Judeo-Christian concept."[12]

Herberg rested his analysis on a general sociological doctrine voiced by Robin Williams in his then widely used discussion, *American Society*.[13] Williams had proposed that "every functioning society has to an important degree a *common* religion."[14] What Herberg argued was that Protestantism, Catholicism, and Judaism, versions of the Judeo-Christian tradition, in their substance were the common religion Williams's sociological doctrine required.

In the three decades since Herberg published his analyses, the American way of life has come under drastic internal criticism as well as received spirited defense. I think it is difficult to maintain that there is now a recognizable spiritual ethos in the culture that is the common religion of this society in anything like the way Protestantism, Catholicism, and Judaism in their presumed commonality were in the immediate postwar era. From this point of view the last decades may be viewed as representing a decisive departure from the century-and-a-half-long tradition of American society centered in a common religion defined in terms of an increasingly broad interpretation of Christianity finally becoming the presumed Judeo-Christian tradition.

As far as I know, no clear thesis has been offered about this basic transformation of American society in the recent decades. There has been a widespread assumption, especially among intellectuals, that the process of secularization explained the development of modern societies in such a way that religion was progressively excluded from positions of influence within them. But that is not exactly what we have experienced in American culture in the last generation. Certainly the incidence of religious behavior and belief has continued uninterrupted on an ascending curve since the founding of the nation. What has happened since mid-century is not a decrease of religious behavior and belief in some absolute sense, but a turn away from what we might term the presumption that religions in their different expressions are in fact one. It is the distinctive aspects of different religions that have been increasingly pronounced since roughly 1955, when Herberg wrote his book.

In *Why Conservative Churches Are Growing*,[15] Dean M. Kelley of the National Council of Churches notes that there were differential rates of growth between the separate religious denominations in the postwar era. As his title suggests, those churches that were demanding or exacting of their members tended to manifest higher rates of growth, indeed often proportioned to the degree of their demandingness. Conversely, those more liberal churches that had looser definitions of membership and required less by way of commitment to church structures showed significantly lower rates of growth, indeed sometimes absolute loss of membership. Kelley's thesis has been debated at some length, but in general the observation on which the book was based does seem to characterize the last several decades of religious life in this culture. What Kelley was pointing to was the significant emergence of distinctive and assertively different religious positions, not content to see themselves as versions of a common religion but intent on forwarding their claims even in literal formulations. This growth of conservative, demanding versions of religious life is a fundamental aspect of the last several decades of church life.

How has Judaism evolved over the course of the last decades? At mid-century one might have projected an increasing assimilation of Judaism to broadly Christian models of religious expression. The vigor of Reform Judaism and the movement of the Conservative branch toward reform in the immediate postwar era suggested that more ancient and distinctive Jewish traditions were losing their hold on members of the community. Yet in the 1980s the field is significantly reversed. The pattern of Jewish development for the last twenty-five years or so has been toward increasing recovery of Jewish practices and beliefs, and a movement away from patterns of general acculturation. In sum, the easy assumptions made by Will Herberg that Judaism was, in some respects, a parallel phenomenon to Protestantism and Catholicism simply failed to acknowledge what would become the distinctive nature of life within the Jewish community in America in the following decades of the century.

Yet a third indication that our world is significantly different from Herberg's is reflected in Martin Marty's tract for the times entitled *The Public Church*.[16] This is, in part, a plea for responsible Roman Catholics, sensitive evangelicals, and the remnants of the old ecumenical church traditions to recognize their common interests in the sphere of public life — in spite of old differences and conceivably continuing clashes of style. That such a perceptive observer of American religious life should take such a minimalist view of the significance of religion for the general society says much about the disappearance of the previous assumption that, first, Christianity or, later, the Judeo-Christian tradition was, in fact, the common religion of the society. Turned around, Marty's argument would be that these three groups are all that remain of the much older and broader perception that a generalized Christianity was indeed at the basis of the common life.

Finally, Richard John Neuhaus's book *The Naked Public Square* has stimulated a number of exchanges in recent months.[17] The argument of the book is that one particular religious tradition will prove dominant within any culture and his is an exhortation to the more vigorous and vital of the different religious traditions in America to contend for a position of hegemony. Neuhaus's concern is not *which* of the candidates for this role should win, whether Roman Catholic, Lutheran, or some other tradition, but that there be one distinctive religious tradition playing a role of generator of values and coordinator of policies, lest the society lose its center altogether.

I am not suggesting that these illustrations necessarily give a consistent picture of what has happened to American culture. But each one of these exhibits does suggest the degree to which in the last twenty-five years the perceived ground rules of the culture have changed. It is simply no longer assumed that there is, or will be, a common religion of the society but rather that there will be contention between a variety of religious positions for influence, if not hegemony, within the society and its culture. In sum, Robin Williams's proposition that every functioning society has a religion seems to have been rejected at least implicitly by most observers of the American religious scene. How may we explain this?

Many argue that secularization explains the increasing removal of religion from places of influence within the culture. That explanation, I have also suggested, probably runs aground on the manifestation of the vigor and vitality, not to speak of the variety, of religious positions within the culture. At least any conventional secularization argument would require a diminished religious vigor in the society rather than the prominence and assertiveness we see around us.

Another argument for making sense of this reversal of Robin Williams's dictum might be the intriguing proposal made by Thomas Luckmann some years ago that within a mature industrial society religious symbols play a different role than in earlier eras.[18] Here religion will be less concerned with public issues and more concerned with private life. Its role will be expressive rather than prescriptive or analytical. Luckmann's thesis might well explain how we could move from an era in which there was a pronounced common religion a quarter of a century ago, to one in which numerous contending religions may struggle for influence but only succeed in displaying the nonexistence of the common religion.

A yet more searching explanation is found in the work of Mary Douglas, who argues that there are very different kinds of social orders. These she charts through her terms *grid* and *group*, signaling definition of social roles on the one hand and collective bonding on the other.[19] She insists that there really are different sorts of societies among the communities of humans on the globe and that the cultures associated with them may have significantly different shapes and significance. It may well be that in the last quarter century American society has moved to place less emphasis upon both grid and group; there may have been a decrease in the strength of group bonds as well as diminished importance of social roles. Under such conditions, the significance of common religion in a society would be radically diminished.

These possible explanations for the apparent confutation of

Robin Williams's dictum within modern American society are not
the only ones available. Even if no particular explanation is persuasive, there is undeniably a fundamental contrast between the
presumption that seemed so natural in the 1950s that there was
a common religion of American society which was in its substance
a generalized Judeo-Christian tradition, and the current broad
perception that there is no common religion in American culture.

In conclusion, it seems to me that what civil religion might
be or what political theology might be in a particular society depends in large part upon whether or not there is a common religion present. Civil religion and political theology shift their
meanings decisively given the presence or absence of this kind of
social reality.

Where there is a common religion, a civil religious tradition
is essentially a specification — perhaps institutionalization — of its
values, symbols, and myths, and may prove to be an effective means
of making broadly based cultural values influential within the
political arena. Absent a common religion, however, and a civil
religion becomes a scarcely veiled revitalization movement, perhaps intensely reactionary in its program, dedicated to returning
a culture to the value complex believed to have dominated a previous time. Far from representing a movement that may be constructive in relationship to the whole society, civil religion in the
absence of the common religion as background seems necessarily
to be highly selective, prejudicial, indeed, one among other religious movements contending for control of the society in question.
So I would argue that attention to the question of common religion in our society will affect the construction to be placed upon
civil religion, and the understanding we might have of it will vary
accordingly.

Somewhat comparable observations may be made about political theology. Where theological traditions bear some relationship to common religions of a society, political theology may work
to rationalize conduct of power by means of transcendent reference. Absent common religion from a social order, however, and
political theology as it speaks for specific programs in the common life becomes increasingly divisive and a source of contention
within the whole. In short, both political theology and civil religion necessarily exist in a dialectical relationship to common re-

ligion, even though that relationship often remains unexplored. In this sense, we return to the fundamental question with which we started: What is the status of common religion in American society? I have proposed that the status of common religion may have shifted decisively within the last several decades. This may mark the end of a long tradition reaching back to late medieval Europe that presumed each territory, however governed, would manifest religious integrity. With the coming of a radically plural religious culture in the recent decades, the United States may well have moved beyond that paradigm. Discussions of both civil religion and political theology have tended to avoid discussion of how each relates to the common religion of society. In the absence of the latter, and in an era of thoroughgoing religious pluralism, we need to think through very carefully how both civil religion and political theology are radically transformed.

NOTES

1. Martin E. Marty, *Righteous Empire: The Protestant Experience in America* (New York: Dial Press, 1970); and Robert T. Handy, *A Christian America: Protestant Hopes and Historical Realities* (New York: Oxford University Press, 1971).

2. Joseph Story, *Commentaries on the Constitution of the United States*, 3 vols. (Boston: Gray Hilliard, 1833), 2:722ff.

3. Ibid., p. 722.

4. Ibid., p. 723.

5. Ibid., p. 724.

6. Philip Schaff, "Church and State in the United States," *Papers of the American Historical Association*, vol. 2, no. 4 (New York, 1888).

7. Ibid., pp. 15–16.

8. Ibid.

9. James Bryce, *The American Commonwealth*, 2 vols. (New York: Macmillan Co., 1914).

10. Ibid., 2:770.

11. Will Herberg, *Protestant-Catholic-Jew* (Garden City, N.Y.: Doubleday & Co., 1955).

12. See the discussion of this much cited incident and passage by Patrick Henry, "And I Don't Care What It Is: The Tradition-History of a Civil Religion Proof-Text," *Journal of the American Academy of Religion* 49, no. 1 (March 1981): 35–49.

13. Robin M. Williams, Jr., *American Society: A Sociological Interpretation* (New York: Alfred A. Knopf, 1951).

14. Ibid., p. 312.

15. Dean M. Kelley, *Why Conservative Churches Are Growing* (New York: Harper & Row, 1972, 1977).

16. Martin E. Marty, *The Public Church* (New York: Crossroads Press, 1981).

17. Richard John Neuhaus, *The Naked Public Square: Religion and Democracy in America* (Grand Rapids, Mich.: Eerdmans, 1984).

18. Thomas Luckmann, *The Invisible Religion* (New York: Macmillan Co., 1967).

19. Mary Douglas, *Natural Symbols* (New York: Pantheon Books, 1970, 1973). Also see the recent study by Richard M. Merelman, *Making Something of Ourselves: On Culture and Politics of the United States* (Berkeley: University of California Press, 1984), which proposes that a loosely bounded culture has superseded earlier patterns of group action.

7

To Be at Home:
Civil Religion as Common Bond

LEROY S. ROUNER

I. THE NEED FOR HOME

THERE IS A VISCERAL human instinct which makes us gravitate toward those of our own kind, and fear the stranger. This yearning of like for like focuses on the natural bonds of blood, land, language, caste/class, and religion. Here are our roots. To be part of this family or tribe; to be familiar with this place of childhood memory; to know this language's local accent and intimate meanings; to have a place, however low, in this community; and to share with others the celebration of belief and commitment, in which the deepest in us meets with the deepest in our fellows—that is what it means to be at home.

Those whose particular bonds are different from ours are outsiders, aliens, strangers. We may be fascinated by them, and occasionally join forces with them, but when their community is opposed to ours—Protestants against Catholics, Tamils against Sinhalese, Arabs against Israelis—what is at stake for us is deeper than economic self-interest or ideological commitment. What is threatened is our cultural home. And we need to be at home in our world.

Hegel once commented that the Roman Empire was the first place where a person could be thoroughly lost. This is an acute observation on the cultural phenomenon we now call pluralism. Individuals from varied traditional backgrounds in Europe, western Asia, and North Africa were told that they were now no longer who they had recognized themselves to be by virtue of their blood, regional, linguistic, class/caste, and religious heritage. Now they were to be Romans, even though Rome was far away, ruled by people who were no kin, who spoke an alien tongue, and worshiped strange gods. More threatening still was the manner in which the force of empire had thrown together all sorts and conditions of folk from different strongly rooted traditional cultures. It was difficult enough to identify oneself with this new Roman heteronomy, but it was almost impossible to feel the common bond now announced between oneself and those of a different traditional culture. Ripped from the womb of one's tradition and thrown into the cultural maelstrom, one was lost because one was no longer at home.

The process of assimilation whereby folk from traditional communal cultures become part of a larger social and political conglomerate culture continues today. Although American interest in Third World development regularly focuses on economy and ideology, the success of nation building in a place like India rests primarily on the extent to which varied ethnic groups can find a common national identity. The Hindu-Muslim conflict is endemic, and the Sikh separatist movement, like similar movements in Tamilnad and Kashmir, is only the most recent attempt on the part of Indians themselves to "quit India." Prime Minister Shastri spoke ruefully of India's "fissiparous tendencies," and Rajiv Gandhi has said that India's future depends on whether enough people of enough influence from enough different traditional communities will finally come to feel at home in this superimposed abstraction called India and identify themselves as Indians, rather than primarily as Tamils or Malayalis or whatever. This is not an easy cultural transition to make.

In a traditional society the community is primary. My sense of myself as an individual is derived from my participation in the community, and the community makes my fundamental life decisions for me. As a man in a traditional society my work is whatever my father's work is; and my wife is chosen for me by my parents, within the caste or class community, with the general consent of the joint family's near relations. Life is tightly constrained. There is very little individual decision-making power, and social behavior is largely prescribed. Tolerance for deviation is minimal. There is much order and little freedom; but one knows where home is. Who I am and where I belong is never a question.

Modern culture, on the other hand, is free from many of these traditional constraints, but metaphysical loneliness is the price modernity pays for its freedom. To be modern is to celebrate individuality and hence, inevitably, to be lonely. Except for family bonds between generations — which count for less with us now than they once did — we have virtually no bonds which are given to us by our world, and are absolutely reliable no matter what. In the modern world we define ourselves by our doing, not our being; so our sense of ourselves is largely self-generated. It has to be a construct, because there is nothing that is simply there, given for us to be. And because we cannot be sure that we can maintain that construct — there are always new decisions to be made — we are fundamentally anxious about ourselves.

The strength of a traditional culture is its assurance of who one is, where one belongs, and what it is one is supposed to do. As a result, there is relatively little metaphysical anxiety in most traditional cultures. The great fear is that one may be "cut off from the land of the living," ostracized from that community which alone can give you the sense of who you are, where you belong, and what you are to do. The payoff is metaphysical security; the price is personal freedom, and alienation from other traditions. Traditional society includes some folk only by clearly excluding others.

The strength of a modern culture is its degree of individual freedom to be and belong and do what one chooses. As a result, there is a relatively high level of metaphysical anxiety, because those issues are always in the making with individual decisions yet to come. The great fear is that one may not "make it," whether that means professional success or personal fulfillment or achievement in any other realm of personal meaning. There is much talk today about a form of social and cultural organization which would have the virtues of tradition's home, as well as modernity's personal freedom. This is a new definition of community. In a traditional culture community means caste or tribe, an exclusive grouping determined by natural givens of blood, region, language, caste/class, and religion. In the modern world, there are small tightly-knit communities such as religious orders and ideological communes like

Brook Farm in the nineteenth century or the flower children communes in the California of the 1960s. For most of us, however, our
primary identity is not with a community. We live in a society,
made up of individuals and institutions. Neither in our personal
freedom nor in our institutional relationships do we experience
community. For a modern society to become a community would
require a strong sense of common identity which is not exclusive,
as traditional bonds are, but inclusive of those who are culturally
alien. It would preserve individual freedom and, at the same time,
give all sorts and conditions of folk a sense of being at home with
one another.

My thesis is that civil religion in America has provided something of that common identity. It is therefore an important paradigm for a pluralistic planetary society which will stop short of
blowing itself up only if it can discover its common humanity as
an identifying bond. My purpose here, however, is to suggest the
way in which civil religion in America has worked to give us at
least a minimal sense of being at home, enough so that the maelstrom of our cultural pluralism becomes tolerable. I also will argue
that Christian theology needs to make a place for civil religion
of this sort because it is those non-Christians who share Christian
values and loyalties who do much of God's work in the world. I
will not enter into the debate about whether such folk are "anonymous Christians" (Rahner). This is one of the major unresolved
issues of contemporary Christian thought. I only observe that the
Christian church is not the sole, or even major, instrument of God's
work in the world. God wants peace on earth, and if we get it,
it won't be the World Council of Churches or the Vatican who
made it possible. Civil religion in America has been a means
whereby Christian loyalties and values have been indigenized and
become effective in a modern, pluralistic society. It behooves Christian thinkers to be less fearful and more grateful for what God
is doing outside the bounds of their control.

I must emphasize that I reject the Moral Majority and all its
works, and I agree with virtually all the criticisms which have been
made about civil religion in America. I agree with Jürgen Moltmann that it can be and often has been a corruption of authentic
Christian faith. I agree also with Richard Neuhaus that civil religion is not really a religion in any socio-historic sense, although

I regret the move which he and Robert Bellah now make to speaking of a public philosophy instead, because this notion does not do justice to the binding power of civil religion. I have therefore discussed civil religion in the context of the American dream, since they are intertwined, both of them vague and visceral notions which drive some of our deep loyalties. I am instructed by John Wilson's warning that loss of a common religion in America may well threaten the possibility of a civil religion as it has functioned creatively in the past. I suspect that he is right, and that, without a strong presence of the church as the keeper of the keys of the Kingdom and as the place where many can celebrate the mystery of God's love for us and saving work among us, civil religion of the type I describe here may not be possible.

II. CIVIL RELIGION AND THE AMERICAN DREAM

The myth of the American dream envisioned a new loyalty to a national idea. America is not a culture; it is a creed (Friedrich). The *metanoia* of the melting pot would supposedly create an individual who, as American, was without definitive regard for his or her racial, religious, or cultural background. All folk were now to be regarded as "endowed by their Creator with certain inalienable Rights." The essential selfhood of the new American would be derived from a new belief in one's right to individual freedom and its opportunities.

The American experiment in nation building was among the most significant political adventures of modernity in the West, because it introduced a radical conception of political community. More decisively than any previous such experiment, it forsook the traditional aristocracies of blood, language, region, class or caste, and religion as the locus of political authority, insisting instead on a secular ideology of personal freedom for the people as the basis for its national life. Liberty was the American watchword. In an unprecedented manner, America sought to extend this liberty to people of various backgrounds, thus giving substance to its ideology. Through free education for all its citizens, equal opportunity would supposedly exist for all. The American mythology thrived on tales of immigrants who arrived penniless, soon to become millionaires by dint of hard work and native wit; and of young backwoods scholars of flawless virtue and unflagging zeal who read books by firelight and grew up to be president.

This lofty idea seemed credible because of the hope for a new life in America's vast, unexplored, virgin land. The virginity of the new land had both theoretical and practical consequences for the American dream.

On the theoretical side it made possible the notion of a new beginning for one's life. In Puritan New England this notion was expressed theologically by analogy to a city set upon a hill, a New Jerusalem, and even, in some Puritan preaching, to a new Eden. In succeeding generations, as this theological ideal became generalized and secularized, the promise of religious freedom was expanded into constitutional guarantees for freedom of movement, freedom of the press, free speech, and freedom of political belief. At that point America became a symbolic land of opportunity where one was challenged to rise to whatever height one's innate capacities might take one.

On the practical side, the ideology of unlimited opportunity and the promise of wealth for the industrious was given substance by the availability of cheap land. All of America was promising, but if one were ambitious and found New York crowded and dirty, one could try an entirely different kind of life in rural Ohio. If the granite boulders in New Hampshire's pastures made farming too backbreaking, the adventurous could and did find rich bottom land in Illinois.

Puritan New England initiated two fundamental motifs of the American dream. One was the trust that one's destiny was guided by a transcendent power, a conviction which undergirded American optimism and idealism. The other was Yankee ingenuity, the imaginative practicality which gave Americans their reputation for inventiveness and productivity. In spite of the prevailing opinion in Boston, however, the definitive event of American life was not what Van Wyck Brooks's too-gentle metaphor called "the flowering of New England." New England burned with a zeal for the transcendent and exhibited remarkable physical and emotional toughness, but it was economically tight-fisted, religiously orthodox, and morally guilt-ridden. For all its gifts, New England knew little of spaciousness. And it was open space and opportunity which inspired the westward movement and eventually defined the American dream.

The spaciousness of the land also made possible the gradual adaptation of various ethnic groups into the American community. Immigrants with a common ethnic background could settle together, transposing their old culture and language for a period, gaining self-confidence and a sense of place before the ceaseless mobility of the New World eroded their traditionalism and gradually worked them into the mainstream of American life.

The myth of the American dream was that this co-equal American, stripped of race, creed, and religion, standing on individual rights, was now free to take advantage of virtually unlimited new opportunity. The story of American national growth is, in no small way, the story of the dream's power. The American enterprise probably could not have been maintained without the American dream, because it provided an effective substitute for the traditional bonds of blood, region, language, class or caste, and religion. For on what basis could these new Americans announce so confidently, flying in the face of all the facts, that "all men are created equal"? With such divergent ethnic loyalties, and such a variety of visceral instincts for what it means to be at home, how could this overpowering land with its confusion of cultures become a homeland? How could a political system which celebrated pluralism and individualism hope to hold this polyglot population together?

Perry Miller regularly reminded his students that the history of American literature is the history of the question: What does it mean to be an American? The American dream was as close as we have come to an answer. Americans are those folk who, in their time, both built a better mousetrap and dreamed a grander dream. And it was the dream that required the mousetrap. American idealism makes American pragmatism a live option. The dream was the quixotic driving force which fueled the westward movement and, in turn, evoked the inventive technology which made expansion practicable.

In providing a national consciousness, the American dream drew on religious themes adapted from Christianity. To be an American was to be part of a pilgrim people in covenant with a transcendent power, a people who had been given a promised land

and a manifest destiny. The outward and visible sign of this inward and spiritual grace was the unprecedented growth and prosperity of the nation. What I am here calling civil religion was the substructure of the dream.

From the point of view of orthodox Christian belief, civil religion has an inevitable tendency to corrupt authentic faith by making the nation and its ideology the transcendent power, in place of the God who judges all things finite. From the point of view of the national community, however, Christian religion had provided a binding ingredient for the nation which was free of traditional religion's exclusivism. In so doing it had posed a new possibility for a genuine community in a post-traditional world. In a world where traditional communities of blood, region, language, caste or class, and religion were now inextricably mixed, the Christian religion had inadvertently provided the terms whereby an intense loyalty could be elicited from various ethnic groups, thus providing a common cake of custom in a pluralistic and individualistic democratic society.

America's pluralistic, individualistic democracy has always lacked visible means of support. What holds this conglomerate together? Why should it work? The American Civil War was a test case where the visceral traditional bond of blood became a fundamental issue in understanding the national enterprise. Was America to be bound by the traditional dominance of one blood community over another, or was the abstract, modern ideology of equality to prevail? Robert Bellah has already pointed out that Lincoln's Gettysburg Address and Second Inaugural were definitive statements of American civil religion on this issue. The notion of "the people" was to predominate and include all sorts and conditions of American folk. Preserving the Union was more important than freeing the slaves for Lincoln because the reality of America's new pluralistic community was more significant than any specific conflict within it.

The magical alchemy never worked as well as our talk about the American melting pot made it seem — the melting pot was probably always more of a salad bowl — but it worked well enough to give a polyglot people a new sense of themselves. The binding ingredient which made it possible was vague and therefore hard to define. It developed over time and was built up out of a common experience of common ventures in education, commerce, and the arts; but it became evident as the idea of America gained self-conscious prestige with its citizenry. One was proud to be an American, loved one's country, and was loyal to its purposes, however ill-defined. Insofar as this was simply the spirit of nationalism and patriotism America was not unusual, and it was as dangerous in America as these self-aggrandizing sentiments always are in nations. But on public occasions when America is celebrated, such as Memorial Day, the Fourth of July, and presidential inaugurals, another deeper note is regularly sounded. These speeches celebrate the sacrifices of those who have died to preserve freedom and the hope for a better tomorrow. The binding ingredient which gives a disparate folk their American identity is not nationalism or patriotism, but loyalty to certain values which transcend the nation and give the nation its purposes and goals — among which are sacrificial love, freedom of the individual, and care for "the people." To call these values a public philosophy does not do justice to their visceral power and their effectiveness in binding a disparate people together. That binding ingredient is what I am calling civil religion. It is a religious loyalty to those values which shape the American dream and confer American identity.

What is the relation between this civil religion and formal, institutional Christianity? Many see civil religion as a threat to Christianity because it can and often does offer itself as a substitute for authentic Christian faith. This was the view of my teacher Reinhold Niebuhr, and has been recently reiterated by my friend and colleague Jürgen Moltmann. My view is that a pluralistic, democratic society cannot exist without such a binding ingredient as civil religion provides. On the other hand, the distinctiveness and root prophetic power of the Christian faith would be lost if the Christian Church were absorbed into a civil religion. Here Moltmann is entirely right to remind us of the tragedy which produced the Nazi-dominated National Christianity in Germany in the thirties. In maintaining its distinctiveness, however, American Christianity has, in fact, made a considerable contribution to the content of American civil religion, as Bellah's original essay pointed out. The early church announced that the new community in Christ was to include Jew and Greek, male and female, slave and free, for all were to be one in Christ Jesus. Here is a guideline for the kind of society Christians seek as a precursor of God's Kingdom. When a pluralistic, democratic society affirms equal human rights and privileges for all sorts and conditions of folk, announcing that "all are to be one" in the new America, the institutional church has evidence of its social influence and reassurance for its hope that God is at work in the world to prepare for the ultimate community of the Kingdom. In this sense, civil religion in America has been the instrument whereby Christianity has become indigenous in our secular democracy.

At the same time, however, the church is properly mindful of civil religion's vagueness, its vulnerability to political demagoguery, and its limitations as a resource for prophetic proclamation. The institutional church will always be the keeper of the keys of the Kingdom, for it is here that the faith is celebrated in its wholeness, and defined in its content. But the church must be mindful of its impotence as servants of God's will in the world. The great Christian tasks of feeding the hungry, caring for the poor and downtrodden, are not accomplished by the church as institution. The actual work of the institutional church in feeding the hungry is tokenism compared to the work of governments and private agencies. The people who are actually doing what God wants done in the world are often not Christian people, yet they form a movement toward goals Christians seek, and their motivation for doing what they do often comes through the ideals and loyalties of civil religion. The best blending of American idealism and pragmatism in recent memory was the Marshall Plan after World War II. It was necessary for a stable world; it was morally right; it was generous in the best American tradition. And it was voted because it embodied the best ideals of American civil religion.

American Peace Corps volunteers, when asked why they are there, regularly mutter vaguely about this being the sort of thing Americans ought to be doing. They speak of their privileges as carrying responsibilities; their desire to help those less fortunate than themselves; and their willingness to make sacrifices in order to do it. Their values reflect American civil religion. Civil religion is an instrument of institutional Christianity in effecting the values with which Christianity seeks to transform the world.

III. DEMOCRACY AND THE GOD OF HISTORY

Reinhold Niebuhr and William Ernest Hocking are the only two American philosophers, to my knowledge, to write a philosophy of history. Hocking's book *The Coming World Civilization* agrees with Niebuhr's work *The Nature and Destiny of Man* in rejecting the liberal notion of progress, but argues for a pattern of meaning, nonetheless, resulting from an accumulation of historical insights. History preserves some achievements. There are certain advances in science and technology which, once achieved, stay achieved. The printing press, modern medical discoveries, and a host of other obvious technical examples are clearly here to stay as long as there is a human culture to employ them. Modern memory bank communications may mean that no technical achievement, however trivial, will ever again be lost — a thought which immediately makes losability a modest value.

More important and complex are those unlosable elements which affect moral and spiritual life. Some religions disappear. Isis and Osiris are gone, even from California. In the great religions which have had such impressive longevity — who can imagine a human culture without Hinduism or reverence for the Tao? — there has been considerable change, growth, and development. But certain moral and spiritual values have become inherently human, and those values have become universal. The inherent value of the individual human being — as knower, as soul, as technical crafter of the natural world, as inherently worthy of dignity — this notion is the chief contribution of modernity to history's store of moral and spiritual unlosables.

Democracy is the political celebration of this insight about the inherent dignity of the individual human being. It is, in part, evidence of the impact of Christian faith on historical process. More than that, it is testimony to eyes of faith that God is indeed at work in our history. Those Christian enthusiasts like Walter Rauschenbusch who thought that they could see the Kingdom of God being established in America forgot that the Kingdom is an eschatological reality. The Kingdom will be established finally only at the end of time. History is the realm of hints and guesses, of foretastes and expectations. Democracy is not the Kingdom. Democracy is only one historical hint of what the Kingdom will mean. It is promise, not fulfillment. It is only the direction of our present historical way, not the revealed nature of our final goal.

For all that, it is not insignificant in the understanding of how God works with us. The critics of democracy are always right that no democratic society fulfills the ideals of its democratic intent. As an empirical reality, it is always a question as to whether any given democratic society is more or less just than a society which does not embody democratic principles. Empirical reality is not the test. The test is intention, purpose, goal. What is the meaning of this particular national enterprise? Sin and self-seeking will always corrupt human enterprise, however grand. To discern the signs of the times, however, we must analyze purposes as well as performance.

American civil religion is the credo of America's purpose. The freedom which American life allows for expression of various beliefs also gives space for those movements which evidence sacrificial care for the hopes of traditional groups other than our own. Participants in the underground railroad of the nineteenth century were largely white people, members of the national establishment of power and influence, who were concerned for the freedom of blacks to be a people of equal right within the national community. Such movements are made possible by a fundamental element of the democratic creed, the need for sacrifice to ensure everyone's freedom.

Within a democratic society it is always a temptation to claim that God is on the side of my cause or my candidate. Such claims always court idolatry. If the biblical story means anything at all it means that chastisement and defeat are also instruments of God's work in the world, and any claim that we know God's will for us at any given time must be made in fear and trembling. Nevertheless, we know something of the Kingdom which is our home, and the prophetic calling to discern the signs of the times has a positive side as well as a negative one. No nation is exclusively God's people — God is not a tribal warlord — but some have caught a vision of loyalty to a purpose and meaning beyond their own national enterprise which is a sign of God's work among God's many peoples to create a genuinely human community. The loyalty to the kind of democratic society which unites various traditions in a spirit of community is such a sign.

The significance of the American experiment in nation building is that it caught something of that vision and embodied it in its civil religion. The vision did not make it immune from retribalization of its dream, as the demonic spirit of manifest destiny has made clear. The idealism of the dream has regularly been used to justify self-seeking in foreign policy, and self-deception at home. Naked power grabbing in the Mexican War and useless slaughter in Vietnam have been justified by appeals to the principles of American civil religion. In the same way, the oppression of black Americans, native American Indians, and Japanese Americans during the Second World War has been obscured or justified to the national conscience by the same nationalistic appeals. The negative criticisms of American civil religion are almost always valid. It is a phenomenon fraught with demonic potential which has too often been realized.

Nor is America the beacon of the world's future, as its civil religion has too often assumed. It has been the culmination of modernity in the West, and its experiment with democracy has been widely influential. The sample of human diversity which it sought to integrate, however, has been limited. In the perspective of the global village American diversity is relatively narrow. The critical test for community building in the postmodern world is no longer the American experiment but the more diverse and difficult Asian experiments in community building such as the current task of the new India. Nevertheless, America is a significant pioneering adventure. That fact is largely lost at present because the left has fallen out of love with its homeland, and the right has celebrated it for mostly wrong reasons.

PART III

The Practice of
Political Theology

8

Political Theology:
A New Paradigm of Theology?

JOHANN BAPTIST METZ

I. THE CRITERIA FOR A NEW PARADIGM

IN ORDER TO EXPLAIN the new political theology I use the concepts of paradigm and paradigm shift introduced to the discussion of theories of science by Thomas Kuhn. Since then, these concepts have been used in a more general sense than in the context of Kuhn's research, and only in this general sense would I like to apply this conceptual pair to theology.

As criteria for a new paradigm of theology I would like to mention tentatively the following:

1. *The capacity for perceiving and dealing with crises stemming from theology's intimate contact with history and society.* The theological hermeneutic corresponding to this capacity can be called the hermeneutic of crisis or the hermeneutic of danger. As an example I would like to point to the beginnings of dialectical theology. Karl Barth developed this dialectical theology in the face of the collapse of the Christian bourgeois culture brought about by the First World War. This is distinct from and even in contrast to the political theology of Carl Schmitt which was written at the same time and can also be understood as a reaction to the crisis of the First World War, but primarily as that national crisis characterized by the collapse of the so-called Second German Reich. This contrast shows that the category of crisis or of danger is by no means unequivocal; rather it gains its distinctive-

141

ness in view of what is to be rescued. Carl Schmitt's political theology is a theology interested in saving a threatened, backward-oriented political utopia. Dialectical theology is a theology interested in saving the Christian message in the face of the collapse of its historical political expression.

2. *The capacity for reduction/concentration*. This capacity is understood first as nonregressive reduction/concentration of over-complexity and overspecialization in which the crises of theology often are suppressed or covered up. This reduction/concentration is also mirrored in a critical challenging of the traditional divisions of labor within theology. This is true of dialectical theology, which, for example, did not take account of the traditional divisions between systematic theology, exegesis, and pastoral theology, or between theology and kerygma. This is also true of the transcendental theology of Karl Rahner, who was often blamed for not sufficiently respecting the traditional boundaries between systematic, practical, and spiritual theology; and it is true of the new political theology as well as of liberation theology.

Second, this capacity refers to the nontrivial reduction of dogma to life, of doxography to biography, because the logos of theology always aims at a way of knowing as a way of living.

This reduction is a concentration on the roots of doing theology. Thus these theologies of crisis can also be called radical theologies, if one understands *radical* as the attempt of theology to grasp its roots. This radicality often gives the impression of a shocking naiveté which, however, can be theologically justified by the hermeneutic of crisis or by the hermeneutic of danger. This hermeneutic, for which perceiving danger constitutes the systematic definition of theology, is simplifying. In the face of danger, praxis returns to pure theory; mysticism returns to logic; resistance and suffering return to the theological understanding of grace and spirit.

These theologies of crisis often go back to suppressed or banned elements of the Jewish-Christian tradition. In dialectical theology and in the new political theology they recall blocked-out memory of apocalyptic over against a modern eschatology which has long since been infected with the sweet poison of an evolutionary flavored, posthistoric world.

3. *The courage to be productively noncontemporary*. The fa-

tal disease of theology is not naiveté but banality. Theology can become banal whenever its commentary on life serves only to repeat that which, without it — and often against it — has already become part of common modern consent. It is appropriate that theological hermeneutics lie in ambush for these commonplaces. It does this by lingering with its traditions and holding its own in the face of them at least a bit longer than modern consent and the anonymous pressure of modern civilization regularly allow. Theology seeks not to reconcile itself meekly with its traditions through subtle modifications, but rather to spell out its tradition as dangerous/subversive memory for the present. This hermeneutic is not a traditionalist hermeneutic. It is not guided by a backward-oriented utopia. Its attempt to rescue is simultaneously an attempt to liberate.

4. *The capacity and the readiness for communicative exchange between theology and life in the church*. There is no hermetic theological history of crisis. The theological history of crisis is always a history of crisis of the church and of believers. A paradigm shift within theology must be nourished by changes in the life of the church. Within liberation theology it becomes especially clear that a paradigm change touches the traditional division of labor, not only within theology, but also within the church system. In other words, there emerges the question of the new loci and bearers of theological activity.

5. *The capacity to perceive and to treat the crisis as an ecumenical challenge*. The theologies of crisis are always theologies which are ecumenically relevant. In the new political theology the crises are so formulated that their productive theological elaboration is ecumenical in its starting point.

II. THREE COMPETING PARADIGMS

Within today's Roman Catholic Church I see primarily three competing paradigms of theology at work: neo-Scholastic, transcendental-idealist, and post-idealist. This post-idealist paradigm is only now beginning to unfold in the new political theology and in the theology of liberation. My own theological work can be understood as a contribution to the developing of this post-idealist paradigm.

In the church as a whole, the neo-Scholastic paradigm still prevails. In the face of the neoconservative social tendencies within the church this paradigm is going through an Indian summer. This paradigm is a defensive and nonproductive confrontation with modernity. It is sufficiently revealing that during the last century the classic work of the neo-Scholastics was entitled "Theology of Pre-Modern Times." The neo-Scholastic paradigm corresponds to a process of spiritual and social isolation of Roman Catholicism that consolidated Catholics in a firm, political Corpus Catholicum, a rather weak imitation of the great Corpus Christianum of the Middle Ages.

The transcendental-idealist paradigm exists thanks to the most penetrating and influential paradigm shift within today's Catholic theology. This paradigm is characterized by a productive confrontation of theology with the challenge of modernity. Here subjectivity questions classical metaphysics and critical confrontations take place with Kant, German idealism, and existentialism, as well as with the social processes of secularization and scientific civilization. This paradigm was given shape by Karl Rahner and fulfills all the criteria for an authentic paradigm change in theology. This paradigm has its ecclesial and social equivalent in new forms of Christian life which result from Vatican II.

In the meantime, however, theology has been confronted with new crises which force us toward a new paradigm which I, for the moment rather helplessly, call post-idealist. I delineate three crises in which the new way of doing theology originates, because they can be worked through neither in the neo-Scholastic nor in the transcendental-idealist paradigm. The first is the Marxist challenge: that is, theology facing up to the end of its cognitive innocence and of a dualistic understanding of history. (See Section IIIA below.) The second is the Auschwitz challenge: that is, theology facing up to the end of idealism and of all systems of meaning which lack historically identifiable subjects. (See Section IIIB below.) The third is the Third World challenge, the challenge of a socially antagonistic and culturally polycentric world, that is, theology at the end of its so-called Eurocentricity. (See Section IIIc below.)

The experience of these crises and the theological confrontation with them in my own thought implies a change of philosophical background: from the transcendental Kant and from Heidegger to the Kant of the primacy of practical reason; from idealism to ideology critique and the post-idealist critique of religion, as well as the attempt of Karl Marx to understand the world as a historical project; to Bloch and Benjamin; to the Frankfurt School; and, finally, to Jewish thought and the long-since blocked-out religious wisdom of Judaism. It became important for me to emphasize the Jewish tradition within Christianity as distinct from the Hellenistic traditions with their ahistoric tendency toward dualism. Beside my companions in the struggle for political theology, names such as Kierkegaard and Bonhoeffer became significant to me without my ever wanting to depart from the spirit and inspiration of the one against whom my criticism was now directed, yet to whom I owe the greatest debt: Karl Rahner. And — once again — perhaps only in the ongoing process of the new liberation theology does it become really clear what is intended by this new paradigm, not only in the field of theology but also in ecclesial life.

IIIa: THE MARXIST CHALLENGE

The first Marxist challenge is in epistemology. According to Marx, all knowledge is bound by interest. This axiom is the basis of his criticism of ideology and religion. Theology has now lost its innocence under the subversive eyes of Marx's ideology critique. This first period of the new political theology is characterized by the attempt to face this challenging situation and nevertheless to remain theology. This theology tried to gain an explicit and systematic awareness of the fact that theology and the church are no longer politically innocent. The political implications of doing theology must be systematically regarded, not because politics expresses the totality of life (in the sense of Carl Schmitt's political theology), but because suspicion against theology has become total.

This new political theology presupposes that the Enlightenment cannot be understood as if it brought forth a completely demythologized and secularized world, in which religion and politics are so separate as to lack any connection. Religion was neither fully privatized, nor politics fully secularized. Politically enlightened societies also have their political religion by means of which they attempt to legitimize and stabilize themselves. We recognize this phenomenon in the form of civil religion in the United States and in the form of what we call bourgeois religion in Europe. They can't be called in any way equivalent; they owe their existence to very different political cultures. When, therefore, German neo-conservatism recommends the introduction of a civil religion in my country, this tends in the last analysis toward a reproduction of traditionalist models of the legitimation of politics through religion — in the style of classical political theology. Both civil religion and bourgeois religion foster a politicization of religion which leads to its strictly societal functionalization.

Political theology criticizes this politicization in two ways. First it criticizes religion which operates as a myth of legitimation and which suspends its truth claim. Second, it criticizes theology which becomes the theology of political religion. The new theology takes the Marxist challenge into account in yet another way. If all knowledge is bound by interest, then not only the content of knowledge but also the bearers and addressees become a constitutive factor in the processes of knowledge. In this sense a question must be raised anew about the appropriate bearers and addressees of theology.

But the central question of the Marxist challenge concerns the truth question. Doesn't Marxism necessarily trivialize the truth question to the question of relevance? No, it puts it in a new form: Are there interests capable of leading to the truth? Interests can only be capable of leading to the truth if they are universal interests or, at least, if they can be universalized. This is because truth must engage all people or it is not truth at all.

The new political paradigm talks about a universal interest which is deeply rooted in the biblical traditions. It is the hunger and thirst for justice, for universal justice, justice for all, the living and the dead. The question of truth and the question of justice are interrelated. The interest in strictly universal justice is one of the presuppositions of truth finding. To that extent, the knowledge of truth has a practical foundation. In this the critical and liberating power of knowing the truth is rooted.

The Marxist discovery is the discovery of the world as a historical project, and of human beings as the agents of their history.

Here Marxism touches and develops another basic theme of Christianity, namely, history. Because we can today compare the great cultures and religions of the world we can see that history is the destiny of Christianity. In distinction from all other great religions of the world, Christianity is guided by the vision of God and history, or even God in history. This becomes immediately apparent if we do not allow the Jewish inheritance in Christianity to be absorbed by the Greek-Hellenistic inheritance which tends toward an ahistoric dualism. And this destiny of Christianity remains able to be seen as long as we do not subject ourselves to an evolutionarily poisoned lassitude about history and surrender ourselves to the anonymous pressure of so-called posthistoricism in our late modernity.

Facing the Marxist challenge, the new political theology understands itself as a theology of history with practical-critical intentions. For this theology there is only one history, since to talk about two histories is not to take seriously enough the gravity and adventure of living in history. There is not actually a history of the world, and beside it and above it a history of salvation. Instead, the history of salvation is that history of the world in which there is also a hope for past sufferings.

The Christian faith in a God for whom past sufferings do not disappear into the abyss of an anonymous, subjectless evolution guarantees the unchangeable criterion of justice in the historical struggle for all men and women and their status as subjects. Wherever our public knowledge is exclusively guided by the fictitious totality of a nonteleological evolution, not only does God become unthinkable but our interest in universal justice also fades away. We lose interest in a strictly universal solidarity and justice which also includes the victims and the defeated of our history. On the shoulders of these forgotten victims we build our paradises, even though these paradises can never make up for those past sufferings. The Christian faith in God is the reliable basis for that strictly universal justice for which the people hunger and thirst, not only today by decree of the spirit of the times but throughout the history of humanity.

The new paradigm attempts to take on the Marxist challenge insofar as it contains an interest in all human beings gaining the status of subjects of their history. But it contradicts the Marxist anthropology by saying that guilt must be considered not as a derivative phenomenon but as an authentic phenomenon within the historical processes of liberation. It cannot be seen as the expression of pure alienation. The denial of guilt is an assault on the dignity of human freedom. To admit guilt in the face of God does not prevent people from becoming fully responsible subjects of their history. On the contrary, wherever guilt is denied or denounced as false consciousness, excuse mechanisms emerge in the face of the painful contradictions of history. The question of guilty and unguilty, just and unjust, cannot be decided by the too-obvious political opposition of friend and foe. Insofar as the Marxist category of class struggle fails to acknowledge the motives of concealment between good and evil and at least implicitly denies the existence of moral guilt, theology cannot accept this category as the basic principle of liberation processes.

However, all other modern analyses are unavoidably structured by a modern sociological theory. These theories are no longer innocent over and against theology. They see themselves, though with varying degrees of explicitness, as so-called metatheories of religion and theology. For them, theology can be analyzed and subsumed within a more general theoretical system. Theology's response to such theories cannot be to seek a foundation and justification in a further attempt to produce a more general pure theory from its own resources. In order to avoid the risk of a speculative infinite regression which would inevitably have to be broken off arbitrarily at some point, it must look for its basis in terms of a return to the subjects of faith and their practice. These are the very sources of crisis and hope. If, for example, the community of believers is regarded as the community which admits and acknowledges the experience of guilt and sin, this community must also present itself as the community of undivided historical responsibility, as the community with an interest in universal justice and liberation. A theology which is aware of the practical and subjective foundation of its wisdom takes firmer hold of the community than the traditional division of labor in the church can imagine or than the ecclesial administration favors. This becomes especially apparent today in the reciprocal influence of liberation theology and the basic communities in the church of Latin America.

IIIb: THE AUSCHWITZ CHALLENGE

Christian theology is not a fateless metaphysics. It is a witness of truth in history: "The Word became flesh." Historical situations are inherent in the logos of theology. Somewhere and somehow I have become aware of a historical situation outside of which I wouldn't have any idea how to get my theological bearings. This situation is "after Auschwitz." Auschwitz represents the crisis of modernity, but above all a crisis of Christian theology. At the outset one must take into account that the catastrophe of Auschwitz, precisely because of its uniqueness, acquires a provocative character. This catastrophe cannot be integrated into history. It directs theology away from the singular "history" to the plural "histories of sufferings," which cannot be idealistically explained but can only be remembered with a practical intention. Because of the way Auschwitz was or was not present in theology, I slowly became aware of the great apathy in theological idealism and its inability to confront historical experience in spite of all its prolific talk about historicity. Obviously there is no meaning of history one can save with one's back turned to Auschwitz; there is no truth of history which one can defend, no God in history which one can worship. Theology must take seriously the negativity of history in its interruptive and catastrophic character.

The catastrophes must be remembered with a practical-political intention so that this historical experience does not turn to tragedy and thus bid the history of freedom farewell. This shows that the political paradigm of theology is due neither to a foolish overactivity nor to the transparent attempt at duplicating the already existing political patterns. It is rather due to the struggle for history in its unfathomable histories of suffering, to history as the constitutionally threatened locus of theological truth-finding.

Theology must risk remembering not only what has succeeded, but also what has been destroyed; not only what has been achieved, but also what has been lost. In this way it is turned against the idea that history is simply the victory of what already exists. This is a dangerous memory and it shows how solidarity with the defeated becomes a universal category of rescue: saving the dignity of history and of human subjects acting and suffering in history.

This theology formulates the God question as the theodicy

question: the deliverance of the victims of our history. How can anyone ask after Auschwitz about one's own salvation outside this perspective? Political theology repeatedly injects this question into public consciousness as a question on which the fate of humanity depends. *Memoria passionis* ("the memory of suffering"), which is a radical biblical category, becomes a universal category of rescue.

> But to forget or suppress this question . . . is to behave in a profoundly inhuman way. For it means forgetting and suppressing the sufferings of the past and accepting without protest the pointlessness of this suffering. In the last resort, no happiness enjoyed by children can make up for the pain suffered by the fathers, and no social progress can atone for the injustice done to the departed. If we persist too long in accepting the meaninglessness of death and in being indifferent to the dead, all we shall have left to offer even to the living will be banal promises. It is not only the growth of our economic resources which is limited, as we are often reminded today, but also the resources of meaning, and it is as if our reserves here are melting away and we are faced with the real danger that the impressive words we use to fuel our own history — words like freedom, liberation, justice, happiness — will in the end have all their meaning drained out of them.[1]

Without this *memoria passionis* life becomes simply an anthropomorphism. The public advertisement for a successor to the human subject who has no memory of past suffering has already begun. *Time* magazine has recently placed a picture of this successor on one of its covers: the robot, a smoothly functioning machine, an intelligence without remembrance, without pathos, and without morals. Thus, in the fight for history and historical consciousness a new front has been opened: the evolutionarily infected lassitude about history, the tending toward a so-called posthistoricity in our late modernity.

After becoming theologically aware of my post-Holocaust situation, I also asked myself what sort of faith it must have been that allowed us to go on believing undisturbed during the Nazi time. Was it not in the end only a purely believed-in faith, a faith without compassion but with a belief in compassion which, under the mantle of believing it was compassionate, cultivated the apathy that allowed us Christians to go on believing with our backs turned to such a catastrophe? I called this type of believing *burgerliche Religion*. The critical use of the concept "bourgeois religion" thus has a solidly theological and not a primarily sociological basis.

Was it not a lack of politically sensitive spirituality which led us into our grievous error? If we had realized that we Christians are also responsible for emerging structures and processes we might have resisted in time. How did we understand our Christianity? As a Christian one can be too pious and too mystical! The one and undivided discipleship of Jesus contains always a mystical *and* a situational political element. They mirror one another, and that is specifically Christian. Naturally "Jesus was neither a fool nor a rebel: but he could obviously be mistaken for either. In the end, he was derided by Herod as a fool and handed over by his own countrymen as a rebel to be crucified. . . . Anyone who follows him . . . must allow for the same possibility of being the victim of such confusion."[2] Theology must not unveil but respect this incognito aspect of Jesus. It belongs to his saving history of passion, and theology has to make clear that the present misery of our Christianity is not that we are too often considered as fools or rebels but, rather, practically never. This theology can reclaim the traditions of this dangerous Jesus in the history of the religious orders, and it can refer today to the new mystical and political experiences of the emerging church and learn from them.

IIIc: THE THIRD WORLD CHALLENGE

The social antagonism in the world becomes central to ecclesial and theological interest in questions of exploitation, oppression, and racism. They demand the formulation of faith in categories of resistance and change. Thus theology becomes political out of its own logos.

In this new ecclesial situation the church finds itself on the way from a culturally monocentric European and North American church to a culturally polycentric universal church. Such tendencies can already be seen in Vatican II. In order to hint at the theological importance of this development, I follow Karl Rahner in dividing theological history into three epochs: first, a short foundational epoch of Judeo-Christianity; second, a long epoch of Hellenistic influence on European culture; and finally, the current epoch of worldwide cultural polycentrism.

Theology and the church are now facing the end of their cultural monocentrism. This end does not mean the dissolution into an arbitrary, contextual pluralism, nor the enthronement of a new non-European monocentrism. The historical development of the West remains inherent to the new cultural polycentrism. Nevertheless, we are concerned here with reciprocal inspiration in developing the life of church and theology. The new paradigm can no longer divide the situation in two. This has, in my opinion, a twofold consequence.

First, European theology has to understand itself as a history of guilt. Frequently we protect ourselves against this guilt by all types of defense mechanisms. With the help of a tactical provincialism we try to safeguard our church and political life against global influence. With an overly routine use of the category *development* we talk about underdeveloped people and cultures of the Third World. We talk of the countries of the Third World as our weakly developed partners, but hardly ever as our victims. Theological awareness of the culturally polycentric world church will teach us to judge ourselves and our own history with the eyes of our victims. Thus theology in the new paradigm must become a politically sensitive theology of conversion. I have critically described a Western Christianity which closes its mind to this experience as bourgeois religion.

Second, our Western theology faces the challenge of a new awakening in and from the poor churches of the world. The new paradigm has to make public this charismatic shock within the universal church. There is a threefold reformational thrust: (1) the development of a new church model in the basic communities which understand themselves to be in connection with the bishops and thus are included in the apostolic succession; (2) the concentration on the Eucharist and discipleship, resulting in a politically sensitive spirituality with a preferential option for the poor; and (3) the theological impulse of liberation theology concerning a new vital unity of redemption and liberation in which the experience of resistance and suffering returns to the experience of grace.

But Roman Catholic theology must not forget that there is

a European dilemma of Catholicism. The Catholic Church accompanied the European history of modern times more or less defensively. It did not really participate in the history of modern freedom or the development of civic enlightenment. Most of the time it resisted them. Were the so-called Catholic times within modern European history not always times of counter-reformation, counter-enlightenment, counter-revolution, and political romanticism? To be sure, one can see in this attitude much sensitivity for the inner contradictions and dangers of the European history of freedom. But who would not also see historic neglects in this situation which makes the conjugation of grace and freedom so difficult, especially for us Catholics? The overcoming of this Catholic dilemma in the late European situation, at least for me, points beyond the occidental-European monocultural church life into a world church which learns how to call for and represent the grace of God as an undivided liberation of humanity and which is willing to pay the price for this historic conjugation of grace and freedom.

Here the new post-idealist paradigm encounters the most acute tensions within today's church. Different visions wrestle with one another over the future of the church and how to be faithful to Vatican II. For me there is a history of the church as a hopeful history and there is also what might be called progress in theology, insofar as we face the described challenges and understand the socially divided and polycentric world church as that learning space in which we find many signs of a Christianity that lays hold of its roots in a new way.

NOTES

1. Johann B. Metz, "Vergebung der Sünden: Theologische Überlegungen zu einem Abschnitt auf dem Synoden dokument 'Unsere Hoffnung,'" *Stimmen der Zeit* 2 (February 1977): 121.

2. Ibid., p. 122.

9

Civil Religion and Political Theology: Politics and Religion without Domination?

MATTHEW L. LAMB

MODERNITY IS NO LONGER what it used to be. Obituaries to the modern age, which began amid the terror and ashes of a war-torn Europe, have increased dramatically as the twentieth century draws to a close. Political theology and civil religion can only be understood within this larger context.

The self-confidence of modernity appears grotesque before the darkness evoked in the Holocaust, the Gulag, and Hiroshima. Thomas Paine expressed this self-confidence when, in his *Common Sense* of 1776, he drew the conclusion that "in all probability, a revolution in the system of government would be followed by a revolution in the system of religion." Today political theologians ask rather how religious institutions can collaborate in moving American politics away from the precipice of nuclear annihilation. Contemporary ecumenical cooperation among world religions, and within Christianity, turns the tables on Paine's conclusion. Today we should ask: Can the ecumenical transformations in the systems of religion be followed by equally peaceful transformations in the systems of government? Can transformations within religious institutions confessing their solidarity with the poor and oppressed, with women and the environment, aid in turning systems of government away from their many addictions to dominative power?

I. PARALLELS BETWEEN CIVIL RELIGION
AND POLITICAL THEOLOGY

A facile mistake would be to identify civil religion in the United States with the modern Enlightenment, concede that it has failed to convert the nation away from the sins of domination, and turn wistfully to political theology for another go at such a national conversion. This misunderstanding overlooks the ambiguities of both.

From 1965 through 1967 Professor Johann B. Metz was lecturing on what he called "a new political theology" which would articulate an understanding of religion and the church as an institutionalized critical or prophetic conscience within modern society. A key element in political theology was the deprivatization of Christian theology. Theology is unavoidably public and political. The first publications in Germany were in 1967, and immediately political theology became a heavily contested and debated notion in both Catholic and Protestant theology in Europe. Metz maintained that the church was hardly fulfilling its prophetic-critical task in modern society when it simply accepted the privatized role modern societies gave religion. There was too much evil and suffering in the modern age for religion to remain silent — churches should be criticizing modernity for the sake of the gospel.[1]

During those same years Professor Robert Bellah was calling the attention of his colleagues and students in the sociology of religion to what had been around but largely unnoticed:

> Few have realized that there actually exists alongside of and rather clearly differentiated from the churches an elaborate and well-institutionalized civil religion in America.[2]

Religion, Bellah argued, had always slipped through the wall of separation between church and state. There was a public or political articulation of religion and a theology in, for example, presidential inaugural addresses. The publication of his article "Civil Religion in America" in 1967 touched off a lively debate in American sociology of religion and related fields. Over recent years, Bellah has also articulated the transformative potential of religion in the United States.[3]

There is another curious coincidence between civil religion

and political theology, as formulated by Metz and Bellah. Whatever one says about the elements of Bellah's and Metz's theories, no one would contest today, as some did two decades ago, the fact that politics and religion are inextricably and critically related. Precisely because religion and politics can mix for both good and evil, how can we discern reasonably and religiously when the mix promotes good, and when it bodes ill?

Both civil religion and political theology are inherently dialectical. They refer to dynamically concrete and contradictory processes operative within histories and societies. Political and religious processes are sometimes complementary and sometimes contradictory ways of rendering transcendence immanent. They complement one another when they both aim at the healing liberation of human life. They become contradictory when one or the other legitimates or fosters domination.

American civil religion was possible only when the European Enlightenment substituted natural religiosity for the revealed religions of Judaism and Christianity. In the United States, the substitution was neither clean nor complete. As Robert Bellah and others have indicated, American civil religion is an amalgam of diverse strands which include republican morality, biblical faith, and liberal humanism. It was this amalgam that led Chesterton to remark that "America is a nation with the soul of a church."

Civil religion in the United States could never reduce Judaism and Christianity to a mix of republican morality and liberal humanism. Biblical faith would always be there to remind the advocates of republican morality and liberal humanism that the just and moral society of which they dreamed ultimately depended upon the gift of the Divine Mystery named God. It is the biblical component of American civil religion which keeps alive apocalyptic fires of radical change.

Simultaneously, however, the irrational and often immoral uses of apocalyptic imagery by Bible-thumping preachers leads one to appreciate the constraints on biblical referents suggested by republican morality and liberal humanism. If the United States in some ways realized the Enlightenment which Europe only imagined, then the dialectic of Enlightenment is also more intensely present in America. That dialectic is marked by contradictions between domination and subject-empowering freedom.[4]

II. THE END OF MODERNITY:
DESTRUCTION OR TRANSFORMATION?

The dialectic of political theology and civil religion goes far beyond any narrow definition of either. There are repressive forms of political theology, just as there are repressive forms of civil religion. Either is repressive to the extent that it would promote the use of religious symbols and values to legitimate or foster economic, political, ecclesial, or other forms of domination. Such a dominative use of religion I call sacralism. Domination and liberation are the key to the dialectic.[5]

The dialectic between civil religion and political theology is a variable of the dialectic operative within each. There are liberating events of civil religion and there are dominative or sacralist events; and likewise with political theology. Indeed, this inner dialectic was more explicit in Metz's articulation of political theology. From the start he opposed his understanding to those political theologies which, from time immemorial, tried to legitimate and sanctify dominative power systems.[6] This dialectic of liberation and domination raises the question: Is it possible to foster political and religious forms of life and organization which are not dominative?

The question is also related to a much more explosive issue: Can humankind survive on this planet in a nuclear age? For the persistent reification of social power and authority as either force or domination has not only deformed and derailed religious traditions and institutions. Such reification of authority has been as constant as warfare throughout history. The terrible fact of this reification is expressed in Max Weber's definition of authority as "the legitimate use of domination."[7]

Can we so transform history that force and massive wars are memories more than monstrous realities? Can we have social authority and power in intelligent and reasonable consensus building and decision, rather than in coercion and domination? These are questions with both religious and rational dimensions. The nuclear arms race has enormously intensified the issues surrounding force and domination. Does humankind have a future? The spectre of a global nuclear winter has shrouded the nuclear arms race in the shadows of possible extinction. Death is no longer an individual fate; it has cast its pale chill over the entire species-being. The Nietzschean "Requiem aeternam Deo" which modern secularism chanted over the ruins of a decadent and dismantled Christendom now echoes back to secularist modernity in the somber tones of a "Requiem aeternam Homini." For millennia humankind has lived by the sword, and now we are beginning to realize that our species may die by it also.

The human drama must change, or make a moral about-face, if it is even going to continue. The human drama has been marked by pell-mell successions of roles which could be designated as winners versus losers. The titanic irony of the nuclear arms race is that it discloses the lethal potential of dominative power as death.

In the sociology of religion the primary social function was to maintain what Peter Berger termed a "sacred canopy" of meaning and value, transcendentally legitimating personal and social living. Forms of both civil religion and political theology have engaged in such legitimization. In such contexts, a major problem for the sociology of religion is the secularization of modernity. Religious transcendence is then invoked as world-maintenance in the face of personal anxieties before the chaos of death.[8]

The nuclear arms race, however, has introduced global dimensions to this anxiety. The sacred canopy is rent by the grotesque possibilities of planetary omnicide. The sacred canopy becomes a sacred discontent with the necrophilic destructiveness of modern secularized societies. The very survival or maintenance of the human species now requires the transformation of modern, technological societies away from such weapons of death.[9]

The dialectic running through both civil religion and political theology has ramifications far beyond either theology or the sociology of religion. Thomas Paine's suggestion that a revolution in the system of government could be followed by a revolution in the system of religion takes on quite a different meaning two centuries later. Paine's tract *The Age of Reason* seems quaint now. It was written at a time when reasonable men [*sic*] could jest about the Christian commandment to love one's enemies as "assassinating the dignity of forbearance, and sinking man into a spaniel."[10] Modern warfare and carnage have intensified the stakes in the *lex talionis* to such a degree that if we start demanding an eye for an eye and a tooth for a tooth there will be no eyes or teeth left. No first use as a declared state policy in the nuclear age seems an eminently rational policy not unrelated to turning the other cheek.

Could it be that a genuine recovery of religious faith might heal and transform an otherwise suicidal instrumental rationality? The objectives of "national security" seem to become increasingly lethal as they are pursued in a nuclear age. Metz's shortest definition of religion as "interruption" seems an overriding imperative when one considers that by responsible estimates world military expenditures now amount to over $78 million every hour, while during that same hour over 1,800 children die for lack of food or elementary vaccines. Weapons, as the American Catholic Bishops recently reported, kill even when they are not fired.[11]

The metaphor for revolutions, as Walter Benjamin intimated, can no longer be the locomotive but must be the emergency brake. Can humankind exercise politics and religion without war or domination? Very quiet and reasonable arguments are being made that the real utopians are those who, despite the mounting evidence of history and statistics, continue to maintain that in this unique instance weapons that are mass produced and heavily deployed will never be used.

Merleau-Ponty might suggest that we are up against the ontological limits of the political. In his *Adventures of the Dialectic* he had seen more clearly than many students of Weber how the latter's liberalism grew out of a reading of history as the natural seat of violence. The practice of resistance during the German occupation seemed, for Merleau-Ponty, to become the master metaphor for a political prudence playing out the Machiavellian derailment of *virtù*.[12] Can there be progress without barbarism?

Now that we wonder how patterns of social domination might end in the universal victimhood of a nuclear winter, perhaps we can begin to hear the cries of the victims so incessantly drowned out by the drums of imperial machismo. As political theologians have suggested, if history has any intelligibility it can be found only in solidarity with the victims.[13] The dialectic between domination and liberation leads both civil religion and political theology to collaborate in moving humankind away from the edge of destruction, back through subversive memories and recovered traditions, to new postmodern or postcritical practices of reason as communicative action in solidarity with the victims of history.

The weapons are all in place. The only event interposed between the world we know and a dreadful experiment in nuclear winter is the passage of electrons along wires igniting enough missiles to eventuate in a 5000-megaton nuclear exchange between the two superpowers. It is humbling to realize that the world of the warriors so easily overwhelms not only religious, philosophical, and poetic wisdom, but quite literally everything we know and love in this world.[14]

Socially and politically, modern secularism has become a reflection of the classical sacralism it initially rejected. Instead of an authoritative Holy Roman Empire we now live in a world of nuclear superpowers which justify their divergent forms of authoritarianism by appeals to national security. Instead of sacralist hierarchic authoritarianisms, we now have secularist bureaucratic authoritarianisms. The disintegration of a divided Christendom had led reformers and counter-reformers to dismantle ecclesial unity but to keep the notion of revealed religion. When these competing sacralisms spawned the wars of religion, the modern quest for pure reason led the rationalists to reject revealed religion and enthrone in its place first a natural religiosity and then a secularist supremacy of reason.

But the dialectic of this Enlightenment was that liberal, egalitarian rational discourse and decision making could hardly be realized in societies distorted by the social injustices of classism, sexism, racism, technocentrism, and militarism. The consequence was that modern secularist liberalism eventually despaired of rational agreement, yet insisted on maintaining respect for individual conscience. Conscience, however, was so privatized that religious, moral, and economic values could not sustain the common good in the republics of representative democracies except through pressure politics relative to the social contract.[15]

Max Weber saw how the claims and counter-claims of competing private religions, private moralities, and private businesses would be at best only adjudicated by bureaucratic techniques. The underlying social Darwinism seemed to assure that modern liberal republics would trace again the trajectory of Rome from a republic to an empire. For, as both Marx and Weber surmised in different ways, the demands of capitalist accumulation, industrialization, and professionalization would increasingly contradict and constrain genuine democracy. Nation-states became engaged in aggressive empire building and militaristic nationalism. These imperial policies mocked the dictates of private conscience in their overriding national security needs for bureaucratically organizing vast economic and military exploits.[16]

Modernity has dead-ended in the World Wars, the Holocaust, countless genocides, the exploitation of Third World countries, the increasing pollutions of the earth's environment, and the terrible specter of nuclear omnicide. "Progress through technology" sounds like the empty gong of a clanging funeral bell. Our modern and enlightened twentieth century has witnessed the slaughter of more human beings by their fellows than any other.[17]

III. JUSTICE AND POSTMODERNITY

Political and liberation theologies are assembling elements of a hermeneutics and dialectics subversive of domination. Memories are subversive because they are so scarred with betrayals and compromises. Long memories are anything but romantically innocent. As never before, critical and conscientious realism is needed in our time.

The dialectical discernment of tradition and betrayal will require the collaborative efforts of many. For there are betrayals of reason as well as of religion. An honestly realistic admission of the need for profound transformations in both religion and reason, in both churches and states, demands extensive collaboration to assure that postmodernity will not devolve into an irrational antimodernity.[18] Thomas McCarthy remarks:

> The discontents of modernity are not rooted in rationalization as such, but in the failure to develop and institutionalize all the different dimensions of reason in a balanced way.[19]

Contributions to developing and institutionalizing the different dimensions of reason can be seen in the many churches risking genuine solidarity with the victims of oppression in their struggles for a new and more just world. The major forms of social injustice are manifestations of domination. To the extent that religiously oriented communities are seeking to overcome those injustices, the possibilities of institutionalizing their criticisms become very real.

To use an analogy, just as the best and brightest minds of the Enlightenment began forming groups and associations which eventually transformed almost every institutional sector of modern society and culture, so the many diverse communities now struggling for a more humane and intelligent world may well be the seeds of profound postmodern transformations. Indeed, one could wager that, only if these and like-minded communities succeed in transforming the institutions of modernity, will there be a future. Communities of faith cooperate with others to transform and heal a world where science has been severed from wisdom, and so seems plunging toward destruction.[20]

Within the perspectives of political and liberation theologies, one could identify five diverse orientations aimed at promoting communities of justice by seeking to heal five major pathologies destroying the very possibilities of community. The five pathologies are sexism, racism, economic oppression or classism, environmental pollution (what might be termed a technocentric denial of our community with the environment), and militarism. Liberation and political theologies, at their best, express the concerns of communities committed to heal and transform the injustices of one or another of these five forms of domination. For a common basic element in all five of these community-destroying pathologies is domination by which genuine cooperation with others, so essential for genuine community, is denied and repressed.[21]

The dead ends of a sacralist Christendom and a secularist modernity provide a *kairos* for Christian theology and Christian churches. Christian faith was distorted and diminished by its sacralist use to enforce and legitimate domination in premodern societies and cultures. Such authoritarian domination destroyed the ecclesial communion which we now must seek to restore through ecumenical cooperation. Human reason has been analogously distorted and diminished by its secularist use to enforce and legitimate domination in modern societies and cultures. Nowhere is this more evident than in the insane and irrational nuclear arms races by so-called sovereign superpowers who each can muster a sense of community only in the hatred or fear of the other, the enemy. We must dominate them before they dominate us.[22]

But the victims of modernity, and those in solidarity with them, contradict the hopes of those who would manage the ever-increasing crises of modernity through more adroit use of the techniques of social engineering and bureaucratic professionalism. The central problem is how to bring about more just and good societies, for only such social transformation will avert the mounting probabilities of ecological and/or nuclear devastation.

Political and liberation theologies concentrate on precisely this central problem insofar as they focus, in solidarity, on those communities concretely striving to transcend classism, sexism, racism, technocentrism, and militarism. This concentration is radically new since it acknowledges the futility of both classical *theoria* and modern *technique* adequately to heal these injustices, and to enable liberating communities to flourish. Simultaneously, however, these contemporary postmodern movements are not a neo-conservative antimodernity. If such theologians, in solidarity with the victims of modernity, have no illusions about modernity as quest for pure reason, they also have no illusions about any restoration in quest of a pure religion in any premodern sacralist guise.[23]

Nor are political and liberation theologians alone in their efforts to promote value-oriented scholarship which advocates justice and peace.[24] Contemporary postempiricist philosophies of science call attention to the fundamental importance, neither of theory nor of technique but of the concrete performance of reason constituted by the raising of ever further relevant questions. This directs attention to the concrete subjects doing science and scholarship, as well as the life-worlds of everyday living, the communal contexts and social institutions within which those subjects do science and scholarship. Hermeneutics, with its emphasis upon tradition and narrative, is central to the philosophy of science now cognizant of the false dichotomies between objectivity and subjectivity, science and ideology, engendered by the modern Enlightenment.

There are a series of functional relations operative among the communities of scientists and scholars engaged in empirical science, hermeneutics, and dialectics. In order to do justice to the praxis of reason operative in the empirical sciences, it is important to complement observation and explanation with interpretive and historical analyses in which the relations to the human life-world are explored. Similarly, in order to do justice to the praxis of reason operative in interpretation and historical reconstruction, their theories need to be complemented by dialectics. True, dialectics without interpretation can be ideologically distorted into a universalizing or totalizing of particular discoveries as though they were the answer to all further relevant questions. Yet interpretation without dialectics cannot engage in the heuristic and critical questioning of latent value conflicts and power complexes whereby the very raising of further relevant questions itself is communally and socially repressed or oppressed.[25]

This brings us to the challenge which the dialectics of political theology and civil religion are posing to social theories and practices. Modern social theories tend to foster dichotomies between community and society. Ferdinand Tonnies described modern industrial socialization as a contraction and dissolution of community. Max Weber systematically exploited this distinction in his highly influential subsequent dichotomies between bureaucracy and charisma, which had an impact on the derivative Troeltschian distinctions between church and sect. Weber was honest about the consequences of these dichotomies. He inclined to view all three ideal-types of authority (traditional, bureaucratic, and charismatic) as forms of legitimate domination. These modern typologies tended to give primacy to extrinsic bureaucratic control techniques as eminently rational.[26]

How can a liberating institutionalization of reason and faith occur if the process itself is misunderstood as dominative? In such a theoretic framework, any movements for liberation, justice, and community could only be understood as charismatic and value-oriented interludes over against the iron inevitability of the bureaucratic institutions of society, which as institutions necessitate the domination upon which feeds the pathologies of classism, sexism, racism, technocentrism, and militarism.

As the eminent British social theorist Anthony Giddens remarks, these dichotomies and ideal-types have intensified the subject/object dualisms which have dogged most areas of modern social analysis and hindered an adequate understanding of how subject-empowering communities of agents actually function in highly complex societies. To correct these inadequacies, Giddens analyzes how all forms of social production and reproduction are constituted by the dialectics of structure and agency whereby the active doings of subjects distance and delegitimate dominative power. Such an analysis indicates the foundational importance of liberative communities empowering subjects in their praxis of transcending social injustice. Contradictions are embedded in dominative power structures whereby it is impossible to negate fully human subjects as knowers and active agents. No matter how alienating past and present social structures were or are, countervailing transformative communities can be nurtured in the present and historically reconstructed where they were operative in the past.[27]

Attention to the communal praxis of reason and the intrinsic relationships between such praxis and justice would carry on the best aspirations of the modern Enlightenment while also uniting them with the premodern religious concerns with wisdom. Classism, sexism, racism, technocentrism, and militarism are not only moral outrages; they are stultifying and irrational alienations from the creative praxis of reason. They are social surds having no intrinsic intelligibility and so can be adequately understood only in the dialectical efforts to transcend their destructive alienation.

Postmodernity will be marked, hopefully, by many communal movements seeking to transcend the irrationalities of classism, sexism, racism, technocentrism, and militarism. Neither an antimodernist authoritarian objectivism nor a modernist relativism can do justice to the interpretive and dialectical empowerment within genuine practices of both religious faith and human reason. Only such practices institutionalized in churches, academies, and societies would assure that the end of the modern age will be a fulfillment of the deepest aspirations of the modern Enlightenment for freedom and justice, and not a terribly lethal dead end.

NOTES

1. The first published article on a "new political theology" was by Johann B. Metz, "Zum Problem einer 'politischen Theologie,'" in *Kontexte* 4 (1967): 35ff.; a year later this was republished in Johann B. Metz, *Zur Theologie der Welt* (Mainz: Grünewald, 1968). For a bibliography till 1973, see Roger D. Johns, *Man in the World: The Theology of Johannes Metz* (Chico, Calif: Scholars Press, 1976). To date Metz's most sustained exposition of his political theology can be found in Johann B.

Metz, *Glaube in Geschichte und Gesellschaft* (Mainz: Grünewald, 1977); translated as *Faith in History and Society*, trans. David Smith (New York: Seabury Press, 1980).

2. Robert N. Bellah, "Civil Religion in America," with commentary and response in *The Religious Situation 1968*, ed. Donald R. Cutler (Boston: Beacon Press, 1968), p. 331; reprinted from *Daedalus* 4 (1967).

3. See Russell E. Richey and Donald G. Jones, eds., *American Civil Religion* (New York: Harper & Row, 1974); Robert N. Bellah, *The Broken Covenant: American Civil Religion in Time of Trial* (New York: Seabury Press, 1975); Jerald Brauer, Sidney E. Mead, and Robert N. Bellah, *Religion and the American Revolution* (Philadelphia: Fortress Press, 1976); Robert N. Bellah and Phillip Hammond, *Varieties of Civil Religion* (New York: Harper & Row, 1980); and the articles of Bellah in *Proceedings of the Catholic Theological Society of America* and in *Religion and the Intellectual Life*. For analysis and comparison of Bellah and Metz, see John Coleman, *An American Strategic Theology* (New York: Paulist Press, 1982). See also Robert N. Bellah et al., *Habits of the Heart: Individualism and Commitment in American Life* (Berkeley, Calif: University of California Press, 1985), for a concluding discussion of "Transforming American Culture."

4. Compare Henry S. Commager, *The Empire of Reason: How Europe Imagined and America Realized the Enlightenment* (Garden City, N.Y.: Doubleday & Co., 1978) with William A. William, *Empire as a Way of Life* (New York: Oxford University Press, 1980) and Philip Berryman, *Religion and Revolution in Central America* (Maryknoll, N.Y.: Orbis Books, 1985). On the dialectic of Enlightenment, see Theodor Adorno and Max Horkheimer, *Dialectic of Enlightenment*, trans. John Cummings (New York: Herder & Herder, 1972).

5. Cf. Alkis Kontos, ed., *Domination* (Toronto: University of Toronto Press, 1975); and Bernard J. F. Lonergan, "Dialectic of Authority," in Bernard J. F. Lonergan, *A Third Collection* (New York: Paulist Press, 1985), pp. 5–12.

6. See Helmut Peukert, ed., *Diskussion zur politischen Theologie* (Mainz: Grünewald, 1968); and Johann B. Metz, "Prophetic Authority," in *Religion and Political Society* (New York: Harper Forum Books, 1974), pp. 173–209.

7. What Talcott Parsons and others translated as "types of authority" is, in the original, *Typen der Herrschaft* ("types of domination") — or what Weber would often designate as "legitimate domination." Max Weber, *Wirtschaft und Gesellschaft*, 2 vols. (Tübingen: J. C. B. Mohr, 1956), vol. 1, chap. 3; for the best English translation see Max Weber, *Economy and Society*, trans. Gunther Roth and Claus Wittlich, 2 vols. (Berkeley, Calif.: University of California Press, 1978), 1: 212ff.

8. Peter Berger, *The Sacred Canopy: Elements of a Sociological Theory of Religion* (Garden City, N.Y.: Doubleday & Co., 1967); and *Facing Up to Modernity* (New York: Basic Books, 1977). Compare with Hans Blumenberg, *The Legitimacy of the Modern Age*, trans. Robert Wallace (Cambridge, Mass.: MIT Press, 1983).

9. See Gregory Baum, "Peter Berger's Unfinished Symphony," in *Sociology and Human Destiny*, ed. Gregory Baum (New York: Seabury Press, 1980), pp. 110–29. On the challenge in the nuclear age, see Gordon D. Kaufman, *Theology for a Nuclear Age* (Philadelphia: Westminster Press, 1985); and Johann B. Metz, *The Emergent Church: The Future of Christianity in a Postbourgeois World*, trans. Peter Mann (New York: Seabury Press, 1981).

10. Thomas Paine, *The Age of Reason* (Secaucus, N.J.: Citadel Press, 1974), pp. 182ff.

11. Ruth L. Sivard, *World Military and Social Expenditures 1983* (Washington, D.C.: World Priorities, 1983); National Conference of Catholic Bishops, *The Challenge of Peace* (Washington, D.C.: USCC, 1982).

12. Maurice Merleau-Ponty, *Adventures of the Dialectic*, trans. Joseph Bien (Evanston, Ill.: Northwestern University Press, 1973), pp. 9–24; and Kontos, *Domination*, pp. 101ff.

13. See Helmut Peukert, *Science, Action, and Fundamental Theology*, trans. James Bohman (Cambridge, Mass.: MIT Press, 1984); and Matthew L. Lamb, *Solidarity with Victims* (New York: Crossroads Press, 1982).

14. Cf. Helen Caldicott, *Missile Envy: The Arms Race and Nuclear War* (New York: Morrow, 1984); Freeman Dyson, *Weapons and Hope* (New York: Harper & Row, 1984).

15. Alasdair MacIntyre, *After Virtue: A Study in Moral Theory* (Notre Dame, Ind.: University of Notre Dame Press, 1981); Bellah et al., *Habits of the Heart*, pp. 297–307; and Robert N. Bellah, "Religion and Power in America Today," *Proceedings of the Catholic Theological Society of America*, vol. 37 (1982).

16. See Weber, *Economy and Society*, vol. 2, pp. 901–1042; Maximilien Rubel, "Marx's Concept of Democracy," *Democracy* 3, no. 4 (Fall 1983): 94–105; and Anthony Giddens, *Capitalism and Modern Social Theory* (New York: Cambridge University Press, 1971), pp. 169–84.

17. Cf. Gil Elliot, *Twentieth Century Book of the Dead* (New York: Charles Scribner's Sons, 1972); also Edith Wyschogrod, *Spirit in Ashes: Hegel, Heidegger, and Man-Made Mass Death* (New Haven, Conn.: Yale University Press, 1985).

18. See Matthew L. Lamb, "Christianity within the Political Dialectic of Community and Empire," in *Method: A Journal of Lonergan Studies* 1, no. 1, pp. 1–30; also Jean-Francois Lyotard, *The Postmodern*

Condition: A Report on Knowledge, trans. Geoff Bennington and Brian Massumi (Minneapolis: University of Minnesota Press, 1985).

19. Thomas A. McCarthy, "Translator's Introduction," in Jürgen Habermas, *The Theory of Communicative Action*, vol. 1, *Reason and the Rationalization of Society*, trans. Thomas A. McCarthy (Boston: Beacon Press, 1984), p. xxxvii.

20. Cf. Bernard J. F. Lonergan, *Method in Theology* (New York: Seabury Press, 1972), pp. 115ff.; David Hollenbach, *Nuclear Ethics: A Christian Moral Argument* (New York: Paulist Press, 1983); and Eli Sagan, *At the Dawn of Tyranny* (New York: Alfred A. Knopf, 1985), pp. 375ff.

21. See Bernard J. F. Lonergan, *Insight: A Study of Human Understanding* (New York: Harper & Row, 1978), pp. 207–44; and *Method in Theology*, pp. 27–55.

22. Lonergan, *Insight*, pp. 231–32; Hannah Arendt, *The Origins of Totalitarianism* (New York: Harvest Books, 1968); and Sagan, *At the Dawn of Tyranny*.

23. See Sergio Torres and John Eagleson, eds., *The Challenge of Basic Christian Communities* (Maryknoll, N.Y.: Orbis Books, 1981); also Frederick G. Lawrence, "The Theology of Basic Christian Communities," in *Lonergan Workshop* (Atlanta, Ga.: Scholars Press, 1985), 4: 177ff.

24. See Matthew L. Lamb, "Die Dialektik von Theorie und Praxis in der Paradigmenanalyse," in *Theologie Wohin? Auf dem Weg zu einem neuen Paradigma*, ed. Hans Küng and David Tracy (Zürich: Benzinger, 1984).

25. See Richard Bernstein, *Beyond Objectivism and Relativism: Science, Hermeneutics, and Praxis* (Philadelphia: University of Pennsylvania Press, 1983); and Anthony Giddens, *Central Problems in Social Theory* (Berkeley, Calif.: University of California Press, 1979), pp. 234–59.

26. See Jürgen Habermas, *The Theory of Communicative Action*, vol. 1, *Reason and the Rationalization of Society*, trans. Thomas A. McCarthy (Boston: Beacon Press, 1984), pp. 216–71, 339–99; See also vol. 2 of the German original *Zur Kritik der functionalistischen Vernünft* (Frankfurt: Suhrkamp, 1981), pp. 449–88.

27. See Giddens, *Central Problems in Social Theory*, pp. 49–197; and Anthony Giddens, *Profiles and Critiques in Social Theory* (Berkeley, Calif.: University of California Press, 1982). Also, relative to the debates on postmodernity, cf. Richard Bernstein, ed., *Habermas and Modernity* (Cambridge, Mass.: MIT Press, 1985).

10

Patriarchy as Political Theology: The Establishment of North African Christianity

MARGARET R. MILES

THERE ARE THREE STAGES in the orthodox resolution of the place of women in Christian churches in North Africa over the two-hundred-year period I am exploring. I want to show that the question about the place of women arose in relation to some of the most characteristic values and interests of the churches of North Africa, traceable in the earliest extant literature of African Christianity. To do so will help us understand the context of some of the arguments and resolutions that today we often take for granted as inevitable, and that some of us have been content to see as decisive.

Church historians agree that the real genius of early North African Christianity was ecclesiastical and practical rather than theological or dogmatic. Conflict within and among Christian groups and the "successful" resolution of this conflict was the particular focus of North African Christianity; the definition and handling of schism and the establishment of church order was the influential feat of catholic Christian groups in the third and fourth centuries. My intention is not to substitute an alternative to the "triumph of orthodoxy" ideology that underlies traditional church historiography, but to suggest that a description of the persistent serious conflict over the roles of women in early North African Christianity not only is legitimate but also provides an important

169

piece of the history of our contemporary concern with issues of church order such as the ordination of women.

One side of the conflict over women's roles is preserved in the extant texts from the two hundred years of North African Christianity for which we have the most evidence. I do not understand this conflict as the gradual establishment of orthodox politics over schismatic politics, but as a conflict in which there were winners and losers. The difference is important; it is the difference between believing that orthodox ecclesiastical politics was scriptural, cosmically correct, and therefore inevitable; and seeing the conflict as caused by the existence of different perspectives and interests.

Moreover, I will not assume that the reasons given by losers in these conflicts were flimsy rationalizations of the wishes of these persons to live ideologically sloppy or sexually permissive Christian lives. Rather, I will try to identify, from the emphases and arguments of their opponents, principled reasons for dissent, legitimized, as we will see, by the earliest North African values and interests. It was these interests and values that gave the question about the place of women its high profile and its poignancy in the struggle over gender roles in North Africa.

We must first identify two intertwined and highly characteristic interests of North African Christianity: martyrdom and the activity of the Holy Spirit.

The beginnings of North African Christianity are shrouded in mystery. We do not know where or how Christianity originated here. The first document of Christianity in North Africa is an account of the trial and martyrdom of six Christians soon after the arrival of the new governor, Vigellius Saturninus, in Carthage.[1] The martyrs — three men and three women — bear native African names and probably came from rural areas surrounding Carthage. Their response to the verdict of condemnation, "Deo gratias," was to ring in the African air throughout the approximately five hundred years of African Christianity, on the lips of martyrs, Donatists, and Catholic bishops. The short *Acta* of the Scillitan martyrs reveals the high value of Christian martyrdom and the power of the martyr, both on earth and in heaven where martyrs are pictured as reigning with God.

Confessors — those who had been condemned to death as Christians — who by the third century were simply called martyrs,

continued to be valued and powerful. The strenuous efforts of
Cyprian, bishop of Carthage in the middle of the century, to limit
and control their power to waive serious offenses of their petition-
ers demonstrate the prestige of the confessors. A century and a
half later, at the beginning of the fifth century, Augustine describes
the liturgical reading of their *Actae* on the anniversaries of local
martyrs and the exuberance with which their birthdays into eternal life were popularly celebrated. Authority and martyrdom were
very closely aligned indeed in North African churches.

The second highly valued interest of North African Christians
was the continuing activity of the Holy Spirit in Christian communities. Again, the earliest Christian documents of North Africa
present a strong picture of ongoing inspiration, prophecy, and sus-
tenance by the Spirit's leadership. The prologue of the *Acta of Saints
Perpetua and Felicitas* repeats themes associated with the power
of the Spirit. Perpetua, a twenty-two-year-old aristocratic Roman
matron, and Felicitas, her slave woman, were martyred on March 7,
203 A.D., in the amphitheater at Carthage. The author of the
Acta — perhaps Tertullian — far from restricting the activity of the
Spirit to the earliest Christianity, writes:

> More recent events should be considered the greater, . . . a
> consequence of the extraordinary graces promised for the last
> stage in time. We hold in honor and acknowledge not only
> new prophecies but new visions as well.[2]

The Montanist movement did not originate in North Africa, but
it had a special resonance there: it identified as essential the present work of the Holy Spirit in the churches, an ancient, scriptural,
and intensely-felt value.

These two values of North African Christianity were not un-
connected. The Holy Spirit was understood to provide both the
training and the support for martyrdom. The authority of the martyr came directly from the Spirit's takeover of her or his personality. Confident of her participation in the power of the Spirit,
Perpetua petitioned the release of her long-dead brother from after-
life suffering, a prayer whose success was shown her in a vision.
She also dreamed vividly and informatively. Her fellow martyr
Saturus also reported a vision which seems to reflect a conflict in
the Christian community at Carthage; in it the bishop Optatus

and the presbyter Aspasius, alienated and spatially distant from one another, pled with Saturus to make peace between them, "for you have gone away and left us thus." Interestingly, an angel in the vision urges the bishop to take a more authoritative role in his congregation: "You must scold your flock. They approach you as though they had come from the games, quarreling about the different teams."[3] This glimpse of internecine conflict allows us to see also the role of the Spirit-filled martyr in orchestrating the reconciliation of antagonists within the churches of North Africa. The martyrs had a great deal of personal and ecclesiastical power.

The high value accorded to martyrdom and to the present leading of the Holy Spirit inevitably led to a sense of equality among North African Christians. Equal courage and commitment were required of women and men, and equal authority and power were bestowed on them; within the Christian community at Carthage, roles were based on personal charisma, insight, and courage. Perpetua, for example, takes a leadership initiative in many of the incidents narrated in the *Acta*. Women may have been attracted to the Christian movement by the opportunities for discovering and using their energy and talent without the restrictions of secular society. We learn from Tertullian's heavy censure of leadership roles for women that many of the attractive and successful Christian communities of North Africa were led by women, especially among the charismatic Montanists. Neither martyrdom nor inspiration by the Holy Spirit was restricted according to gender roles.

I

Tertullian is the only North African Christian leader who wrote pointedly against the leadership of women in Christian churches. In his time — the end of the second century and the beginning years of the third — his vitriolic invective against women leaders in Christian groups gives us a sense of the appeal of dissident groups, both for women, whose talents and personalities could be explored without restriction in these groups, and for men.[4] Moreover, the situation in which early Christians questioned and sometimes jettisoned their gender role conditioning was one in which they expected an imminent end of their world, either through the apocalyptic return of Christ or through their personal apocalypse in martyrdom.

Tertullian's writings reveal the presence of conflict over gender issues in the Christian community. Conversion to Christianity brought with it, for women as for men, a strong sense of liberation from the conventional patterns of late Roman corporate life. But gender role expectations were one of the least malleable because most inaccessible carryovers from a Christian's former life. "It is not permitted for a woman to speak in church," Tertullian repeats, quoting Paul, "but neither is it permitted her to teach, nor to baptize, nor to offer, nor to claim to herself a lot in any manly function, not to say in any sacerdotal office."[5]

But women *were* speaking in churches, prophesying, even baptizing, Tertullian himself tells us. To be sure, these were "heretical" women, but we know too little about their doctrines to be able to say with assurance that their differences with the catholic Christians were primarily doctrinal. Tertullian also repeats Paul's idea of patriarchal order as Christian order against Carthaginian consecrated virgins who felt themselves exceptions to Paul's general injunction against women because of their total commitment to Christ and the Christian community: "On the ground of her position, nothing in the way of public honor is permitted to a virgin."[6] In exegeting the Genesis text on the naming of woman by man (Gen. 2) Tertullian says that woman is "a second human being made by God for man's assistance." Consecrated virgins must regard themselves as continuing to share this status: "If 'the man is head of the woman', of course he is head of the virgin too, from whom comes the woman who has married; unless the virgin is a third generic class, some monstrosity with a head of its own."[7]

For male ecclesiastical leaders, the enthusiastic participation of women in North African Christianity was a problem. In each of the three contexts in which we examine their responses to Christian women, we will see the acute discomfort of men culturally conditioned to expect docility and submissiveness from women. The issue of women's dress focused the ongoing conflict between male leaders and women who were feeling empowered to new energy and activity. Not until the end of the fourth century, when patriarchal order had been solidly established, did male ecclesiastical leaders stop trying to control women's dress. By Augustine's time dress was a matter of indifference. But Augustine's indifference, either to differentiating Christians from pagans or to protecting men from the distracting beauty of women, rests on the secure establishment and full theological rationalization of patriarchal order. The rantings of Tertullian come from a vastly different reality, one in which the "confusion" of gender roles threatened the power of a fragile male episcopate.

The Carthaginian context of conflict over the roles of Christian women is crucial if we are to interpret accurately Tertullian's sarcastic attack on the women he addresses as "handmaidens of the Lord, fellow servants, sisters."[8] Although the two books of Tertullian *On Women's Dress* probably represent a minority opinion in the Carthaginian Christian community, we can, by examining these texts, recover information about the attitudes and practices against which he inveighs. Both books were written during Tertullian's catholic period, but they reflect his already strong discomfort with that Christian community. Although it is unlikely that he was ever a priest, he claims a Spirit-directed authority in order to tell Christian women what their attitude should be to clothing, finery, and cosmetics.

These texts reveal, first, a disagreement over the issue of acculturation versus separation. Some women were apparently arguing that a distinguishing drabness of dress was not called for in a Christian woman. The "salt of the earth" model, in which Christians flavored from *within* the secular world, espoused by Tertullian's opponents, is vehemently rejected in Tertullian's promotion of a separatist stance in relation to secular culture. In evaluating this conflict of interpretations on the role of the Christian in society, it is important to think of a rather wide area of late Roman culture as neither Christian nor pagan but simply secular, a common arena of economic, political, and social interaction. The confusion and disagreement evident in early Christian authors about what a Christian's appearance and behavior should be in this secular arena indicate that it was not at all easy to sort out which parts of life were directly relevant to the Christian life, requiring Christians to look and act differently from other people. Whether Christians should serve in the army, which professions Christians might follow, and how Christian women — men are not discussed — should look, as well as many other questions, are addressed very differently at different times and in different locations by Christian authors. It was not clear which areas of life required distinctive Christian behavior.

Second, Christian women felt restored to spiritual integrity so that appearances were no longer significant. Tertullian describes Christian women as saying: "To me it is not necessary to be approved by men; for I do not require the testimony of men: God is the inspector of the heart."[9] Freedom from the constant attention to reputation required of Roman women must have been one of the benefits for women of Christian faith. Tertullian snatches it away from them. No argument is too farfetched or involuted to support his insistence that consecrated virgins must be veiled, and other women should "remove all traces of natural grace by concealment and negligence."[10] Natural beauty, he writes with an uncharacteristic generosity, is not to be censured; it is, however, to be feared.[11] The word is revealing: by whom should women's beauty be feared? It is the salvation of males that Tertullian is protecting; men's salvation is at stake:[12]

> I beseech you, be you mother, sister, or virgin-daughter . . . veil your head: if a mother, for your sons' sakes; if a sister, for your brothers' sake; if a daughter, for your father's sake. All ages are imperiled in your person.[13]

Even more specifically, Tertullian himself had what his most recent biographer called a "natural sensitivity to feminine beauty."[14] Tertullian is more forthright than his biographer; he tells us in *The Resurrection of the Flesh* that in his youth he was an adulterer.[15] Tertullian, painfully aware of his "natural sensitivity," is concerned about his own salvation.

Tertullian's assumption that women care for their appearance only in order to please men is a familiar one. Moreover, he argues for the logical validity of projection; he can be confident, he says, that he recognizes a woman's motivation by the way he is affected by a woman's appearance. If a man is aroused by looking at a particular woman, that woman means to arouse him: "Seeing and being seen belong to the self-same lust."[16] Some of the Carthaginian consecrated virgins wore veils on the street but removed them in church since they felt themselves safe from intrusive gazes among the Christian community. This gesture of trust and Christian freedom Tertullian also rejects: "They fear strangers," he writes, "let them fear the brethren also."[17]

Ironically, one of the authoritative values of Christian North Africa, guidance by the Holy Spirit, is invoked against women who have been empowered by their equal accessibility to the leading of the Spirit.[18] According to Tertullian, however, the special province of the Holy Spirit is "the direction of discipline,"[19] and predictably, "those who heed the present prophecy of the Spirit" agree with Tertullian. It is the Spirit's authority that guarantees the legitimacy of Tertullian's judgments on matters not mentioned in scripture. Quoting 2 Tim. 3:16 from memory, Tertullian makes a telling error; instead of "all scripture is given by inspiration of God and is useful for . . . instruction," Tertullian writes, "all that is useful for edification is divinely inspired."[20]

A further methodological principle governs Tertullian's claim to authority. Not only are present prophetic utterances in matters of discipline decisive, but Tertullian claims the right to unlimited generalization from these inspired utterances:

> No enunciation of the Holy Spirit ought to be confined to the subject immediately in hand merely, and not applied and carried out with a view to every occasion to which its application is useful.[21]

The universalization of his personal point of view is painfully evident in Tertullian's identification of his own opinion with truth: his feeling that consecrated virgins should be veiled is, he writes, an observation prescribed by truth, which remains the same without influence of "space of times, influence of persons," or "privilege of regions."[22] Identification of truth with his own view gives Tertullian a heavy advantage; he can conclude: "Whatever savors of opposition to truth, this will be heresy."[23]

Although Tertullian was a dissident in the catholic Christian community and ultimately left this communion, on this issue his views have been highly influential. Indeed, too much has been made of a separation of Tertullian's "orthodox" period from his Montanist period. His harsher opinions of women cannot be comfortably cubbyholed to his Montanist period.[24] Even though these opinions may have contributed to his departure from the catholic Christian community, they carried the perennial authority of skillful rhetoric and a male voice. Tertullian's opinions on matters as close to the bone as gender hierarchy are continuous through his church hoppings.

II

Approximately fifty years after Tertullian's treatises on women's dress, the "woman question" appears to be unresolved in North Africa. It is, however, demonstrably in process of resolution by the establishment of patriarchal order. Cyprian, bishop of Carthage in the mid-third century, no longer ranted against women taking leadership roles in the churches. Apparently by mid-third century a male ecclesiastical hierarchy can be taken for granted in African catholic communities; indeed, by now this feature of church order serves to distinguish catholic communities from schismatic Christian groups. Tertullian, threatened by the attraction to North African Christians of communities in which women were allowed to preach, celebrate, baptize, and teach, had heightened his rhetorical bombast. Cyprian called Tertullian "the master" and read his writings daily; he was indebted to Tertullian's opinions and arguments, but Cyprian no longer felt sufficiently threatened to denounce women leaders. Another aspect of the participation of women in the Christian community is more prominent in the writings of Cyprian.

Like Tertullian, Cyprian wrote a treatise on the dress of consecrated virgins. Cyprian's treatise is very informative about the attitudes and activities of mid-third-century consecrated virgins in the Carthaginian churches. We can glimpse, for example, why virginity was an attractive option for women. We can also see some familiar motifs, like male efforts to control the behavior and dress of women. The honored role of consecrated virgin carried the attractive potential of a much greater degree of personal autonomy and independence than did the secular possibilities for women in the late Roman world. In the secular world a young wife remained in the jurisdiction of her father until she reached the age of twenty-five; a woman who was not married by age twenty-five was placed under the formal supervision of a legal guardian.[25] Late Roman satirists repeatedly report the quaint

Roman belief that an unsupervised woman was dangerous to herself and society.

Until Constantine's legislation in the fourth century, the legal position and social relationships of consecrated virgins were ambiguous. As our contemporary, the late Joan Kelly, pointed out, it is in times of social ambiguity that women are able to create new roles and expand the range of old ones. Cyprian's treatise reinforces the impression of new roles and relationships within a community of Christian women. In the middle of the third century, vows of virginity consisted of private resolution without public ceremony or official ratification. There is no evidence that vows of poverty and obedience were included at this time. A consecrated virgin might continue to live at home, spending much of her time in prayer and charitable activities. Or she might live in a small community of similarly committed women associated with a local parish. We must keep in mind the highly informal nature of both vows and living arrangements. What we will examine in this context is a struggle between a bishop and some committed Christian women over the right to define their lifestyle and activities.

What picture of these women's lives do we get from Cyprian's writings? First, *virgines subintroductae*, consecrated virgins who lived with — but did not have sexual intercourse with — clerics are still in evidence. Women and men, living and working together in relationships that rejected the gender conditioning of their society, felt that the need to communicate and rapidly spread the gospel required new kinds of relationship. This practice, which originated in the excitement of the Christian missionary movement, is mentioned as early as the second-century *Shepherd of Hermas*. Repeatedly, and well into the fifth century, local and ecumenical councils condemned the practice, thereby attesting its continuation.

Cyprian's *Epistula* 4 demands that these relationships be discontinued. In vain consecrated virgins volunteered to undergo medical examinations to prove their continued virginity;[26] Cyprian finds cohabitation too dangerous to be permissible. Speaking of women, he writes: "Not only is there the weakness of their sex (*sexus infirmus*), but they are still at a vulnerable age (*aetas adhuc lubrica*) and ought to be guided completely by our direction and control."[27] Cyprian's parable of God as jealous husband of the virgin living with another man is not subtle: "Christ is our Lord and our Judge: when he observes his own virgin who has been vowed to him and dedicated to his holy estate lying with another man, imagine his rage and his fury and the punishments he threatens to exact for such unchaste associations."[28]

Apparently these relationships were often simultaneously loving, meaningful, and nonsexual, if we are thus to understand the willingness of some of the consecrated virgins to prove their virginity by medical examination. Cyprian, as a bishop, had, however, the power to demand that such relationships cease. Indeed, in his situation, in which his authority was frequently threatened, his control of the consecrated virgins of his diocese may have been a key to strengthening his authority.

It was not a threat to the salvation of these women that lies closest to Cyprian's heart; rather, "it is our duty to take pains to ensure by every possible means that every one of our brothers can escape his spiritual sword and the approaching day of his judgment."[29] Although, he says, the responsibility for these relationships is with his clerical brothers, the punishment he threatens is for the women who live with them. They are to be warned, Cyprian writes, that their "life and salvation"[30] will be "taken away" if they refuse "to obey their bishops and priests" in this matter.[31]

Second, another aspect of Cyprian's struggles with celibate women is revealed in *The Dress of Virgins*. Freedom from the authority of a husband or father seems to have been at least a part of the attraction of the celibate life. In a society in which women had few options for an independent autonomous lifestyle, the community of celibate women must have provided such an opportunity. Cyprian gives us a picture of the activities of celibate women in his objections to their behavior. Since they had neither renounced possessions nor vowed obedience they felt that their clothing, cosmetics, and grooming were a matter of personal taste. They liked a good party, too; Cyprian complains that their attendance at typical bawdy Carthaginian wedding parties might threaten their vow of virginity, which must be "guarded with anxious fear."[32] And since they felt no sense of shame, nor did they "look immodestly" at anyone, they saw no problem with bathing at the integrated public baths.

They acted, it must be surmised, somewhat more freely than

did dutiful daughters and married women. Cyprian mentions "notorious and detestable gossip" about them that caused the church "frequently to bewail her virgins."[33] But again, as with the women who were living as *subintroductae*, Cyprian's concern is not primarily for the women themselves. Rather he insists repetitively that their freedom is causing men problems. Berating consecrated virgins who used makeup with "causing another's ruin,"[34] Cyprian insists that the women will be accountable for those they have "ruined":

> Without perhaps losing your own soul, you nevertheless ruin others and offer yourself [as] a sword and a poison, as it were, to those who behold you; you cannot be excused on the ground that your mind is chaste and pure.[35]

He speaks sternly to virgins, Cyprian says, for their own good and because he cares for them so much. He explicitly compares himself to God in chastising in order to correct: "Now if God chastises whom he loves, and chastises that he may correct, brethren also, and priests particularly, do not hate but love those whom they chastise."[36] The figure of the Roman *paterfamilias* is the model Cyprian has in mind when he admonishes, "Listen, virgins, as to a father, . . . listen to one who is faithfully watching over your advantages and interests."[37] If one of the attractions of celibacy for women was freedom from a *paterfamilias* who held their practical destinies in his hand, denial of their ability for self-definition and the imposition of yet another paternal authority, that of the Christian bishop, cannot have pleased the women to whom it was addressed. We may surmise that Cyprian's command, "Be such as the hand of the Father has fashioned you,"[38] carried for them all the ambiguity that we can detect in it.

Cyprian's problem with Christian women is different from that of Tertullian. Women are no longer mentioned as occupying leadership roles in Christian groups. Yet the control of groups of celibate women associated with local churches has become a focus of the bishops' power. Cyprian's letters and treatises suggest that the fragile power of a mid-third-century bishop, in Cyprian's case a power already questioned by ecclesiastical rivals, could be strengthened and demonstrated by the successful assertion of the authority of a *paterfamilias* over celibate women.

III

The final situation in North African Christianity that we will explore is that of Augustine, bishop of Hippo Regius in the beginning of the fifth century. Augustine's situation and problems are different from either those of Tertullian, in early third-century Carthage, or Cyprian, in mid-third-century Carthage. Augustine's authority among the North African Catholic churches was secure. But the society was not. Following the unbelievable sack of *Roma eterna* in A.D. 410, the shock waves quickly spread to North Africa, itself the location of internal political upheaval and threatened barbarian invasion.

Augustine's philosophical and theological work from 410 on can be understood partly as a massive attempt to support and promote the stability of Roman culture under the Christian emperor. His answer to the perilous slipperiness of what he thought of simply as civilization was the theological rationalization of a pervasive hierarchical orderliness. Almost thirty years before he wrote *The City of God* he outlined, in his treatise *On Continence*, three hierarchical pairs: spirit and flesh, husband and wife, and Christ and the Church. In about A.D. 420, writing in the sober wake of the sack of Rome, he needs only to add to these paradigms "ruler and people" to have a comprehensive model of human life from individual to society. "Of these," he wrote in A.D. 395, "the former cares for the latter in each case, and the latter waits upon the former. All are good when among them, some, excellently as superiors, and others, fittingly as subjects, preserve the beauty of order."[39]

Augustine's model of human being as hierarchically structured — body controlled by soul, soul controlled by God — both reflected and, in turn, came to be reflected by Western Christian society. His idea of the proper relationship of husband and wife provides an example of what he saw as the necessarily hierarchical structure of society. The subordination of women is central to Augustine's attempt to prescribe for the social and political instability of his time. In late Roman culture, Augustine saw an extension of his anthropological model in a necessary and inevitable subordination of some people to others. In the slippery world of the newly sacked city of Rome, he specifically urged that this hierarchical model be accepted as the lesser of the social evils. Although in Book 19 of *The City of God* he describes social inequality as part of the evidence that human beings exist in a fallen state, a state of punishment, Augustine does not criticize this order but counsels respect for dominance and subordination on every level of society, from families to kingdoms. Social inequality, Augustine says, is the result of the anxious craving of the few for dominance over the many. "God did not wish the rational being, made in God's own image, to have dominion over any but irrational creatures, not human over human, but human over the beasts." Nevertheless, the "ordered harmony" Augustine advocates for society begins in the mini-society of the home where "the husband gives orders to the wife, parents to children, and masters to servants."[40]

Conspicuously missing from Augustine's program for ordered harmony under the permanently unsettled and unsettling conditions of this human pilgrimage is any glorification of inequality; but neither could he envision social arrangements in which dominance and subordination would not be necessary for peace. His is the rationalization that has been used throughout the history of the Christian West to justify dominance and subordination: the one who gives orders, Augustine writes, must consider himself the "servant," caring for the needs of those to whom orders are given; he must act from "dutiful concern," not from "lust for domination."[41]

Augustine's model of society is human being, a complex organism in which orderliness is necessary for life on the physical level and the body's subordination in value and activity to the soul is never questioned, even — or especially — when he calls the body the spouse[42] of the soul. Likewise, in the family and in society, Augustine sees only the inevitability of dominance and subordination; his model of body and soul does not — as it certainly might — provide him with a model of interdependence.

In Augustine's writings we do not find anything faintly resembling the rantings of Tertullian against women leaders; no women leaders are in sight. Nor do we find Tertullian's and Cyprian's concern about women's dress and the control of potentially autonomous women. Consecrated virgins by Augustine's time took vows which stipulated their obedience as well as virginity. He still wrote treatises addressed to virgins and widows, but the questions he takes up are those of attitudes, not of behavior. The spiritual danger of pride, of being puffed up because of their special gift of virginity, does not seem to have had political dimensions with the consecrated virgins Augustine addresses. One still senses something of the anxiety provoked by women not directly in the jurisdiction of a male in his careful instructions to celibate women. And there is still the sense of unattached sexuality as simultaneously miraculous and dangerous, but the more extreme metaphors of Tertullian and Cyprian do not appear in Augustine's advice. He explicitly rejects Cyprian's metaphor of God as jealous husband: "He is not the kind to whom someone may lie about you and cause him to fly into a jealous rage."[43]

Augustine's horizons have widened from the relatively small embattled and persecuted Christian communities of the third century, and his treatment of the place of women reflects this altered context. It is women's place in the society and the world which occupies him, not primarily in the Christian churches. Yet women and their roles are still crucial to his prescription for the maintenance of society. Submission, docility, obedience — these are the virtues urged on wives, consecrated virgins, and widows alike. The humility of the virgin must parallel the submissiveness of the wife, "thinking how she may please her husband."[44]

It is striking that Augustine promotes these virtues on women so frequently and so insistently, while men's temptations to tyranny on every level of society do not receive anything like the constant injunctions addressed to women's attitudes and behavior. In the A.D. 401 treatise, *The Good of Marriage*, Augustine discusses the question of why the patriarchs of the Old Testament were permitted to take more than one wife. His discussion reveals rather than states his attitude that unexamined domination is less to be feared than insubordination:

> It was permitted for one husband to have several wives, [but] it was not permitted for one woman to have several husbands, even for the sake of offspring. . . . For, by a hidden law of nature things that rule love singularity; things that are ruled, indeed, are subjected not only each one to an individual master, but also, if natural or social conditions allow, many of them are not unfittingly subjected to one master . . . just as many souls are properly subjected to the one God.[45]

"Things that rule love singularity"; again the rationale demonstrates the implicit identification of the male with God: "just as many souls are properly subjected to the one God." Augustine has learned a great deal from his African forefathers; their attitudes appear again and again in the different social and textual context in which Augustine used them. In Augustine's writings, the "woman question" has been fully resolved, philosophically and theologically rationalized in a form that will remain for 1500 years of Western Christian history.

These three stages in the development of the Christian churches and society reveal that patriarchal order was not, as we may have come to think of it, inevitable, God-ordained, and scripturally based. It was the gradual implementation of women's subordination, in churches and in society, over women who understood Christian faith to render obsolete the gender stipulations of their culture, who experienced the freedom of Christ specifically as freedom for the cultivation of a lifestyle and spiritual life undefined by males.

We are today faced with the challenge of a reinterpretation of these early struggles over the involvement of Christian women in the Christian churches. We must question whether Christian churches can continue to confine and limit women's roles and participation. The nuclear world in which we live gives us a sense of peril and urgency similar to that created in the early churches by an expected imminent eschatological limit to human life and work. Like early Christians, we live in a time in which the churches and the world desperately need to engage to the fullest the talent and energy of each Christian person. We are challenged, as were the earliest Christian communities, to service based on talent, regardless of gender, and to the establishment of the equality and dignity of every person. We are challenged to envision and create communities of love and service that reject our individual and cultural gender conditioning in the interest of working as speedily as possible to prevent nuclear war, to promote political and economic justice, and to further global peace. Recognizing and acknowledging the extent to which the political essence of Christianity has been patriarchal order, we must reappropriate the struggle, begun so long ago, for gender equality and we must give this struggle a different outcome in our perilous world.

NOTES

1. "Passio Sanctorum Scillitanorum," in *The Acts of the Christian Martyrs*, ed. Herbert Anthony Musurillo (Oxford: Clarendon Press, 1972).

2. "Passio SS. Perpetua et Felicitas," in *Acts of the Christian Martyrs*, ed. Musurillo.

3. Ibid., p. 13.

4. Elizabeth Schüssler Fiorenza, *In Memory of Her* (New York: Crossroads Press, 1983), p. 54. Schüssler Fiorenza has written: "The acid polemics of the fathers against the ecclesiastical leadership of women and against their teaching and writing books indicate that the question of women's ecclesiastical office was still being debated in the second and third centuries C.E. It also demonstrates that the progressive patriarchalization of church office did not happen without opposition but had to overcome various early Christian values and praxis that acknowledged the leadership claims of women."

5. Tertullian *De virginibus velandis* 9. Hereafter cited as VV.

6. Ibid., 9.

7. Ibid., 5.

8. Tertullian *De cultu feminarum* 2.1. Hereafter cited as CF.

9. Ibid., 2.13.

10. Ibid., 2.2.

11. Ibid.

12. Ibid.

13. Tertullian, VV, 16.

14. Timothy D. Barnes, *Tertullian: A Historical and Literary Survey* (Oxford: Clarendon Press, 1971), p. 137.

15. Tertullian *De resurrectione carnis* 59.3.

16. Tertullian, VV, 2: "Eiusdem libidinis est videri et videre."

17. Ibid., 13.

18. Ibid., 17.

19. Ibid., 1.

20. Tertullian, CF, 1.3.: "Et legimus omnem scripturam aedification habilem divinus inspirari."

21. Ibid., 2.

22. Ibid., 1.

23. Ibid., 13.

24. Tertullian, CF, 2 (A.D. 196–97); CF, 1 (A.D. 205–6); VV (A.D. 208–9); only the last of these writings falls firmly within Tertullian's Montanist period.

25. Schüssler Fiorenza, *In Memory of Her*, p. 314.

26. Cyprian *Epistula* 4.3.1.

27. Ibid., 4.2.1.
28. Ibid., 4.3.2.
29. Ibid., 4.3.3.
30. That their *Christian* life is what is meant here is clear from ibid., 4.4.3.
31. Ibid., 4.4.2.
32. Cyprian *De habitu virginum* 2.
33. Ibid., 20.
34. Ibid., 13.
35. Ibid., 9.
36. Ibid., 1.
37. Ibid., 21.
38. Ibid.
39. Augustine *De continentia* 23.
40. Augustine *De civitate Dei* 19.14.
41. Ibid., 19.15.
42. Ibid., 15.7.
43. Augustine *De sancta virginitate* 55.56.
44. Augustine *De bono conjungali* 11.13.
45. Ibid., 17.20.

11

Black Theology as
Public Theology in America

JAMES H. CONE

MORE THAN EIGHTY YEARS ago W. E. B. DuBois wrote in *The Souls of Black Folk* his classic statement of the paradox of black life in America.

> It is a peculiar sensation, this double-consciousness, this sense of always looking at one's self through the eyes of others, of measuring one's soul by the tape of a world that looks on in amused contempt and pity. One ever feels his twoness — an American, a Negro; two souls, two thoughts, two unreconciled strivings; two warring ideals in one dark body, whose dogged strength alone keeps it from being torn asunder.[1]

The two warring ideals that DuBois described in 1903 have been at the center of black religious thought from its origin to the present day. They are found in the heated debates about integration and nationalism and in the attempt to name the community — beginning with the word *African* and using at different times such terms as *colored, Negro, Afro-American*, and *black*.

The two warring ideals in black religion are *African* and *Christian*. Black religious thought is not identical with the Christian theology of white Americans. Nor is it identical with traditional African beliefs, past or present. It is both — but reinterpreted for and adapted to the life situation of black people's struggle for justice in a nation whose social, political, and economic structures are dominated by a white racist ideology. It was the African side of black religion that helped African-Americans to see beyond the white distortions of the gospel and to discover its true meaning as God's liberation of the oppressed from bondage. It was the Christian element in black religion that helped African-Americans to reorient their African past so that it would become useful in the struggle to survive with dignity in a society that they did not make.

Although the African and Christian elements have been found throughout the history of black religious thought, the Christian part gradually became dominant. Though less visible, the African element continued to play an important role in defining the core of black religion, thus preventing it from becoming merely an imitation of Protestant or Catholic theologies in the West.

Of course, there are many similarities between black religious thought and white Protestant and Catholic reflections on the Christian tradition. But the dissimilarities between them are perhaps more important than the similarities. The similarities are found at the point of a common Christian identity, and the dissimilarities can best be understood in light of the differences between African and European cultures in the New World. While whites used their cultural perspective to dominate others, blacks used theirs to affirm their dignity and to empower themselves to struggle for justice. The major reason for the differences between black and white reflections on God is found at the point of the great differences in life. White theology is largely defined by its response to modern and postmodern societies of Europe and America, usually ignoring the contradictions of slavery and oppression in black life. Black religious thought is the thinking of slaves and of marginalized blacks whose understanding of God was shaped by the contradictions that white theologians ignored and regarded as unworthy of serious theological reflection.

ROOTS OF BLACK RELIGIOUS THOUGHT: SLAVERY

The tension between the African and Christian elements acted to reorder traditional theological themes in black religion and to give them different substance when compared to other theologies in Europe and America. Five themes in particular defined the character of black religious thought during slavery and its subsequent development: justice, liberation, hope, love, and suffering.

No theme has been more prominent throughout the history of black religious thought than the justice of God. African-Americans have always believed in the living presence of the God who establishes the right by punishing the wicked and liberating their victims from oppression. Everyone will be rewarded and punished according to their deeds, and no one can escape the judgment of God, who alone is the sovereign of the universe. Evildoers may get by for a time, and good people may suffer unjustly under oppression, but "sooner or later . . . we reap as we sow."[2]

The "sooner" referred to contemporary historically observable events: punishment of the oppressors and liberation of the oppressed. The "later" referred to the divine establishment of justice in the next world where God "gwineter rain down fire" on the wicked and where the liberated righteous will "walk in Jerusalem just like John." In the religion of African slaves, God's justice was identical with the punishment of the oppressors, and divine liberation was synonymous with the deliverance of the oppressed from the bondage of slavery — if not now then in the not yet. Because whites continued to prosper materially as they increased their victimization of African-Americans, black religious thought spoke more often of the "later" than of the "sooner."[3]

The themes of justice and liberation are closely related to the idea of hope. The God who establishes the right and puts down the wrong is the sole basis of the hope that the suffering of the victims will be eliminated. Although African slaves used the term *heaven* to describe their experience of hope, its primary meaning for them must not be reduced to the pie-in-the-sky, otherworldly affirmation that often characterized white evangelical Protestantism. The idea of heaven was the means by which slaves affirmed their humanity in a world that did not recognize them as human beings.[4] It was their way of saying that they were made for freedom and not slavery.

Black slaves' hope was based on their faith in God's promise to protect the needy and to defend the poor. Just as God delivered the Hebrew children from Egyptian bondage and raised Jesus from the dead, so God will also deliver African slaves from American slavery and in due time will bestow upon them the gift of eternal life. That was why they sang:

> Soon-a-will be done with the trouble of the world;
> Soon-a-will be done with the trouble of the world;
> Going home to live with God.

Black slaves' faith in the coming justice of God was the chief reason why they could hold themselves together in servitude and sometimes fight back, even though the odds were against them.

The ideas of justice, liberation, and hope should be seen in relation to the important theme of love. Theologically God's love is prior to the other themes. But in order to separate black reflections on love from a similar theme in white theology, it is important to emphasize that love in black religious thought is usually linked with God's justice, liberation, and hope. God's love is made known through divine righteousness, liberating the poor for a new future.

God's creation of all persons in the divine image bestows sacredness upon human beings and thus makes them the children of God. To violate any person's dignity is to transgress "God's great law of love."[5] We must love the neighbor because God has first loved us. And because slavery and racism are blatant denials of the dignity of the human person, God's justice means that God "will call the oppressors to account."[6]

Despite the strength of black faith, belief in God's coming justice and liberation was not easy for African slaves and their descendants. Their suffering created the most serious challenge to their faith. If God is good, why did God permit millions of blacks to be stolen from Africa and enslaved in a strange land? No black person has been able to escape the existential agony of that question.

In their attempt to resolve the theological dilemma that slavery and racism created, African-Americans turned to two texts — the Exodus and Ps. 68:31.[7] They derived from the Exodus text the belief that God is the liberator of the oppressed. They interpreted Ps. 68:31 as an obscure reference to God's promise to redeem Africa: "Princes shall come out of Egypt, and Ethiopia shall soon stretch forth her hands unto God." Despite African-Americans' reflections on these texts, the contradictions remained between oppression and their faith.

BLACK RELIGIOUS THOUGHT,
THE CIVIL RIGHTS MOVEMENT,
AND MARTIN LUTHER KING, JR.

The withdrawal of the black church from politics and its alliance with the accommodation philosophy of Booker T. Washington created the conditions that gave rise to the civil rights movement: the National Association for the Advancement of Colored People (NAACP) in 1909, the National Urban League (NUL) in 1911, and the Congress for Racial Equality (CORE) in 1942. These national organizations, and similar local and regional groups in many parts of the United States, took up the cause of justice and equality of blacks in the society. They were strongly influenced by ideas and persons in the churches. Civil rights organizations not only internalized the ideas about justice, liberation, hope, love, and suffering that had been preached in the churches; they also used church property to convene their own meetings and usually made appeals for support at church conferences. The close relation between the NAACP and the black churches has led some to say that "the black church is the NAACP on its knees."

Due to the deradicalization of the black church, progressive black ministers found it difficult to remain involved in the internal affairs of their denominations. Baptist ministers, because of the autonomy of their local congregations, found it easier than the Methodists did to remain pastors while also being deeply involved in struggles for black equality in the society. Prominent examples included Adam Clayton Powell, father and son pastors of Abyssinian Baptist Church in New York. Adam, Jr., made his entry on the public stage by leading a four-year nonviolent direct action campaign, securing some ten thousand jobs for Harlem blacks. In 1944 he was elected to Congress.

Adam Clayton Powell, Jr., embraced that part of the black religious tradition that refused to separate the Christian gospel from the struggle for justice in society. In his influential *Marching Blacks*, he accused the white churches of turning Christianity into "church-ianity," thereby distorting the essential message of the gospel which is equality and brotherhood.

> The great loving heart of God has been embalmed and laid coolly away in the tombs we call churches. Christ of the manger, the carpenter's bench, and the borrowed tomb has once again been crucified in stained-glass windows.[8]

Other influential thinkers of this period included Howard Thurman and Benjamin E. Mays. Howard Thurman wrote twenty-two books and lectured at more than five hundred institutions. He also served as dean of Rankin Chapel and professor of theology at Howard University; dean of Marsh Chapel and minister-at-large of Boston University; and minister and co-founder of the interdenominational Fellowship Church of San Francisco. His writings and preaching influenced many, and *Life* magazine cited him as one of the twelve great preachers of this century. Unlike most black ministers concerned about racial justice, liberation, love, suffering, and hope, Thurman did not become a political activist; he took the inward journey (the title of one of his books), focusing on a spiritual quest for liberation beyond race and ethnic origin. He was able to develop this universalist perspective without ignoring the urgency of the political issues involved in the black struggle for justice.[9]

Benjamin E. Mays, ecumenist and long-time president of Morehouse College, also made an important contribution to black religious thought through his writings and addresses on the black church and racism in America. He chaired the National Conference on Religion and Race in 1963.[10] Mays was an example of a black religious thinker who found the black church too limiting as a context for confronting the great problems of justice, liberation, love, hope, and suffering. Like Thurman and Powell, Mays regarded racism as anti-Christian, an evil that must be eliminated from the churches and the society.

No thinker has made a greater impact upon black religious thought or even upon American society and religion as a whole than Martin Luther King, Jr. The fact that many white theologians can write about American religion and theology with no reference to him reveals both the persistence of racism in the academy and the tendency to limit theology narrowly to the academic discourse of seminary and university professors.

Much has been written about the influence of Martin King's graduate education upon his thinking and practice, especially the writings of George Davis, Henry David Thoreau, Mahatma Gandhi, Edgar S. Brightman, Harold DeWolf, G. W. Hegel, Walter Rauschenbusch, Paul Tillich, and Reinhold Niebuhr.[11] Of course, these religious and philosophical thinkers influenced him greatly, but it is a mistake to use them as the primary basis for an interpretation of his life and thought. Martin King was a product of the black church tradition; its faith determined the essence of his theology.[12] He used the intellectual tools of highly recognized thinkers to explain what he believed to the white public and also to express the universal character of the gospel. But he did not arrive at his convictions about God by reading white theologians. On the contrary, he derived his religious beliefs from his acceptance of black faith and his application of it to the civil rights struggle.

In moments of crisis, Martin King turned to the God of black faith. From the beginning of his role as the leader of the Montgomery bus boycott to his tragic death in Memphis, Martin King was a public embodiment of the central ideas of black religious thought. The heart of his beliefs revolved around the ideas of love, justice, liberation, hope, and redemptive suffering. The meaning of each is mutually dependent on the others. Though love may be appropriately placed at the center of his thought, he interpreted it in the light of justice for the poor, liberation for all, and the certain hope that God has not left this world in the hands of evildoers.

Martin King often used the writings of Tillich, Niebuhr, and other white thinkers to express his own ideas about the interrelations of love and justice. But it was his internalization of their meaning in the black church tradition that helped him to see that "unmerited suffering is redemptive." While the fighters for justice must be prepared to suffer in the struggle for liberation, they must never inflict suffering on others. That was why King described nonviolence as "the Christian way in human relations" and "the only road to freedom."[13]

To understand Martin King's thinking, it is necessary to understand him in the context of his own religious heritage. His self-description is revealing:

> I am many things to many people; civil rights leader, agitator, troublemaker, and orator, but in the quietness of my heart, I am fundamentally a clergyman, a Baptist preacher. This is my being and my heritage for I am also the son of a Baptist preacher, the grandson of a Baptist preacher, and the great-grandson of a Baptist preacher. The church is my life and I have given my life to the church.[14]

The decisive impact of the black church heritage upon King can be seen in his ideas about justice, liberation, love, hope, and suffering. Martin King took the democratic tradition of freedom and combined it with the biblical tradition of justice and liberation as found in the Exodus and the prophets. Then he integrated both traditions with the New Testament idea of love and suffering as disclosed in Jesus' cross, and from all three, King developed a theology that was effective in challenging all Americans to create the beloved community in which all persons are equal. While it was the Gandhian method of nonviolence that provided the strategy for achieving justice, it was, as King said, "through the influence of the Negro church" that "the way of nonviolence became an integral part of our struggle."[15]

As a Christian whose faith was derived from the cross of Jesus, Martin King believed that there could be no true liberation without suffering. Through nonviolent suffering, he contended, blacks would not only liberate themselves from the necessity of bitterness and feeling of inferiority toward whites, but would also prick the conscience of whites and liberate them from a feeling of superiority. The mutual liberation of blacks and whites lays the foundation for both to work together toward the creation of an entirely new world.

In accordance with this theological vision, he initially rejected black power because of its connotations of hate, and he believed that no beloved community of blacks and whites could be created out of bitterness. King said that he would continue to preach nonviolence even if he became its only advocate. It is significant that King softened his attitude toward black power shortly before his assassination and viewed its positive elements as a much needed philosophy in order to eradicate self-hate in the black community, especially as revealed in the riots in the cities. He began to speak of a need to "teach about black culture" (especially black philosophers, poets, and musicians) and even of "temporary separation,"[16] because he realized that without self-respect and dignity black people could not participate with others in creating the beloved community.

A similar but even more radical position was taken in regard to the war in Vietnam. Because the Civil Rights Act (1964) and the Voting Rights Bill (1965) did not affect significantly the life-chances of the poor, and because of the failure of President Johnson's war on poverty, King became convinced that his dream of 1963 had been turned into a nightmare.[17] Gradually he began to see the connections between the failure of the war on poverty and the expenditures for the war in Vietnam. In the tradition of the Old Testament prophets and against the advice of many of his closest associates in black and white communities, King stood before a capacity crowd at Riverside Church and condemned America as "the greatest purveyor of violence in the world today."[18] He proclaimed God's judgment against America and insisted that God would break the backbone of U.S. power if this nation did not bring justice to the poor and peace to the world. Vicious criticisms came from blacks and whites in government, civil rights groups, media, and the nation generally as he proclaimed God's righteous indignation against the three great evils of our time — war, racism, and poverty.

During the severe crises of 1966–68 King turned, not to the theologians and philosophers of his graduate education, but to his own religious heritage. It was the eschatological hope, derived from his slave grandparents and mediated through the black church, that sustained him in the midst of grief and disappointment. This hope also empowered him to "master [his] fears" of death and to "stand by the best in an evil time."[19] In an unpublished sermon preached at Ebenezer Baptist Church he said:

> I've decided what I'm going to do; I ain't going to kill nobody . . . in Mississippi . . . and . . . in Vietnam, and I ain't going to study war no more. And you know what? I don't care who doesn't like what I say about it. I don't care who

criticizes me in an editorial; I don't care what white person or Negro criticizes me. I'm going to stick with the best. . . . Every now and then we sing about it: "If you are right, God will fight your battle." I'm going to stick by the best during these evil times.[20]

It was not easy for King to "stand by the best," because he often stood alone. But he firmly believed that the God of black faith had said to him: "Martin Luther, stand up for righteousness. Stand up for justice. Stand up for truth. And lo, I will be with you, even until the end of the world."[21]

Martin King combined the exodus-liberation and cross-love themes with the message of hope found in the resurrection of Jesus. Hope for him was not derived from the optimism of liberal Protestant theology but rather was based on his belief in the righteousness of God as defined by his reading of the Bible through the eyes of his slave foreparents. The result was the most powerful expression in black history of the essential themes of black religious thought from the integrationist viewpoint.

Centuries ago Jeremiah raised a question, "Is there no balm in Gilead? Is there no physician?" He raised it because he saw the good people suffering so often and the evil people prospering. Centuries later our slave foreparents came along and they too saw the injustices of life and had nothing to look forward to, morning after morning, but the rawhide whip of the overseer, long rows of cotton, and the sizzling heat; but they did an amazing thing. They looked back across the centuries, and they took Jeremiah's question mark and straightened it into an exclamation point. And they could sing, "There is a balm in Gilead to make the wounded whole. There is a balm in Gilead to heal the sinsick soul."[22]

BLACK RELIGIOUS THOUGHT, BLACK POWER, AND BLACK THEOLOGY

From the time of its origin in slavery to the present, black religious thought has been faced with the question of whether to advocate integration into American society or separation from it.

The majority of the participants in the black churches and the civil rights movement have promoted integration, and they have interpreted justice, liberation, love, suffering, and hope in light of the goal of creating a society in which blacks and whites can live together in a beloved community.

While integrationists have emphasized the American side of the double consciousness of African-Americans, there have also been nationalists who rejected any association with the United States and instead have turned toward Africa. Nationalists contend that blacks will never be accepted as equals in a white racist church and society. Black freedom can be achieved only by black people separating themselves from whites — either by returning to Africa or by forcing the government to set aside a separate state in the United States so blacks can build their own society.[23]

The nationalist perspective on the black struggle for freedom is deeply embedded in the history of black religious thought. Some of its prominent advocates include: Bishop Henry McNeal Turner of the African Methodist Episcopal Church; Marcus Garvey, the founder of the Universal Negro Improvement Association; and Malcolm X of the religion of Islam. Black nationalism is centered on blackness, a repudiation of any value in white culture and religion. Nationalists reversed the values of the dominant society by attributing to black history and culture what whites had said about theirs. For example, Bishop Turner claimed that "we have as much right biblically and otherwise to believe that God is a Negro . . . as you . . . white people have to believe that God is a fine-looking, symmetrical, and ornamented white man."[24] Marcus Garvey held a similar view:

> If the white man has the idea of a white God, let him worship his God as he desires. . . . We Negroes believe in the God of Ethiopia, the everlasting God — God the Father, God the Son, and God the Holy Ghost, the One God of all ages.[25]

The most persuasive interpreter of black nationalism during the 1960s was Malcolm X, who proclaimed a challenging critique of Martin King's philosophy of integration, nonviolence, and love. Malcolm X advocated black unity instead of the beloved community, self-defense in lieu of nonviolence, and self-love in place of turning the other cheek to whites.[26]

Like Turner and Garvey, Malcolm X asserted that God is black; but unlike them he rejected Christianity as the white man's religion. He became a convert initially to Elijah Muhammad's Nation of Islam and later to the worldwide Islamic community. His critique of Christianity and of American society as white was so persuasive that many blacks followed him into the religion of Islam, and others accepted his criticisms even though they did not become Muslims. Malcolm pushed civil rights activists to the left and caused many black Christians to reevaluate their interpretation of Christianity.

> Brothers and sisters, the white man has brainwashed us black people to fasten our gaze upon a blond-haired, blue-eyed Jesus! We're worshiping a Jesus that doesn't even *look* like us! Now, just think of this. The blond-haired, blue-eyed white man has taught you and me to worship a *white* Jesus, and to shout and sing and pray to this God that's *his* God, the white man's God. The white man has taught us to shout and sing and pray until we *die*, to wait until *death*, for some dreamy heaven-in-the-hereafter, when we're *dead*, while this white man has his milk and honey in the streets paved with golden dollars right here on *this* earth![27]

During the first half of the 1960s, Martin King's interpretation of justice as equality with whites, liberation as integration, and love as nonviolence dominated the thinking of the black religious community. However, after the riot in Watts (Los Angeles) in August 1965, some black clergy began to take another look at Malcolm's philosophy, especially in regard to his criticisms of Christianity and American society. Malcolm X's contention that America was a nightmare and not a dream began to ring true to many black clergy as they watched their communities go up in flames as young blacks shouted in jubilation, "Burn, baby, burn."

It was during the James Meredith "march against fear" in Mississippi (June 1966, after Malcolm's assassination in February 1965) that some black clergy began to question openly Martin King's philosophy of love, integration, and nonviolence. When Stokely Carmichael proclaimed black power, it sounded like the voice of Malcolm X. Though committed to the Christian gospel, black clergy found themselves moving slowly from integration to separation, from Martin King to Malcolm X.

The rise of black power created a decisive turning point in black religious thought. Black power forced black clergy to raise the theological question about the relation between black faith and white religion. Although blacks have always recognized the ethical heresy of white Christians, they have not always extended it to Euro-American theology. With its accent on the cultural heritage of Africa and political liberation "by any means necessary," black power shook black clergy out of their theological complacency.

Separating themselves from Martin King's absolute commitment to nonviolence, a small group of black clergy, mostly from the North, addressed the black power movement both positively and critically. Like King and unlike black power advocates, these black clergy were determined to remain within the Christian community. This was their dilemma: How could they reconcile Christianity and black power, Martin King and Malcolm X?

Under the influence of Malcolm X and the political philosophy of black power, many black theologians began to advocate the necessity for the development of a black theology, and they rejected the dominant theologies of Europe and North America as heretical. For the first time in the history of black religious thought, black clergy and theologians began to recognize the need for a completely new starting point in theology, and they insisted that it must be defined by people at the bottom and not the top of the socio-economic ladder. To accomplish this task, black theologians focused on God's liberation of the poor as the central message of the gospel.[28]

To explicate the theological significance of the liberation motif, black theologians began to reread the Bible through the eyes of their slave grandparents and started to speak of God's solidarity with the wretched of the earth. As the political liberation of the poor emerged as the dominant motif, justice, suffering, love, and hope were reinterpreted in its light. For the biblical meaning of liberation, black theologians turned to the Exodus, while the message of the prophets provided the theological content for the theme of justice. The gospel story of the life, death, and resurrection of Jesus served as the biblical foundation for a reinterpretation of love, suffering, and hope in the context of the black struggle for liberation and justice.

As black theologians have reread the Bible in the light of the struggles of the oppressed, the idea of the suffering God has become important in our theological perspective. Our theological imagination has been stirred by Jürgen Moltmann's writing about *The Crucified God* as well as by Luther's distinction between the "theology of glory" and the "theology of the cross." But it has been the actual suffering of the oppressed in black and other Third World communities that has been decisive in our reflections on the cross of Jesus Christ. As Gustavo Gutierrez has said, "We cannot speak of the death of Jesus until we speak of the real death of people." For in the deaths of the poor of the world is found the suffering and even the death of God. The political implications of Luther's insight on this point seemed to have been greatly distorted with his unfortunate emphasis on the two kingdoms. Many modern-day Lutheran scholars are even worse, because they turn the cross of Jesus into a theological idea completely unrelated to the concrete historical struggles of the oppressed for freedom. For most Lutheran scholars, the theology of the cross is a theological concept to be contrasted with philosophical and metaphysical speculations. It is a way of making a distinction between faith and reason, justification by grace through faith and justification by the works of reason.

But when the poor of North America and the Third World read the passion story of the cross, they do not view it as a theological idea but as God's suffering solidarity with the victims of the world. Jesus' cross is God's election of the poor by taking their pain and suffering upon the divine person. Black slaves expressed this theological point in such songs as "He Never Said a Mumblin' Word" and "Were You There When They Crucified My Lord?"

Modern-day black theologians make a similar point when they say that God is black and that Jesus is the Oppressed One. Our rejection of European metaphysical speculations and our acceptance of an apparently crude anthropomorphic way of speaking of God is black theologians' way of concretizing Paul's saying that

God chose what is foolish in the world to shame the wise, God chose what is weak in the world to shame the strong, God chose what is low and despised in the world, even the things that are not, to bring to nothing the things that are. (I Cor. 1: 27–28, RSV)

Another characteristic of black theology is its deemphasis, though not complete rejection, of the Western theological tradition and its affirmation of black history and culture. If the suffering of God is revealed in the suffering of the oppressed, then it follows that theology cannot achieve its Christian identity apart from a systematic and critical reflection upon the history and culture of the victims of oppression. When this theological insight impressed itself upon our consciousness, we black theologians began to realize that we have been miseducated. In fact, European and North American theologians have stifled the indigenous development of the theological perspectives of blacks by teaching us that our own cultural traditions are not appropriate sources for an interpretation of the Christian gospel. Europeans and white North Americans taught us that the Western theological tradition as defined by Augustine, Aquinas, Luther, Calvin, and Schleiermacher is the essential source for a knowledge of the Christian past. But when black theologians began to concentrate on black culture and history, we realized that our own historical and cultural traditions are far more important for an analysis of the gospel in the struggle of freedom than are the Western traditions which participated in our enslavement. We now know that the people responsible for or indifferent to the oppression of blacks are not likely to provide the theological resources for our liberation. If oppressed peoples are to be liberated, they must themselves create the means for it to happen.

The focus on black culture in the light of the black liberation struggle has led to an emphasis upon *praxis* as the context out of which Christian theology develops. To know the truth is to do the truth, that is, to make happen in history what is confessed in church. People are not poor by divine decree or by historical accident. They are made poor by the rich and powerful few. This means that to do black liberation theology one must make a commitment, an option for the poor and against those who are responsible for their poverty.

Because black theology is to be created only in the struggles of the poor we have adopted social analysis, especially of racism and more recently of classism and sexism, as a critical component of its methodology. How can we participate in the liberation of the poor from poverty if we do not know who the poor are and why they live in poverty? Social analysis is a tool that helps us to know why the social, economic, and political orders are arranged as they are. It enables us to know not only who benefits from the present status quo, but what must be done to change it.

In our struggle to make a new start in theology we discovered, to our surprise and much satisfaction, that theologians in Asia, Africa, and Latin America were making similar efforts in their contexts.[29] The same was true among other ethnic minorities in the First World and among women in all groups.[30] Black theology has been challenged to address the issues of sexism[31] and classism in a global context, and we have challenged them, especially Latin Americans and feminist theologians of the dominant culture, to address racism. The focus on liberation has been reinforced and deepened. What many of us now know is that a turning point has been made in the theologies of black and Third World communities as radical as were Luther, Schleiermacher, and Barth in the sixteenth, nineteenth, and twentieth centuries in Europe. Let us hope that the revolution in liberation theology will change not only how we think about God, but more importantly what we do in this world so that the victims might make a future that is defined by freedom and justice and not by slavery and oppression.

NOTES

1. W. E. B. DuBois, *The Souls of Black Folk* (1903; reprint ed., Greenwich, Conn.: Fawcett Premier Books, 1968), pp. 16–17.

2. A concise statement of the major themes in black religious thought during and following slavery is found in a 1902 sermon of an ex-slave and Princeton Theological Seminary graduate, Francis J. Grimke. See Francis J. Grimke, *The Works of Francis J. Grimke*, ed. Carter G. Woodson, 4 vols. (Washington, D.C.: Associated Publishers, 1942), 1: 354.

3. For an interpretation of the slaves' idea of justice and liberation, see James H. Cone, *The Spirituals and the Blues* (New York: Seabury Press, 1972), especially chap. 3. See also Albert J. Raboteau, *Slave Religion* (New York: Oxford University Press, 1978); Vincent Harding, *There Is a River* (New York: Harcourt, Brace, Jovanovich, 1981); and Gayraud S. Wilmore, *Black Religion and Black Radicalism*, rev. ed. (Maryknoll, N.Y.: Orbis Books, 1983).

4. For a fuller discussion of the idea of heaven in slave religion, see Cone, *The Spirituals and the Blues*, chap. 5. See also John Lovell, Jr., *Black Song* (New York: Macmillan Co., 1972), especially pp. 310–12, 315–74.

5. Grimke, *Works of Grimke*, p. 354.

6. Ibid.

7. For an interpretation of these texts, see Albert J. Raboteau, "'Ethiopia Shall Soon Stretch Forth Her Hands': Black Destiny in Nineteenth-Century America," The University Lecture in Religion at Arizona State University, January 27, 1983.

8. Adam Clayton Powell, Jr., *Marching Blacks*, 2nd ed. rev. (New York: Dial Press, 1973), p. 194.

9. Some of Howard Thurman's most influential writings include *Deep River* (Mills College, Conn.: Eucalyptus Press, 1945); *The Negro Spiritual Speaks of Life and Death* (New York: Harper & Row, 1947); *Jesus and the Disinherited* (New York: Abingdon-Cokesbury Press, 1949); and *The Search for Common Ground* (New York: Harper & Row, 1971).

10. For an account of that conference, see Mathew Ahmann, ed., *Race: Challenge to Religion* (Chicago: Henry Regnery Co., 1963). Influential works by Benjamin E. Mays include *The Negro's Church* (with Joseph W. Nicholson) (New York: Institute for Social and Religious Research, 1933); *The Negro's God* (Boston: Chapman & Grimes, 1938); *Seeking To Be Christian in Race Relations* (New York: Friendship Press, 1957); and *Born to Rebel* (New York: Charles Scribner's Sons, 1971).

11. See especially Kenneth L. Smith and Ira G. Zepp, Jr., *Search for the Beloved Community: The Thinking of Martin Luther King, Jr.* (Valley Forge, Pa.: Judson, 1974); John J. Ansbro, *Martin Luther King, Jr.: The Making of a Mind* (Maryknoll, N.Y.: Orbis Books, 1982).

12. The importance of the black religious tradition for King's theology has not received the attention that it deserves from scholars. See James H. Cone, "Martin Luther King, Jr., Black Theology—Black Church," *Theology Today*, January 1984. See also the important essay of Lewis V. Baldwin, "Martin Luther King, Jr., The Black Church, and the Black Messianic Vision," *Journal of the Interdenominational Theological Center* (forthcoming). David Garrow's definitive biography on Martin King is soon to be published under the title of *Bearing the Cross: Martin Luther King, Jr., and the Southern Christian Leadership Conference, 1955–58*. It will show the important role of the black church tradition in his life and thought.

13. See Martin Luther King, Jr., "Nonviolence: The Christian Way in Human Relations," *Presbyterian Life*, February 1958; "Nonviolence: The Only Road to Freedom," *Ebony*, October 1966.

14. Martin Luther King, Jr., "The Un-Christian Christian," *Ebony*, August 1965, p. 77.

15. See Martin Luther King, Jr., "Letter from Birmingham Jail," in Martin Luther King, Jr., *Why We Can't Wait* (New York: Harper & Row, 1963), pp. 90–91.

16. The best sources for King's affirmative emphasis on black power and pride are his unpublished speeches on the "Pre-Washington Campaign," recruiting people for the Poor People's March to Washington. See especially his addresses at Clarksdale, Miss. (March 19, 1968), p. 7; Eutaw, Ala. (March 20, 1968), p. 3; Albany, Ga. (March 22, 1968), pp. 5ff. Most of King's unpublished papers, addresses, and sermons are found at the Martin Luther King, Jr., Center for Nonviolent Social Change in Atlanta, Ga.

King affirmed the need for "temporary segregation" in an interview article, "Conversation with Martin Luther King," *Conservative Judaism* 12, no. 3 (Spring 1968): 8–9.

17. On many occasions, Martin King talked about his dream of 1963 being turned into a nightmare. The most informative reference in this regard is his "Christmas Sermon on Peace," delivered in Ebenezer Baptist Church in Atlanta, Ga., on December 24, 1967. See Martin Luther King, Jr., *The Trumpet of Conscience* (New York: Harper & Row, 1967), pp. 75–76. See also similar comments at an Operation Breadbasket Meeting at Chicago Theological Seminary on March 25, 1967, and also during his appearance on the Arlene Francis Show on June 19, 1967. These sources can be located at the King Center Archives.

18. See Martin Luther King, Jr., "Beyond Vietnam," a pamphlet published by Clergy and Laity Concerned, a 1982 reprint of his April 4, 1967, speech at Riverside Church in New York City, p. 2.

19. The most reliable sources for Martin King's theology are the unpublished sermons at the King Center Archives. They include "A Knock at Midnight," All Saints Community Church, Los Angeles, Calif. (June 25, 1967); "Standing by the Best in an Evil Time," Ebenezer Baptist Church, Atlanta, Ga. (August 6, 1967); "Thou Fool," Mount Pisgah Baptist Church, Chicago, Ill. (August 27, 1967); and "Mastering Our Fears," Ebenezer Baptist Church, Atlanta, Ga. (September 10, 1967).

20. King, "Standing by the Best in an Evil Time," p. 7.

21. King, "Thou Fool," p. 14. This sermon recounts King's "conversion experience," that is, his existential appropriation of the faith he was taught during his childhood. There is no doubt that the "kitchen experience," as it might be called, was the turning point in King's theological development.

22. This quotation, taken from "Thou Fool," concludes many of King's sermons.

23. For an excellent introduction to black nationalism, see Alphonso Pinkney, *Red, Black, and Green: Black Nationalism in the United States* (Cambridge: At the University Press, 1976). See also John H. Bracey, Jr., August Meier, and Elliott Rudwick, eds., *Black Nationalism in America* (Indianapolis, Ind.: Bobbs-Merrill, 1970).

24. Henry McNeal Turner, *Respect Black: The Writings and Speeches of Henry McNeal Turner*, ed. Edwin S. Redkey (New York: Arno Press, 1971), p. 176.

25. Marcus Garvey, *Philosophy and Opinions of Marcus Garvey*, ed. Amy Jacques-Garvey (New York: Arno Press, 1968), p. 44.

26. The best introduction to Malcolm X's philosophy is still Malcolm X, *The Autobiography of Malcolm X*, with the assistance of Alex Haley (New York: Grove Press, 1965).

27. Ibid., p. 222.

28. For an account of the origin of black theology, see James H. Cone, *For My People: Black Theology and the Black Church* (Maryknoll, N.Y.: Orbis Books, 1984). See also Gayraud S. Wilmore and James H. Cone, eds., *Black Theology: A Documentary History, 1966–1979* (Maryknoll, N.Y.: Orbis Books, 1979). The best narrative history of black theology by one of its creators is Gayraud S. Wilmore, *Black Religion and Black Radicalism*, rev. ed. (Maryknoll, N.Y.: Orbis Books, 1983). The earliest published books on black theology were James H. Cone, *Black Theology and Black Power* (New York: Seabury Press, 1969); and *A Black Theology of Liberation* (Philadelphia: Lippincott, 1970). They were followed by J. Deotis Roberts, *Liberation and Reconciliation: A Black Theology* (Philadelphia: Westminster Press, 1971); and Major Jones, *Black Awareness: A Theology of Hope* (Nashville, Tenn.: Abingdon, 1971).

29. For an account of black theologians' dialogue with theologians in Africa, Asia, and Latin America, see Wilmore and Cone, *Black Theology: A Documentary History*, pp. 445–608, and Cone, *For My People*, pp. 140–56. See also my essays in the volumes that have been published from the conferences of the Ecumenical Association of Third World Theologians: "A Black American Perspective on the Future of African Theology," in *African Theology en Route*, ed. Sergio Torres and Kofi Appiah-Kubi (Maryknoll, N.Y.: Orbis Books, 1979); "A Black American Perspective on the Search for Full Humanity," in *Asia's Struggle for Full Humanity*, ed. Virginia Fabella (Maryknoll, N.Y.: Orbis Books, 1980); "From Geneva to São Paulo: A Dialogue between Black Theology and Latin American Liberation Theology," in *The Challenge of Basic Christian Communities*, ed. Sergio Torres and John Eagleson (Maryknoll, N.Y.: Orbis Books, 1981); "Reflections from the Perspective of U.S. Blacks," in *Irruption of the Third World: Challenge to Theology*, ed. Virginia Fabella and Sergio Torres (Maryknoll, N.Y.: Orbis Books, 1983); and "Black

Theology: Its Origin, Method, and Relation to Third World Theologies," in *Doing Theology in a Divided World*, ed. Sergio Torres and Virginia Fabella (Maryknoll, N.Y.: Orbis Books, 1985).

30. The dialogue between black theology and other ethnic theologies in the United States has taken place in the context of the Theology in the Americas. For an interpretation of this dialogue, see Cone, *For My People*, chap. 7; see also Sergio Torres and John Eagleson, eds., *Theology in the Americas* (Maryknoll, N.Y.: Orbis Books, 1976); and Cornel West, Caridad Guidote, and Margret Coakley, eds., *Theology in the Americas: Detroit II Conference Papers* (Maryknoll, N.Y.: Orbis-Probe, 1982).

31. See especially Wilmore and Cone, *Black Theology: A Documentary History*, pp. 363–442; Cone, *For My People*, chap. 6; and James H. Cone, *My Soul Looks Back* (Nashville, Tenn.: Abingdon, 1982).

12

Christianity, Political Theology, and the Economic Future

JOHN B. COBB, JR.

MY THESIS IS THAT political theology should expand so as to include theoretical reflection on political economy, and that when it does so it will be led away from both capitalism and socialism. This double thesis will be defended in two parts. The first part surveys the role played by political theology thus far and the need to take further steps. The second part discusses some of the questions that the political theologian should ask and argues for specific answers as being appropriate to Christian faith.

I. TOWARD A CHRISTIAN ECONOMIC THEORY

The demise of the social gospel did not mean the loss of Christian interest in public affairs, but it did mean the return to an individualistic understanding of salvation. Concern for others was again seen as an outgrowth of an inward change in the Christian's heart. The hard-won insight into human solidarity faded into the background.

In the United States we are indebted to black theology, Latin American liberation theology, and German political theology, and in a different way to feminist theology, for renewing our awareness that the salvation we seek is, in Dorothee Sölle's words, the indivisible salvation of the whole world. As a white North Atlantic male it seems best for me to refer to what I have learned from these movements as political theology.

By political theology I have been reminded that in biblical terms salvation from a nuclear holocaust is not a secondary by-product of personal salvation, but is itself an instance of salvation. Similarly, work toward empowering people to deal with their own problems is quite directly salvific work, not merely an expression of something more fundamental.

This is not to depreciate what happens in the interior experience of individuals — quite the contrary! Sustained commitment to God's work of global salvation is urgently needed, and such commitment does not arise simply from the recognition of the global crisis. It involves a deep reorientation of one's total existence of the sort that is properly called regeneration. It involves also a critical self-examination informed by the analysis of how we are all products of our social and economic class and its interests as well as of our race and gender. It thus leads to repentance. It intensifies the awareness of our inability to purify ourselves from active involvement in our own distortions of vision, and it accentuates our awareness that we can be justified only by grace. It accents the knowledge that if there is to be salvation for the world the initiative lies with God, and that our best work is to allow God to align our purposes to the divine ones.

But political theology rightly calls us to integrate our attention to the mixture of sickness and health to be found within us with response to God's call to participate in the work of salvation for all. That will require that we do what we can to draw others into this work. Evangelism in a quite traditional sense is central to our calling. But attention to God's call will warn us against a proselytizing that makes for self-centered converts worse than ourselves.

Understood along these lines I consider myself a political theologian. Important as psychological and existential needs are, they must not be allowed to distract us from the call to take part in the indivisible salvation of the whole world.

Political theology has helped us to recover a biblical doctrine of salvation. It has also shown us how profoundly our social situation in the North Atlantic white churches has distorted our reading of the gospel. It has reminded us of the global horizons within which economic and political policies should be formed and of the bias for the poor that characterizes the prophetic tradition in which

Jesus stood. It has thereby provided a point of view from which the church can protest the sins of governments and individual Christians can protest the sins of the church.

But if political theology carries us this far, it must carry us farther still. It is not enough to denounce every act of governments and churches because they all fall short of the full demand of the gospel. To denounce everything undercuts the power of all denunciations. Nations and churches must act in an imperfect world. They must choose among actual options. To be reminded of the sinful element in every choice is helpful in countering the self-righteousness that corrupts even the best choices, but it is not enough. If some choices are really better than others from a Christian point of view, that fact must be clarified and those choices must be commended despite their ambiguity.

The inadequacy of that political theology which maintains its distance from policy formation has been shown recently in the critical response of the neoconservatives, ably represented in this country by Michael Novak and the Institute for Religion and Democracy. They do not deny that Christians should deal with the great public issues of our time. They do not disagree about the need to consider the whole world. They do not lack concern for the masses of poor people who are now suffering. But they also point out that rhetoric in favor of the poor benefits them little unless there are goods for them to possess and food for them to eat. Hence, the question the Christian should ask most emphatically, in their view, is how to increase the production of the goods and services needed by all.

Novak asks a second question as well, for he sees that Christians cannot accept a purely economic definition of the goals of a political economy. Christians prize human freedom as well. Hence, Novak urges that Christians must ask how increase of production can be correlated with the growth of free institutions. When these questions are asked, capitalism appears as the one great hope for humanity.

When political theologians call for global sensitivity to the poor, they bring into consciousness the enormous suffering of the poor involved, first, in the imperialism associated with the industrialization of the First World and, second, with the industrialization of the Third World countries and their incorporation into the

First World capitalist system. Hence, the general impact of their work has been to intensify criticism of international capitalism. But little has been said to counter the arguments of Novak and other neoconservatives that the only hope for the poor involves their short-term sacrifices for the sake of long-term growth through which their descendants will prosper. If the neoconservatives are correct in their analysis, then pointing with distress to the suffering and lack of freedom of masses of people in this interim period is an act of sentimentality that has to be overruled in the councils of responsible politicians.

Novak's position can be appropriately challenged at two levels. First, those who share the conviction that industrialization and advanced technology are essential for the relief of human suffering can argue in favor of a different economic system. The implication of the critique of capitalism on the part of political theologians is usually to the effect that socialism is to be preferred as the political context for industrialization. Sometimes democratic socialism is explicitly advocated.

Unfortunately, it is hard to find any full development of this argument. Too often the case for socialism consists exclusively of pointing out the evils of capitalist development. The question that must be addressed is whether socialism in fact offers a better way. If one is to defend this claim, one cannot appeal to orthodox Marxism, since Marx himself saw a historic role for capitalism in the process of industrialization. Only after this process had led to the maturation of an industrial economy was socialism to be brought into being. This may be relevant to decisions of the First World nations, some of which have nationalized a significant segment of their industries and become democratic welfare states. But this does not help us directly if we seek a model of socialism as the engine of technological modernization. For this we must look to the Soviet Union or China.

In *Pyramids of Sacrifice* Peter Berger has provided us with an insightful comparison of two important models of economic development. The Brazilian model is committed to capitalism. It aims to make Brazil a prosperous industrialized nation by the end of the century. To that end it commits Brazil to rapid industrialization at the expense of the immediate welfare of the majority of the people. By keeping wages low and creating a favorable environment for investment, it has attained a rapid rate of growth. But only 15 percent of the people clearly profit from this. The vast majority are relatively and even absolutely worse off. Unemployment has increased. Millions have died of malnutrition and related causes directly correlated with their economic plight. Belief that the prosperity of the few will spread to the many is sustained only by faith that the stages of economic growth in Western Europe must repeat themselves in Brazil.

China provides Berger's second model. It is by far the most important socialist experiment in development in our generation. Berger points out that China, too, is committed to industrialization and advanced technology. Measured by these standards its progress has been very slow as compared with Brazil. Further, for ideological reasons the revolution has taken the lives of millions who actually resisted or were charged with resistance. China has, however, attained a remarkable approximation to economic equality, has abolished hunger, and has generally improved the lot of the majority of its people.

Berger's book raises the challenge to Novak at the second level. Is industrialization, or modernization in general, worth the sacrifice it requires? May it not be that peasant societies, for example, are of inherent worth, such that their forced destruction remains unjustified? Are modern industrial societies so healthy and happy that it is evident that enormous sacrifice is justified in attaining them?

These are difficult questions, and I wish that Berger's raising of them had been more widely effective. Governments everywhere seem to be committed to modernization regardless of the cost. Berger implies that any effort to intervene in a society for the sake of those who live in it is inherently elitist and misguided. I find this formulation extreme and specifically disagree with some of his negative comments on Freire's efforts to empower peasants to shape their own destinies. But I am very sympathetic with his doubts about the inherent advantages of modernization.

At the same time, I am impressed by the achievements of Taiwan, Singapore, and South Korea, and in a different way by China and Cuba. Perhaps in time it will appear that the sacrifice imposed on the poor of those countries for the sake of rapid modernization will be vindicated. I do not know. If the same pattern of development could be repeated in all of southern Asia, Africa, and Latin America, it could be argued that the sacrifice of a generation is not too high a price to pay.

But I am convinced that no such massive transformation of the planet is possible. I do not mean only that the social, cultural, and economic obstacles are enormous. I mean also that there are physical limits. The planet cannot sustain overall the level of industrialization attained in the countries mentioned, much less the level of industrialization reached in ours. The resources are insufficient and the biosphere cannot accept the increased punishment that this would inflict. Long before the envisioned prosperity became universal among the descendants of the now exploited poor, catastrophes would have befallen all of us. Hence there is profound deception at work in calling for sacrifices now for the sake of the future. The hoped-for future will never come.

This means that the goal for the global economy must be reconceived radically. If Christians are called to think about political economy in new ways, are we called also to propose a Christian economics? There are at least three senses in which that would be a false goal.

First, it might be understood that a Christian economics affirmed ideals that are unique to Christians, so that only Christians would be attracted to it. Such an economics could then be effected in a religiously pluralistic society only through Christian coercion of others. Even if this were possible, it would be completely wrong. The values to be realized in the economics supported by Christians must be ones that many other people would also support — values that can be affirmed and defended without any specific appeal to the Christian faith.

Second, it might be understood that only one set of economic principles can be justified from Christian faith, so that all who disputed the proposed theory would be *ipso facto* denied an equal claim to be Christian. That, too, would be disastrous. Any new proposal must win its way in a discussion with Christian capitalists and Christian socialists that in no way imputes insincerity or invalidity to their claims to find warrants for their views in Christian history.

Third, another danger of calling an economic theory Christian is that Christians may try to picture it as purer and better than it will ever be. In fact, its theoretical assumptions will never be perfected, and the theory will always be faulty. Even more obviously, any serious attempt to embody it will be caught in all the ambiguous historical forces that pervade every human society. We do not want a repetition of the medieval and early Calvinist identifications of specific social forms as constituting a Christian society.

But if we can avoid these misunderstandings, then there is a sense in which we should be able to speak again of a Christian economic theory. That is, we should strive to determine which among competing assumptions for economic theories are most acceptable to Christians.

II. SOME CHRISTIAN ASSUMPTIONS FOR ECONOMIC THEORY

I propose five types of questions to ask about economic writings, indicating my judgment as to answers called for today by Christian faith.

First, what is the horizon in which problems are seen? Many treatises take contemporary First World economies as the horizon of their interest. In general the span of history they consider is fairly brief. They argue from what has happened in the past generation or two to what will happen in the next generation. Milton Friedman's writings, such as *Capitalism and Freedom*, are important examples of this genre.

A few studies broaden their horizons so as to include the Third World trading partners of the First World. *Facing the Future* published by the Organization for Economic Cooperation and Development does this and makes projections into the twenty-first century. Still fewer broaden their horizons to the whole planet and take a chronologically long view. Herman Kahn in *World Economic Development* has done this.

I believe that most Christians will join me in thinking that judgments about present policy should be set in the broadest context possible. If God cares for all, we cannot be indifferent to the consequences of economic developments in the United States or the First World for all other people. Also we cannot be satisfied to concern ourselves only with the short term.

Somewhat independent of the question of horizon, there appears a second consideration. From what point of view are events seen? Is the concern with what happens to the First World economies or with all economies? Or is the focus not so much on the economies as on ordinary people? Is the human world viewed as set over against the planet or as intrinsic to the biosphere?

The tendency of economists is, naturally, to focus on the economic system as such, and to measure its health chiefly by growth. The physical world is a resource base which is almost completely invisible in many economic treatises. This is characteristic of *Facing the Future* and *World Economic Development*. They see economic growth as the only solution to human problems and are committed to the view that, whatever the environmental stresses, they can and must be accepted and dealt with in the process of growth. Lester Brown, on the other hand, views the economy in terms of the available resources of land and water, minerals and plants. He calls for the adjustment of economic planning to the realities of this physical base.

Despite two centuries or more in which many Christians have adopted the dualism and anthropocentrism of the Enlightenment, most today recognize the need to treat the global economy in the context of the global physical reality. There remain many technical questions as to how much food, fiber, and firewood the planet can produce and how much industrialization is compatible with a sustainable biosphere. But that these questions must be asked has become clear. Christians cannot view the economic system as something autonomous and self-justifying apart from the whole of creation of which it is a part.

The perspectives of Kahn and the authors of *Facing the Future*, on the one side, and of Lester Brown, on the other, do not exhaust the possibilities. Susan George, for example, in *How the Other Half Dies*, writes about what is going on now from the perspective of the poor, especially the poor of the Third World. The result is a quite different picture focusing more directly on the consequences for human beings of the dominance of the profit motive in the corporations that control food. This book embodies the perspective called for by most political theologians. It will certainly make its claim on the Christian reader.

But in focusing upon the exploitation of global poor by the

actual workings of the capitalist system, George narrows the chronological horizon. And as usually happens when this is done, the natural world largely disappears from view. An adequate perspective from the Christian point of view will need to fuse that of the world's poor and that of the physical environment. It will then have to introduce such additional considerations as those of race and gender. The attainment of an adequate perspective for viewing our global possibilities and problems is thus a complex one. We are helped by such work as that of Tissa Balasuriya in *Planetary Theology*, as well as by much that has been done in the World Council of Churches, where the presence of so many voices discourages too narrow a closure of perspective.

In addition to horizon and point of view, there is also the question of ontology. That is many-faceted, but I shall focus on just one central question, the question of relations. Are relations always external, or are there genuinely internal relations? That is, can a relation be constitutive of what a thing is?

If relations are external to the things they relate, then the world is made up of self-contained entities each of which can be understood in its separation from all the others. There will also be the question of how they are related to one another, but since these relations will have no fundamental effect on the relata, this will remain a secondary question. Primary will be the question of what each thing is in itself. On the other hand, if relations are constitutive of what things are, then when one views an entity apart from its relations one is considering the entity not as it actually is but rather quite abstractly. The real entity is what it is by virtue of its relations to other things.

Classical economic theory has assumed that relations are external, that concrete things are self-contained and separable from their relations. The focus here is on the understanding of human beings. This theory treats individuals as self-existent and only incidentally bound up in families and communities. *Homo economicus* is a self-enclosed individual who calculates self-interest rationally.

Socialist theory criticizes this individualism, but it does not clearly affirm the alternative ontology of internal relations. Instead it relocates the substantive individuals at the level of classes. Individual persons cease to be significant agents in their own right, and their fate has importance only as representative of the class. Between classes, on the other hand, relations are external.

There is, of course, a great difference among ontologies in terms of where the true individuals are located. But the issue to which I want to direct attention is a different one. Are the true individuals self-contained and related to one another only externally? Or are their mutual relations constitutive of what they are? If the latter is the case, then there are no units that can accurately be understood apart from the communities that they constitute with one another. The interests of individual persons or of individual classes cannot be separated from the interests of the total community, and the interests of the human community cannot be separated from the interests of all living things.

The ontology of external relations that shapes both capitalist and socialist theory inevitably leads to viewing relations among the units as competitive. In capitalism it is individual persons who compete. In socialism it is classes. Capitalist theories are skilled at showing that the competition which, for socialists, should exist only between classes in fact exists between individuals even in socialist societies. Socialists are skilled at showing how the competition among entrepreneurs emphasized in capitalist theory is easily replaced by solidarity once class interest is threatened. Neither theory accounts for all the facts.

Of course, both theories do illumine much of what transpires. One weakness of each theory is that it underestimates the truth in the other. An adequate theory must reckon with both. But that is hardly possible if the basic ontological model is one of external relations. With that model there must be some unit that is related to other things only externally and whose parts are not themselves true individuals. Such status cannot be attributed both to individual persons and to classes.

With a model of internal relations, on the other hand, all this changes. The individual person is largely constituted by relations to others. The complex patterns of relations order individuals into societies of many overlapping types. Economically defined classes are among the most important of these. But ethnic, cultural, linguistic, religious, and national societies are also important. Individual persons are individual foci of relations and also, to some degree, constitute themselves as transcending them.

No one is simply the product of society. That means also that there is an element of the individuality emphasized in capitalist theory that can and does express itself in pure self-interest. But it is equally true that individual persons can and do subordinate private interest to that of groups to which they belong or, more accurately perhaps, identify their personal interest with the advancement of the group. Class solidarity is a fact. So is national solidarity.

There is, of course, a great deal of competition both among individuals and among classes. There is also competition among religions and most strikingly of all among nations. The model of internal relations does not deny this. But the model of internal relations does deny that there are ontological grounds for the priority of competition over communal feeling. Indeed, it suggests that the extent to which competition dominates in our world is partly the result of models and theories that encourage it. Less competitive societies are possible.

The point is that a model of internal relations emphasizes that the well-being of any one entity is largely dependent on the well-being of those with which it is most closely associated. Capitalist theoreticians often concede that the units of competition are not really individual human beings but rather families or households. But this concession is not allowed to affect the basic model. Actually, however, even within capitalist society many workers realize that their welfare is bound up with the success of the companies for which they work and some managements understand that the total well-being of those who work for them is an important factor in the success of the companies. Economic units come in all shapes and sizes and are constantly shifting. Within the economic unit cooperation replaces competition to a considerable extent.

None of this discounts the importance of competition. It only points out that the competition is not limited to that between individuals or between classes. Who will compete with whom is not ontologically determined. The reality is normally a very complex pattern of competition and cooperation determined by equally complex patterns of identification or belonging as well as by purely private self-interest.

A fourth area for questioning economic theories is their anthropologies. What has been said about ontology impinges on this, but certain features of traditional Christian anthropology need to be brought more explicitly to the fore. I refer especially to Christian teaching about sin and grace.

Capitalist thinking is grounded in an anthropology that corresponds with the Christian doctrine of original sin. This is its strength. Sin as self-centeredness and selfishness is a pervasive feature of human existence. We are all motivated by the chance to get ahead. Also, greed, as the desire for possessions and for enhanced consumption, regardless of the availability of goods for others, plays an enormous role in most cultures. By accepting this as the basic reality about human beings, capitalist theory has attained a realism that enables it to survive and prove itself again and again.

There is, however, a radical break between capitalist anthropology and Christian anthropology beyond this shared analysis. Capitalist anthropology holds that this condition of universal selfishness is not so much to be confessed as to be celebrated. It turns out that, when it is unapologetically recognized and acted upon, the result is not mutual destruction but the welfare of all. Universal selfishness turns out to be the principle of salvation!

Christian theology has taken a different view. Pervasive human sinfulness is the reason, in Christian thought, that human beings cannot save themselves by their own efforts. We are wholly dependent on grace. And this grace is not the "invisible hand" of capitalism that transforms the results of selfishness into the general good but a working of divine power that breaks the stranglehold of self-centeredness in human life.

Christians discern this grace everywhere. It produces civil virtues in all societies. At the very least it widely transforms purely private self-centeredness into group loyalties of various sorts. Among Christians it is expected to open up the possibility of truly disinterested action for the sake of God and God's world. It is in this working of grace that salvation is to be sought.

Christian teaching is also in opposition to that of socialist theory. There it is assumed that human self-centeredness and selfishness are the product of certain social structures and would disappear once a socialist society is established. Individual human nature is either virtuous or purely neutral. Sin is the result of social evil; it is not its source. Christians share with capitalist theorists in the expectation that within socialist societies private selfishness will manifest itself. That this happens is by now sufficiently apparent that socialist governments have been forced to modify the collectivist policies based on their theory in favor of others that take advantage of the energies released when individuals are allowed to benefit privately from their initiative and hard work.

This does not mean, however, that socialists are wrong in discerning a close connection between social structure and selfish individuals. Anthropologists point out that among tribal peoples the individualism presupposed by private selfishness does not exist. In Christian vision the universality of sin expresses not our created condition but our fallen one, and there is hope for a radically new age.

The self-refutation of capitalist theory is not as clear. Capitalists can point to the great increase in production that has occurred where free enterprise motivated only by the desire for private gain has been given the opportunity to work. They can argue that the undeniable suffering that accompanies this growth is a small price to pay for the eventual benefits when the standard of living of the whole society is raised dramatically.

The issue is complex, but the Christian must ask two questions. First, has the measure of success undeniably achieved in First World countries been due basically to the element of free competition that has been allowed or to the combination of such competition with political actions motivated at least in part by compassion for the suffering of the many and the desire to moderate the extreme inequalities generated by pure economic freedom? Second, is the economic success of the First World countries bought at too high a price?

My own judgments are probably clear. First, the concern for distribution, an expression of grace, is essential to a happy economic outcome of a capitalist economy. Today it is widely argued that in the interest of justice and equity entrepreneurs have been too hemmed in, and the major pressures now are toward relaxation of restrictions on their actions and their profits. Given the usually presupposed goal of economic growth, this may be correct. For example, the GNP of a number of countries is likely to grow faster if capitalists are given greater latitude and if their taxes are reduced. But this leads to the second question. What price—

economic, ecological, and social — is paid by the other peoples of the world and by future generations everywhere for economic growth in the First World? I believe this price is too high — much, much too high.

In sum, the recognition of individual selfishness and its positive importance for production has been an important contribution of capitalist theory. It is doubtful that any economic system that fails to take this seriously will be practicable. Also, the unleashing of individual initiative motivated by selfish economic interests does lead to the increase of production and thus to the increase of available goods. But thus far success in some parts of the world has been at the cost of increasing misery in other places. And the goal of overcoming misery globally by vast increase of industrialization is illusory. Grace, expressed in compassion, has always been essential to moderate the suffering caused by economic competition. Today the continuation of that competition, far from leading us toward salvation, will bring us to self-destruction. Our hope must be that growing recognition of the suicidal nature of our present program of self-salvation can enlist the energies of selfishness into a new identity with all living creatures in a shared struggle for a healthy survival on this planet. In this way the disinterestedness which Christians have seen as a special mark of grace can be brought into cooperation with the identification with groups and communities which common grace has always effected universally, as well as with the individual selfishness that is original sin. But that will require quite new thinking about the economy.

There is a fifth question which Christians must address to economic theories. Political economists are concerned with values. The question is, What is good or valuable?

There are two ways to approach this question. One is for economists or Christians to decide what people really should have and then seek to devise a system that will produce these true goods. The other is to trust individuals to know what is good for themselves and to devise a system that will produce what individuals want, namely, what they will pay for.

Capitalist theory adopts the latter alternative. Its understanding of human sinfulness makes it skeptical of the ability of any one group in society to decide what is really good for others. The more individuals can make these decisions for themselves the better. Hence it celebrates the free market where goods can be offered and all are free to select what they want to buy given the limitations of their purchasing power.

Capitalist theoreticians know that some limits must be imposed. If some people desire to destroy others, the society cannot allow them free access to the means of implementing their desire. Hence, no one advocates a totally free market. But restriction in terms of what is widely agreed to be harmful is quite different from the attempt to determine positively what people should have. Capitalist theory aims to leave these choices to the buyer.

Should Christians support this basic decision of capitalist economic theory to avoid judgments as to what people truly need and leave the decisions to the marketplace? There is much to commend this. It encourages individual responsibility and thus personal development toward maturity. It avoids the danger of imposing the prejudices of the few upon the many. It leads to continual improvement of goods and services as judged by their consumers.

On the other side, it underestimates human sinfulness and is based too much on the nonrelational ontology that underlies the whole theory. It underestimates human sinfulness, first, with regard to how those with the power to do so will persuade people to want what they do not need and the purchase of which will harm them. Advertising is not motivated by desire for the well-being of the consumer or for the dissemination of factual information. Far more of society's resources go into this way of shaping "needs" than into the dissemination of accurate information.

It underestimates human sinfulness, second, in respect to decisions made to purchase goods even when there is accurate understanding of what is happening. Sin consists not only in seeking one's own good at the expense of others but also in seeking immediate gratification at the expense of long-term benefits. Because we are bound together in all sorts of ways, because the choice of immediate gratification is often at the expense of the larger society as well as of the individual's future, society has an interest in the discouragement of sin. For example, the eating of junk food by children has economic effects not borne exclusively by them or by their parents. The same is true of cigarette smoking by adults. The issue takes on greater seriousness when we consider automobiles and factories. Society has a stake in healthful air and is therefore justified in forbidding the manufacturing of unnecessarily polluting vehicles.

No one supports a free enterprise that ignores questions of public health. What may be new, however, is the dawning awareness of how tightly we are bound together. Whereas in the development of the capitalist system it seemed that individuals could make decisions about their businesses and about their purchases with only incidental effects on others, now we are beginning to realize that every decision has effects on the whole society.

For example, today many international corporations are considering relocation of heavy industry to developing countries where wages are low and labor is tightly controlled by military governments. On capitalist principles this is often a wise move. Also, those who believe that unrestrained capitalism is the source of salvation for Third World countries will point to such moves as important steps in development. But decisions of this sort have such major effects upon both the country from which the industry is moved and the one to which it moves that they cannot be left entirely to the financial interests of the companies involved. The United States, for example, must ask how important it is to be relatively self-sufficient in basic heavy industry. It must ask whether unemployment can be kept within acceptable bounds if such movement of industry takes place. The answer may be that no restriction need be imposed. But it cannot be assumed that political and social consequences of economic decisions are mere "externalities."

The issues become even more apparent when we consider the effects of industry on the environment. Recently the Environmental Protection Agency issued a report indicating that the consumption of fossil fuels is leading to a warming trend which will soon begin to melt the Arctic icecaps and raise ocean levels everywhere. Enormous funds will have to be spent over the years to protect coastal cities. Some will have to be abandoned. Meanwhile weather patterns will change, with now productive agricultural areas becoming too dry and hot and sub-Arctic ones becoming productive. Social dislocations will of course be enormous. There will be shifts in the relative power of nations.

In view of these prospects it is clear that industrialization in general, at least insofar as the combustion of fossil fuels is involved, is a matter of concern for everyone. We cannot afford to work with a model that initially ignores such matters, introducing them only later as "externalities."

These are only samples. But they are sufficient to indicate that the scope of unwanted effects of economic decisions is global and long-term. This may be treated as simply an expansion of long-accepted public concern for health. But the expansion is so great that the difference of degree becomes one of kind. Instead of viewing as primary the free market with free producers and free consumers hedged in only here and there by necessary restrictions, we will have to think of what kind of economy the planet can tolerate and how much freedom can be allowed producers and consumers within that economy. Christians will share with capitalist theories in the desire to have as much freedom as possible, but we cannot accept the policies that are now encouraged by these theorists. New theories are needed.

This paper is a call for new theories and a suggestion of some of the considerations important to their formation. It does not itself offer any economic theory. I wish I were able to do so. I hope that I can make some progress in this direction. But it is unrealistic to think that a Christian theologian can go far. Only economists know enough to do so.

At the same time economists cannot and should not pursue this task alone. The discipline of economics, like all academic disciplines, has focused attention on some matters and neglected others. The point of this paper is that most economic theories need wider horizons, more adequate perspectives, a more accurate ontology, a more balanced anthropology, and a better understanding of the relation of freedom and social responsibility. The kind of thinking that is needed cannot be done without the full cooperation of economists, but it requires also political theorists, sociologists, anthropologists, ecologists, and representatives of many other disciplines. Indeed, no combination of disciplines will suffice. It requires a nondisciplinary approach which draws not on the disciplines as such but on some aspects of what they have learned. It requires something that Christians should be able to help provide — an inclusive concern for God's interconnected world.

Author Index

Subject Index